THE MAIL ORDER FOOD GUIDE

by Ann Tilson

and Carol Hersh Weiss

Simon and Schuster : New York

Designed by Irving Perkins
Manufactured in the United States of America
1 2 3 4 5 6 7 8 9 10

Library of Congress Cataloging in Publication Data

Tilson, Ann.
  The mail order food guide.

  Includes index.
  1. Food industry and trade—United States—
Directories.   2. Mail-order business—Directories.
I. Weiss, Carol Hersh, joint author.   II. Title.
HD9003.T54   380.1'45'664   77–22395
ISBN 0-671-22810-2
ISBN 0-671-23077-8 Pbk.

Acknowledgments

Special thanks to Aphrodisia, 28 Carmine Street, New York, New York for allowing us to reprint many of its superb recipes. Thanks also to the following for sharing their recipes with us:

Ahlers Organic Date and Grapefruit Garden
Daisyfresh Yogurt Company
Durham Meat Company
Euro-Veal Farms, Inc.
Jane Giulieri and Marybeth Carlile
The Great Valley Mills
Happy Dragon Chestnuts
Anton Josephson Company
Joyner Smithfield Hams
L. L. Lanier & Sons
McArthur's Smokehouse
Marin French Cheese Company
"Mr. Artichoke," Boggiatto Packing Company
Pan American Coffee Bureau
Parprikas Weiss
Scandinavian Foods
Schaller & Weber, Inc.
Seaweed Ltd.
Smithfield Packing Company, Inc.

The Sonoma Cheese Factory
Sternberg Pecan Company
Sugarbush Farm
Surma, *How to Have a Ukrainian Christmas*
Vermont Country Store and Grist Mill
Thousand Island Apiaries
  and
U.S. Department of Agriculture
U.S. Department of Commerce

Our personal thanks to:
Lois Strodl Brand
Barrie Chi
Judy Francis
Minh Chau Gallagher
Vera Hamid
Judith Hasselbrack
Linda Friedman Siegel
Joan Lebow Wheeler
  and our editor Dee Ratterree
  and especially and with love to:
Edna and Stanley Hersh
Janet and John Wattendorf

For BRET *and* NORMAN *who know that "life can be sustained by bread and water, but is given a sharp, upward boost by caviar and champagne"; and for* GILLIAN *and* MARTA *who love peanut butter and lox.*

CONTENTS

INTRODUCTION

SZECHUAN shrimp, bagels, and tandoori chicken are warming hearts and stomachs in meat-and-potato country while *The New York Times* proclaims grits are "moving north to appear on some very chic menus." Cooks across the country have more on their shopping lists these days than Shake 'n Bake and Instant Breakfast. The proliferation of cookbooks, television cooking shows, classes, and the many unusual restaurants that are opening in all parts of the country attest to the food revolution that is affecting the nation —and it is moving at more than an escargot's pace.

If specialty cooking ingredients are hard to find in your neighborhood, *The Mail Order Food Guide* tells how you can bring culinary delights from around the world to your door—the exotic, the unusual, the finest, and sometimes, the cheapest—farmhouse cheeses from England, Southern country hams smoked according to secret family recipes, freshly roasted, prime-quality coffees, garlicky sausages, produce from family farms, fish and shellfish, stone-ground flours, ethnic spices, and giant wheels of aged cheddars. Even those who have access to the immense variety of foods available in large cities can order by mail some of the otherwise difficult-to-obtain foods described in this book— regional specialties such as pale-rosy-pink and delicately smoked salmon from the Pacific Northwest, spicy Southwestern chili, a juicy-sweet, fresh-picked Hawaiian pineapple, succulent Florida stone crabs, a New York kosher salami, and an entire New England clambake, seaweed and all.

Some readers will order food by mail out of necessity—there may just not be a place in town to buy Indian spices, egg roll wrappings, or stone-ground whole wheat flour. Others will find luxury items which make special gifts, such as a sachertorte flown in its own little wooden crate from Vienna, or a pound of fresh beluga caviar, or a complete lox and bagel breakfast or a freshly ground peanut butter. Instead of going to Chinatown and being assaulted by an overwhelming array of cans and jars of alien vegetables and dried who-knows-what, the mail-order shopper can use this book to send for a long listing of Chinese ingredients, browse through it, comparing what is listed with recipes in a favorite cookbook, and then order confidently by mail what is needed.

To prepare this book, we contacted—by letter— several thousand businesses involved in mailing food. Over a thousand again we reached by telephone. The sources range from large concerns to home kitchens, to family-run farms to small ethnic shops filled with barrels of dried beans and spices, sausages and cheeses dangling from the ceiling, counters laden with freshly baked pastries. We have tried to gather what is best representative of the many types of foods that can be mail-ordered and the regions and countries from which they come. The descriptive text, or lack of it, should not influence the reader in choosing a source for his or her favorite food. Most of the places will send catalogs and price lists, a few for a nominal charge; others have no printed information available but are willing to mail their products and are experienced in doing so.

The prices given are current as of 1976 and are, of course, subject to change. Always write to request current prices and catalogs before ordering food.

Some shops have received more than one listing. This does not mean that they are in any way superior to those listed only once. It is just that we thought the foods offered to be interesting or unusual enough to mention in one or several chapters. Obviously, there is much overlapping. Spices can be found primarily in the "Coffee, Tea, and Spice" chapter, but Indian spices, for example, appear in the "Ethnic Foods" section as well. Flours and grains are featured in Chapter 1, but also constitute a large part of the stock in almost all health food stores and many ethnic shops as well.

Researching this book involved unequal amounts of energy, drudgery, persistence, tact, good humor, and much pleasure. We came to expect the unexpected as we discovered all the exciting foods available from a great number of sources. We talked to farmers in the Midwest, ranchers from Montana to Texas, commercial fisheries, wild rice gatherers in Minnesota, buffalo ranchers in Wyoming, meat packinghouses in Chicago, an elderly lady putting up jams in her kitchen, a beekeeper, a Greek baker, a cheese importer, a cheesemaker—and many fruitcakes. We hope you will have as much fun using this book as we have had in compiling it.

We would be happy to hear about any further sources for mail order food. Please write to us c/o Simon and Schuster, 1230 Avenue of the Americas, New York, N.Y. 10020

ANN TILSON AND CAROL HERSH WEISS

TO many, this chapter may be worth the whole book. The sources provided here should not only satisfy the needs of every avid bread baker in search of fine-quality grains and grain products, but also please pastamakers and rice and bean enthusiasts. As James Beard points out in *Beard on Food*, "Proper hard-wheat bread flour is not easy to find in this country, but well worth the searching." The very best hard-wheat flour, as well as a vast array of other hard-to-find items, can be ordered directly from the millers listed in this chapter.

There are coarsely ground meals and grits and cracked or whole grains processed by cool, slow stone grinding. You will find every variety of flour necessary to create different textures in bread—yellow or white cornmeal to make a crumbly sweet bread, fine millet to produce a crunchy texture, or rolled oats for a more chewy character. The many sources for rice offer white or brown varieties in short and long grains. Wild rice, gathered from the shores of lakes and streams, is available from several sources in northern Minnesota.

Special whole grain mixes for pancakes, cakes, and all kinds of breads are prepared with interesting combinations of grains by millers. Mixes to make wild rice pancakes, whole wheat angel food cake, and French crusty rolls are among a variety of ready-to-make foods. Traditional breakfast cereals such as steel-cut oats, samp, organic crushed wheat, and cracked wheat can be found here, as well as all types of granola and other mixed cereals.

Included in this chapter are several sources for beans and seeds, since millers of grains often process and stock a large inventory of both. Of course, these are also available from companies listed in the "Fruit and Vegetable" chapter, as well as in the "Health Foods" and "Ethnic Foods" chapters.

Birkett Mills, Penn Yan, New York 14527. Free price list.

Birkett Mills, better known as Wolff's Family Foods, is a large manufacturer of buckwheat products. Stone-ground flours, pancake mixes (4 pounds under $2), brown groats, also known as kasha (case of six 1-pound boxes, a little over $3), and cereal are available by the pound in sacks and bales. Flours: buckwheat, dark and light (5-pound sack less than $2), whole wheat and rye (2 pounds less than $2), and unbleached pastry (5 pounds under $1) can be ordered. Wheat germ is freshly milled as ordered (3 pounds just over $1). There is nothing added to any of the flour and groat products during the milling process. A 32-page *Kasha Cookbook* can be ordered for $1.

Righteous Corn Bread

    3 tablespoons melted butter or oil
    2 beaten eggs
    2 cups yogurt
    2 cups yellow cornmeal
    1 teaspoon salt
    3 teaspoons baking powder
    ¼ cup wheat germ

Melt butter or oil in 9-by-11-inch pan. Beat eggs in mixing bowl, add yogurt. Add dry ingredients, then fat. Stir only to blend. Pour into pan in which fat was melted. Bake at 400° F about 30 minutes.

Brown County's Old Country Store, The Nashville House, Nashville, Indiana 47448. Free catalog.

The little brown jug is filled with Hoosier sorghum, small crocks hold white clover honey, and the apple butter ($1.50 per pint) is baked, the old-fashioned way. These items can be sent to city folk along with stone-ground, whole-grain flours and meals which include whole wheat graham flour, whole rye flour, white grits and white and yellow cornmeal (all 5 pounds for $4.75 postpaid). There are also 2 pancake mixes, whole wheat and wild rice. If the squirrels don't get them first, the Country Store will have some wild forest nuts from the Brown County hills.

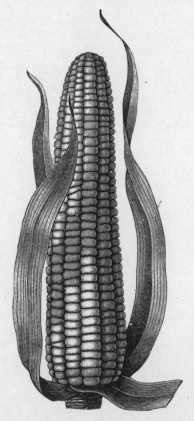

Chico-San Inc., P.O. Box 1004, Chico, California 95926. Free catalog.

Organically raised short-grain brown rice in amounts from 1 to 100 pounds can be ordered directly from this California grower. Details of Chico-San's organic farming methods are fully described in its catalog. Sweet brown rice, a more glutinous variety with a higher protein content, is also grown, both just over $3 for 5 pounds. The two are stone-ground together to make rice flour (just over $1 per pound). Other products made from brown rices include rice cream, also about $1 per pound, a whole-grain cereal which can be used also as a thickener in cooking, and rice cakes, brown rice and sesame seed biscuits available in 3 varieties: plain-flavored and with millet or buckwheat (about 70¢ for 4 ounces). Chico-San also sells nonrice products, including whole-grain noodles such as whole wheat spaghetti and buckwheat spaghetti. Black soybeans (under $3) and small, red, Japanese, imported azuki beans (under $2) are offered by the pound.

Conrad Rice Mill, P.O. Box 296, New Iberia, Louisiana 70560. Prices on request.

The Rice Mill offers 1-pound bags ($4.95 postpaid) of Konriko Louisiana Wild Pecan Rice. This product is not wild rice, but a long-grain rice with a natural pecan flavor and aroma.

Deer Valley Farm and Farm Store, R.D. 1, Guilford, New York 13780. Free catalog.

The Carstens, owners of Deer Valley Farm, are great enthusiasts of naturally grown grains, beans, and seeds. Whole wheat kernels for milling or cereal, soft-wheat kernels for pastries or cereals, and whole wheat kernels for sprouting, all range from 30¢ to 35¢ a pound. Beans are available in many varieties. There are red marrow beans (good for baking), about 60¢ a pound; yellow or green soybeans (for cooking and sprouting), from 40¢ to 60¢ a pound; and turtle soup (black) beans, about 75¢ a pound. Open pollinated corn in yellow or white varieties can also be ordered, about 30¢ a pound. Flours made from the farm's own naturally grown, stone-ground grains include unbleached white flour, milled from spray-free Montana spring wheat—one for bread and one for pastry, about 35¢ a pound; whitmerwheat flour, about 40¢ a pound; and rye flour in either course or fine grain, about 35¢ a pound. From a wide choice of cereals and meals you can order eight-grain blended meal, made of wheat, corn, flax, rye, barley, millet, and sunflower seeds, about 65¢ a pound; and ready-to-serve cereals such as soya-date, about 99¢ for 14 ounces, and cream of rye, about 89¢ a package. You will also find items such as rice baking mix, about $1 a pound; baking powder, 29¢ for 4 ounces; and sourdough starter in an earthen jar, about $3.

E. L. Floura, Wild Rice Distributor, Blackduck, Minnesota 56630. Free price list.

The Flouras have a small family business which they operate from their home in northern Minnesota. Mr. Floura learned how to pick wild rice from his father when he was a boy and now his children are learning the art. The Flouras sew their own white-canvas, plastic-lined bags in which the rice is packed, and imprint the bags with a wild rice label by silkscreen. A minimum order is 5 pounds, at $4.20 per pound, and includes a 16-page cookbook on request. Prices are less on larger quantities ($3.90 per pound for 10 pounds; $3.65 per pound for 25 to 50 pounds). A free sample will be sent along on request.

The Great Valley Mills, Quakertown, Bucks County, Pennsylvania 18951. Free catalog.

An old-fashioned store located in Pennsylvania Dutch country, Great Valley Mills has a wide variety of area specialties, including a nice choice of grains and related products. Whole-grain flours, pumpernickel rye meal, graham flour, and brown rice flour (all between $1.40 and $2.50 for 3 pounds) are a few of the Great Valley Mills products. Scotch oatmeal, in fine ($1.00 per pound) or coarse (75¢ per pound) texture, and Irish oatmeal (about $2.00 for 3 pounds) are shipped, as are other breakfast foods.

Ready mixes for griddle cakes, waffles, and muffins come in flour varieties such as buckwheat, unbleached, and whole wheat—all under $1.00 per pound. A 20 percent discount is allowed on all flours, cereals, and meal packed in paper bags of 24 pounds each.

There is also a selection of smoked meats, preserves, Dutch butters, and condiments. Smoked hams from corn-fed hogs are cured with spiced vinegar and sugar and smoked for two weeks over apples and hickory wood (ready to eat, 12 to 14 pounds, $32.00). Canadian bacon is sold in rindless slabs or sliced. Other smoked meats are tongue (3 pounds, $6.50), dried beef ($2.75, ½ pound), and Pennsylvania Dutch scrapple (3-pound cans, $3.75). Besides Lebanon bologna, a specialty in this area, a beer bologna and a ring bologna are also available; all are pure beef and cost about $2.00 for a midget size. Shipping charges are additional. Telephone orders accepted (215) 536-3990.

The Hicks Wild Rice Company, Cohasset, Minnesota 55721. Free brochure.

The Hicks Wild Rice Company is the national distributor for Chippewa Brand wild rice. The fancy grade of rice comes in 1-pound cartons or bags and a minimum order of 2 pounds ($9.50 or $9.30) is required. There is a sampler package which includes ½ pound of wild rice, 1 pound of wild rice pancake mix, and a tin of "Pow Pow Pops," a French-fried, wild-rice cocktail bit ($5.75 ppd).

Outasight Pancakes

2 cups whole wheat pastry flour
1 cup powdered milk (optional)
1 cup wheat germ
2 teaspoons salt
4 teaspoons double-acting baking powder
3 cups yogurt
¼ cup vegetable oil
4 eggs

Sift dry ingredients into a mixing bowl. Add the rest of the ingredients and stir until just mixed. Drop from a large spoon onto a moderate griddle lightly greased.

Leon R. Horsted, Whole Grain Foods, Route 2, Waunakee, Wisconsin 53597. Price list 10¢, plus self-addressed stamped envelope.

Because of his long experience raising and retailing organic foods, Leon Horsted believes he is able to judge what is truly organic. He also knows sources that because of their smallness cannot advertise nationally. Such products appear on his price list. Per pound costs are reasonable for flours such as buckwheat (30¢), corn (40¢), rice (75¢), millet (55¢), unbleached hard Minnesota white flour (28¢), and Wisconsin pastry wheat flour (20¢). There are meals (corn, 35¢, and oat, 45¢), hulled sunflower kernels ($1.40), barley (68¢), whole soybeans (60¢), and Horsted's own white popcorn (40¢). Other natural food items include carob products and honeys, sauerkraut (89¢ per quart) and sea salt (26 ounces for 55¢). Shipping charges are additional but in his newsletter (published 4 times a year, 20¢ per issue, free to regular customers), Mr. Horsted notes that each summer his family takes to the road visiting parts of Wisconsin, Minnesota, South Dakota, and Iowa. Customers in these states might be able to arrange direct delivery of their orders.

L & L Health Foods Company, Route 1, Box 197, Fairview, Oklahoma 73737. Free price list.

From L & L Health Foods Company you can order grains, seeds, dried fruits, and nuts—raw shelled peanuts, pecan halves, and almond or walnut meats. Grains include whole kernels, oats, meals, and cereals. Most are sold in quantities of 2 to 10 pounds. (Whole kernel wheat and rye kernels, about $9 for 100 pounds, $1 for 10 pounds, and whole wheat flour are also available in bulk amounts.) You will find garbanzo, mung, pinto, and soybeans, and such seeds as flax, sesame, and alfalfa. Among a limited selection of dried fruits there are pitted cherries, apricots, and raisins. Other natural foods listed here are carob (powder and candy bar), safflower oil, and yeast flakes. All items are as nearly naturally grown as L & L is able to obtain.

Letoba Farms, Route 3, Box 180, Lyons, Kansas 67554. Free brochure.

From the breadbasket of the world is available a great selection of Letoba Farms basic whole grains, meal, and flours. Whole-grain wheat—what the people of Letoba Farms call a nutritional bargain—(5 pounds about $1.00), raw wheat germ (5 pounds about $2.00), and wheat bran made of four to six outer layers of the kernel (2 pounds about 50¢) are among the selection, as well as rye, soft spring wheat, corn, pearled barley, and two kinds of millet (the unhulled white prosso and the yellow "bead"

Milwaukee Rye Bread

1½ cups cold water
¾ cup cornmeal
1½ cups boiling water
1½ tablespoons salt
1 tablespoon sugar
2 tablespoons shortening
2 cups mashed potatoes
1 package yeast
¼ cup lukewarm water
6 cups rye flour
2 cups hard white flour
1 tablespoon caraway seed

Stir cold water into cornmeal until smooth. Place over fire, add boiling water, and let cook, stirring constantly, about 2 minutes, to a mush. Add salt, sugar, and shortening, and let stand until lukewarm. Add potatoes and yeast dissolved in lukewarm water, and then the rye and white flour and caraway seed. Mix and knead to a smooth, stiff dough, using white flour on board to mold. Place in bowl, cover, and set in warm place to rise until it doubles in bulk. Shape into 3 or 4 loaves; place in greased pans. Let rise to top of pans, place in 375° F oven and bake for about an hour or until bread shrinks from sides of pan.

hulled)—all are between $1.20 and $2.00 for 5 pounds. Rice varieties available are long- and short-grain (under $4.00 for 5 pounds), brown and wild rice (under $2.00 per pound).

Versatile and sometimes hard-to-find grain products include dark wheat meal, a cream-of-wheat style made from the whole kernel of wheat, and cracked wheat, a medium-sized grind often used in cereals and added to many prepared dishes. Also available are bulgur wheat pilaf or bulgur with soy added for additional protein—all under $1.00 for 2 pounds.

Six grain flakes, used as cooked cereal, in granolas, baked goods, and as extenders, can be ordered. These are quickly cooked under dry radiant heat and then rolled and flattened so the flake contains the whole kernel along with the whole nutrient value. They average between 35¢ and 45¢ per pound.

Other products carried at Letoba Farms are sorghum grits (2 pounds for 60¢), a combination of the sorghum grains and soybean; ultrasoy (5 pounds for $2.00), a textured, vegetable protein product; and beans for sprouting. These include mung beans, lentils, wheat, triticale, alfalfa, and yellow soybeans. Soybeans must always be cooked, toasted, or sprouted before eating to destroy enzymes that interfere with digestion.

Triticale flour (5 pounds for $1.30), with a distinctive and nutty taste, and "trit-i-kay-lee," named from its parents—*Triticum*, the Latin generic for wheat, and *Secale*, for rye—are among 9 varieties of stone-ground flours that can be ordered.

Minnehaha Wild Rice, 420 WCCO Radio Building, Minneapolis, Minnesota 55402.

It isn't really rice but it is wild, and it can be ordered in 1-pound packages ($6.85 ppd) from Minnehaha Wild Rice. A discount is offered on orders of 5 pounds ($29.50 ppd) of this highly prized grain which was once one of the staples in the diet of the Sioux and Chippewa Indians.

The Nauvoo Milling Company, Nauvoo, Illinois 62354. Prices on request.

Nestled next to the Mississippi River is a small enterprise where whole grain is ground on a stone mill. Most of the milling produces 2 finely ground whole wheat flours: bread flour made from a high-protein northern hard wheat and cake flour from a local soft wheat. Also made is cracked wheat and cornmeal. Some of the flours are combined into mixes: a whole wheat angel food cake mix; a pancake mix made from whole-grain wheat, corn, and rye flours; and other mixes such as corn bread, chocolate cake, hot roll, muffin, or nut bread. Nauvoo Milling will ship 5-pound orders to individuals and is able to ship orders of more than a ton to groups buying together. As an example, 5 pounds of flour are under $1.50; 10 pounds, just over $2.50. Shipping charges are additional.

WILD RICE

Wild rice is an aquatic grass, high in vitamin B. It is found mainly along the shores of rivers and streams in shallow water. Ripe rice, as it is called, is harvested by teams in canoe-like boats poled from the rear, with the front man knocking the rice from its stalk into the boat. About 20 percent of a crop is actually harvested; the rest falls to the water to seed for future crops, and only about 25 percent of the harvested crop is culled for the finished product. Understandably the price is high.

A. Scheresky, Box 10, Glen Ewen, Saskatchewan SOC 1CO, Canada. Free price list.

Mr. Scheresky's farm, 640 acres of grain-producing land, is set among groves of aspen poplars in southeastern Saskatchewan. Although many products such as oats, barley, and millet are grown there, the Canadian Wheat Board does not permit shipments outside Saskatchewan of anything but millet.

Naturally grown, hulled, finely ground flour and millet meal sells for a little over 30¢ per pound by the 50-pound pack. Five-pound quantities also can be ordered at a slightly higher cost per pound. Orders are shipped collect via Motorways for fastest service, unless otherwise specified.

Vermont Country Store, Inc., Weston, Vermont 05161. Catalog 25¢.

Freshly baked bread and cookies are available from Vermont Country Store's own bakery. Whole-grain bread is made from stone-ground, 100 percent whole-grain wheat meal and is so popular that some of the store's regular customers drive fifty miles to buy it (3 loaves, $2.75). Jumbo cookies, also made from whole meal, measure 4 inches in diameter and are sold in boxes containing 15 assorted varieties, $4.00.

A dozen cereals made from a mixture of whole grains includes samp cereal, a concoction of coarse cracked corn and wheat; Vermont lumberman's mush, a soft cereal of corn, wheat, and oatmeal; and Vermont Country Store's own high-nutritional breakfast food, a combination of wheat germ, cracked sunflower and pumpkin seeds, raisins, skim milk powder, chopped nuts, date sugar, sesame seeds, apple, and banana flakes.

Meal and flour varieties available are oat flour, a ground

oatmeal flour for use in making oatmeal bread and cookies; pancake or muffin meal made of whole-grain corn, wheat, and rye; and pastry wheat flour, sometimes called graham flour after Dr. Sylvester Graham, who advocated it for good health. All meals, flours, and cereals come in 2-pound bags ($1.40) or 5-pound bags ($2.50), except for the high nutrition breakfast food which is $1.95 per pound. Shipping charges are additional.

Walnut Acres, Penns Creek, Pennsylvania 17862. Free catalog.

Many ready-to-eat breakfast cereals such as puffed millet, granolas in flavors like maple-almond and apple-cinnamon, by the pound or in individual serving packets, and dozens of hot cereals are among the grain products produced by Walnut Acres from its own organically grown grains which are kept in refrigerated bins. In addition to the more standard flours, you can find bran flakes, carob flour, potato flour, and a twelve-grain flour. Almost all are under $1 per pound. Walnut Acres' own pancake and bread mixes, in varieties such as buckwheat, rice pancake and baking mix, and a wheatless mix come with recipes. Baking aids include the less common single-acting baking powder (61¢ per pound). Breads are baked twice weekly and shipped only on those days. Varieties include whole wheat, crushed wheat, raisin, rye, and soya carob. Prices are reasonable, with six 1¼-pound loaves costing less than $5. There is also a full line of Erewhon organic pastas. Walnut Acres has been growing, shipping, and preparing natural foods for mail order for over a quarter of a century.

Wilson Milling, Wesley K. Wilson, P.O. Box 481, La Crosse, Kansas 67548. Free price list.

From Kansas, known for its fine wheat and grains, comes Wilson's organically grown wheat. The wheat is the strong gluten, high-protein, hard winter variety. In 23-pound bags, Wilson Milling sells whole wheat berries (under $4.00), stone-ground whole wheat flour (just over $5.00), and cracked whole wheat cereal (about $11.00). Also raised and sold in 7-pound bags are whole soybeans ($1.59), mung beans ($4.11), and raw, stone-ground soybean flour ($2.22). The whole wheat and beans are cleaned, graded, and ready for the grinder. The flour is stone-ground just prior to shipping. Wilson recommends that whole wheat and soy beans be kept in a dry place or refrigerated; the flours should be kept under refrigeration.

EXPERIMENTING WITH FLOURS

In making bread, many flours can easily be substituted for the wheat and white flours used in most basic recipes. Whole wheat and unbleached white flours have a high gluten content necessary to give dough elasticity and the final baked product an airy quality. Therefore, only one-half the required amount of these flours is usually substituted. Each flour will lend a different taste and texture to your bread. For example:

When using mealy-textured grains, the addition of a little *rye flour* will help make the dough more workable.

Small amounts of *barley flour* will give the dough moisture and a slightly sweet flavor. (Toast in the oven or on top of the stove before using for best flavor.)

Rolled oats will give the bread a chewy texture and a sweet flavor.

Cornmeal will create a crumbly and somewhat crunchy texture and a sweet flavor.

Soy flour is usually added to other flours for its high-protein content. This is best done by blending soy flour with liquids instead of adding soy directly to white flour.

Potato flour will lend moisture to bread and helps keep the bread from becoming stale too quickly.

To substitute the following flours in place of 1 cup of unbleached white or whole wheat flour use:

½ cup barley flour
¾ cup buckwheat flour
1 cup corn flour
¾ cup cornmeal
⅔ cup oat flour added to ⅓ cup wheat or white flour
1½ cup rolled oats
⅝ cup potato flour
1¼ cup rye flour
¾ cup soy flour or 2 tablespoons soy flour added to each ⅞ cup of wheat or white flour

2. BREAD

WHAT could be nicer than to have a home-made loaf of bread in the mailbox every morning? It is entirely possible. We have searched out bakers and ethnic shops that are quite used to the idea of shipping their unusual breads and other goods to dedicated customers all over the country. Danish pumpernickel, Jewish rye, and breads made from cracked wheat, oats, or rye are among an interesting selection of breads baked in all shapes and sizes. Sourdough bread can be air-shipped from San Francisco, and if you are fond of baking with sourdough, that too is available. Real water bagels can be shipped directly from New York. And if you are inclined to do your own baking, you will find a great variety of bread and muffin mixes made from stone-ground whole grains.

Although we have listed in this chapter major sources for bread and bread-related goods, these items can also be ordered from many millers listed in the "Grains" chapter and from some natural food suppliers who also maintain their own bakeries. The latter sources are listed in the "Health Foods" chapter.

N. Alioto's Pacific Fair Restaurants, Fisherman's Wharf, 155 Jefferson Street, San Francisco, California 94133. Prices on request.

What is it that makes San Francisco sourdough bread so unique? Attempts at duplication have been made with the exact recipe used in San Francisco, yet no one has been able to equal the texture or flavor. The most prevalent explanation is the distinctive San Francisco weather, but the question is still a mystery. Until the problem is solved, Frank Alioto will make this delicious bread more readily available by UPS air shipment; 6 loaves for $11 includes delivery. Telephone orders are accepted at (415) 776-7300.

Bachman Foods, Inc., Gift Division, Eighth and Reading Avenues, P.O. Box 898, Reading, Pennsylvania 19603. Free catalog.

If you want to order a wastebasket, charcoal bucket, planter, or umbrella stand by post, Bachman is the place to get it. All come filled with some combination of pretzels: Bavarian Dutch, thin pretzels, cheese sticks, bite-sized pretzels, pretzel logs, nutzels, or corn chips, popcorn, cheese twists, and taco chips. The true pretzel freak might appreciate the plain cardboard carton filled with 8 pounds of bite-sized pretzels ($4.25, plus shipping) or the plain cardboard carton filled with 180 individually wrapped extra-thin ($5.25, plus shipping) or cheese pretzels ($6.25, plus shipping).

G. H. Bent Company, 7 Pleasant Street, Milton, Massachusetts 02186. Prices on request.

Common crackers are a staple in many New England homes, and according to the eighty-seven-year-old patriarch of the Bent Company, they have been on the market since 1801. Mr. Pierotti goes to the factory every morning and says that when he bought the business he didn't know one flour from another.

The hard water crackers contain flour and water only and no salt. They are often eaten toasted with cheese. Common crackers are used for chowders and stuffings and come packaged in bags; the hard water crackers, in boxes—both about $1 each.

Danish Mill Bakery, 1682 Copenhagen Drive, Solvang, California 93463. Free price list.

Family recipes once used in Copenhagen bakeries are used today by the Petersens in Solvang, known as California's "Little Denmark." A large, old-fashioned Danish pumpernickel bread can be shipped anywhere for between $2.50 and $3.50 depending upon the destination. The Petersens also mail their tubs of butter cookies. Packed by hand, fresh from the oven, a tub of 12 of each of 6 types runs about $3.00, plus postage. The containers and packaging process have been perfected over the years so that the cookies are not damaged during shipment and stay fresh for several weeks.

Dimpflmeier Bakery Ltd., 216 Dixon Road, Weston, Ontario M9P 2M1, Canada. Free price list.

Preserving the tradition of past generations, Dimpflmeier Bakery Ltd. produces old-fashioned, German-style breads and assorted baked goods. A German immigrant who learned the art of breadmaking as a youth, Alphons Dimpflmeier has been baking breads in Canada for fifteen years in authentic, old-style German stone ovens. Holzofen bread, Munich City bread, and Monastery bread, a few of the varieties made from traditional German recipes, can be ordered in 1-, 2-, 3-, 4-, and 10-pound loaves. Mr. Dimpflmeier makes rolls, shortcake, and, of course, strudel. The products are air-shipped throughout Canada and the United States. Breads are made without preservatives and have a shelf life of about ten days.

Giulieri and Carlile, 9 Fawn Creek Court, Pleasant Hill, California 94523. Prices on request.

Giulieri and Carlile put out an attractive little recipe book which comes with its own packet of dehydrated sourdough starter ($4 ppd). Starter is a combination of flour, water, and wild yeast cells and was used by the early pioneers. This particular starter had its origin in the Pyrenees Mountains, and was brought to Wyoming by a Basque sheepherder; it is about ten years old. Some starters are passed from generation to generation and are believed to become more flavorful with age. One known to the authors of the cookbook is three hundred years old and still working fine.

The cookbook has many interesting recipes, ranging from basic French bread to Italian panettone, Russian koulitch, and Swedish sugar twist cookies. The cookbook also has tips on caring for the starter, directions for making your own, and instructions for freezing. The sheepherder starter is also available separately, with just basic instructions. (See Pancake recipe that follows.)

Gourmet Appetizers, Inc., 203 East Houston Street, New York, New York 10002. Prices on request.

Freshly baked New York water bagels and bialys (15¢ each) can be ordered from Gourmet Appetizers. The difference between the two: a bagel is first cooked in water before being baked, while a bialy (a Jewish English muffin) is baked only. If you think a bagel is a bagel, Joe Haber, the shop's owner, will disagree. He says, "A real bagel must be made in New York just as San Francisco sourdough bread cannot be duplicated elsewhere. It's the

---

Sourdough Potato Pancakes

  6 medium potatoes, grated
  1 medium onion, grated
  2 eggs, beaten
  ¼ cup starter
  1 teaspoon salt
    Dash pepper
  1 tablespoon oil or bacon drippings

Squeeze water from grated potatoes and mix with onions. Add eggs, starter, salt, and pepper, and then oil. Mix lightly and drop 2 tablespoons at a time on a hot, greased griddle. Fry golden brown on both sides.

New York water that makes the difference; bagels made anywhere else just don't have the same flavor or consistency." Joe also recommends his Jewish rye and pumpernickel bread baked in 1-pound oblong loaves (70¢ each).

Hearty Mix, 1231 Madison Hill Road, Rahway, New Jersey 07065. Free price list.

Hearty Mix produces fortified flour mixes, made without chemical preservatives, for breads, pancakes, biscuits, muffins, doughnuts, and fruitcake. The company started with the purpose of making a "geriatric" bread for the elderly and the ill, who need more nutrition packed into their usually lowered diet (a tea-and-toast diet in many instances). The original product was buttermilk bread; available now as well are Italian bread mix with whole wheat, bran–wheat germ muffin mix, and whole wheat, buttermilk doughnut mix with bran, among a selection of a dozen different mixes. All products are packed in 1½- or 3-pound bags. The price is the same for all products—$3.50 for 3 pounds, either two 1½-pound bags or one 3-pound bag. The price includes postage and shipping costs.

Herter's Inc., Route 2, Mitchell, South Dakota 57301. Catalog $1.

Several bread mixes are among the food items offered by Herter's, an emporium of outdoor and sporting equipment. There is a French bread mix; a high-gluten, low-starch sourdough mix; and "Meet Bread Mix," which is made from 25 percent vegetable protein so that a slice of the bread is equivalent to the same amount of cooked beef in protein content. (All mixes about $2.50 for 5-pound boxes.) Also sold is a French wild rice crepe mix, Alaskan sourdough pancake mix, and rice flour (5 pounds

```
┌─────────────────────────────────────────┐
│                                         │
│  FREEZING SOURDOUGH STARTER             │
│                                         │
│     The freezing of starter is very     │
│  successful if it is frozen at the peak │
│  of its thick, bubbly stage. It can be  │
│  kept frozen up to a year.              │
│                                         │
└─────────────────────────────────────────┘
```

for $2.29). A unique item is Herter's liquid sourdough concentrate in a bottle costing under $1.00. Herter's also sells wild rice and a special "duck marsh," long-grained brown rice put up in 1-pound "vermin proof cans." One can stuffs 2 mallards, 2 pheasants, 3 teal, or 2 cottontail rabbits for less than $1.00.

The Jolly Farmer, East Lempster, New Hampshire 03605. Free price list.

The Jolly Farmer stone-grinds all of its own flours. Two lines are offered: organic flours and lower-priced natural flours for those who do not require an organic item but enjoy a fresh-ground, wholesome product. Dated 2-pound bags of flour include four kinds of wheat flour, light (89¢ or 59¢) and dark (65¢ or 55¢) rye flours, bran flakes, yellow cornmeal (65¢ or 49¢), cracked wheat (89¢ or 59¢), all-purpose white, and pastry white flour (89¢ or 63¢). The white flours are unbleached and darker in color than commercial white flour, as some bran and wheat germ remains. (The higher prices are the organic line.)

The ingredients in the baked breads—whole wheat, four-grain, cracked wheat, raisin, white, rye, and salt-free—are clearly stated. There are no additives. For an unknown reason the organic loaves come unsliced, the natural ones sliced. Customers can take advantage of case prices and mix varieties (natural bread about $7.50, for sixteen 1-pound loaves; organic bread, twelve 1½-pound loaves, about $10.00). There are also 5 varieties of natural cookies made from stone-ground flours: chocolate chip, oatmeal raisin nut, molasses crinkles, snickerdoodles, and peanut butter crunchies—6 packages, about $3.00 (natural). Doughnuts are another specialty: plain and powdered and chocolate chip. The Jolly Farmer offers an introductory sampler of its Natural Line products, which includes a bag of whole wheat flour, 2 kinds of bread, plain doughnuts, granola, and cookies at an introductory price of $2.99. Shipping charges are additional.

Nichols Garden Nursery, 1190 North Pacific Highway, Albany, Oregon 97321. Free catalog.

Two kinds of sourdough bread starter are available from Nichols. One is Oregon-pioneer, hop-yeast starter, which was used by the early Oregon settlers and then was taken to Alaska in the gold rush of 1891 where it became the basis of Alaskan sourdough. The other is a French lactic sourdough starter. Both come with directions and recipes ($2.00 a jar). Nichols also sells an economy 1-pound jar of bakers' yeast for about $2.50, which is the equivalent of $4.00 worth of yeast in the usual small packets.

Toufayan Bakery, Inc., 9255 Kennedy Boulevard, North Bergen, New Jersey 07047. Free price list.

A dry falafel mix (under $1) can be ordered from this company, along with several of its ready-baked items. Pita, the hollow bread of the Middle East, comes made either with enriched white flour or stone-ground whole wheat flour. Vinegar is added as a natural preservative; no fats or chemicals are used. Both cost 70¢ a package. Also available are sesame bread sticks (70¢ for ½ pound) and pitos, which are sesame-sprinkled dough rings—sort of a giant bagel. They come white or whole wheat at under a dollar for 5 rings.

Vermont General Store and Grist Mill, Inc., Woodstock, Vermont 05091. Free brochure.

Almost everyone agrees that home-baked bread is delicious, but there is less unanimity on the question of whether it is worth the trouble. The Vermont General Store has taken out much of the work by developing a line of bread mixes containing all the necessary ingredients premixed. Only water and yeast need to be added. There is a graham quick bread mix, honey oatmeal mix, and a three-grain mix (wheat, corn, and rye) which bakes into a medium brown flecked loaf. All come in 24-ounce packages, each making 3 loaves—$1.49 each, plus 25¢ shipping. Also available are pancake waffle mixes to which milk, eggs, and vegetable oil are to be added. These include wheat and cornmeal mix and buckwheat buttermilk mix. There is also a bran muffin mix and a cornmeal and rye muffin mix. (Pancake and muffin mixes, $1.69, plus shipping.) The grains used in all the Vermont Country Store products are stone-ground whole grains.

For additional sources, see:

A —my dear child—the first
letter—is here:

One that in many a word does
appear.

3. FRUITS AND VEGETABLES

STRAIGHT from the farmer to you: tree-ripened fruit, unsulfured dried fruits, organically grown vegetables, and nuts and seeds beyond the common varieties. Sources for these unusually fresh foods range in size from small family operations to major growers and importers who supply the wholesale trade and service the individual by mail order. There are fresh pineapple from Hawaii, giant shallots from California, Jerusalem artichokes from Tennessee, limes by the lug from Miami, and lychee nuts from Florida's Merritt Island. Citrus can be ordered from Israel, Texas, Oregon, and the major producing states, Florida and California. You will find sweet oranges that range from thick-skinned, easily segmented navels with nutlike flavor to delicious Florida juice oranges. There are native mandarins of Florida, such as the tangelo, and grapefruit varieties such as the seedless Marsh and the juicy Duncan. Local varieties of fresh fruits and vegetables picked in their prime come from family-operated orchards and farms all over the country. Apples, numerous in variety, are available from New England and Wisconsin orchards in such hard-to-find grafts as northern spy, Macon, and McCowan.

Whole dates for munching, date pieces for cooking, and date confections can be ordered from Southern California's date-growing valleys. They are available in grades from choice to extra fancy, and in quantities from flats to small family packs. The selection is vast. Varieties range from the dry, chewy Deglet Noor, the most common of the group, to the large, moist, extra-fancy Medjhool, the richest and most prized of the family. Dried fruits of all kinds are also offered. There are familiar types such as apples and prunes, as well as less common choices like papayas and cherries. Dried fruits come packed in fancy gift arrays, in combination with fresh fruits and nuts, and in bulk boxes (the latter being the least expensive and a good purchase, especially for backpackers). Dried fruits are naturally more expensive than fresh fruits, since it takes, for example, 5½ pounds of fresh apricots to yield 1 pound when dried.

Whether you are interested in fresh or dried fruits, vegetables, or seeds, most sources will ship in bulk, as well as small-sized containers and gift assortments. You will find shopping from these sources a close approximation to visiting roadside stands throughout the country. Farmers and growers are friendly and easy to deal with. Many will send along notes on their theory of crop raising, the latest crop news, and their favorite recipes.

Ahlers Organic Date and Grapefruit Garden, P.O. Box 726, Mecca, California 92254. Free brochure.

This farm is one of the many green oases that spot Southern California's desert region, an area well-known as a date-growing paradise. Ahlers grows and processes its crops organically and naturally. "As soon as our dates are picked we put them on hardware cloth trays in single layers and set them on metal table tops in the sun. This takes care of the dates on both sides without turning them. At 100 to 110 degrees F in the clear air and hot sun for three to four hours dates are cleaned and cured."

Four popular varieties of dates are grown at Ahlers': the Halawi, the Khadrawy, and the Zahidi, and the Deglet Noor. "Thrifty" group orders are encouraged, since dates as dried fruit shipped out of state are given lower rates by truck, and date prices are less on bulk orders. Prices range from $27.00 for 20 pounds, including shipping in California ($30.00 elsewhere) to 3 pounds for $6.25 in California ($7.95 outside). Dates, with their own natural sweetness, are made into coconut date bars and snowballs, a combination of dates, walnuts, and unsweetened coconut—both about $11.00 a box. No sugar is added to either item. For making your own confections, Ahlers has ground sugar dates which come accompanied by recipes for such goodies as matrimonial bars and coffee date chiffon pie.

Organically grown, white Marsh seedless grapefruit is Ahlers' main citrus crop; however, some kinnows, tangelos, and lemons are available from February until the end of March.

All Organics, Inc., 15870 Southwest 216th Street, Miami, Florida 33170. Free brochure.

This farm specializes in growing mangoes and avocados without chemical fertilizers or pesticide sprays. Maxicrop seaweed is used for spraying, since it has nutritional and insect-repellent qualities. All Organics writes that it occasionally uses a fungicide because of tropical climate conditions, but that it washes off. Fruits are shipped by the 16-pound box to your door via UPS for about $11. Mangoes are in season only during July, August, and September, and avocados from July through February. If exotic fruits or limes are of interest, inquire about them. The farm has some, but the supply is limited. Fruit is shipped each Monday as available.

Refrigerator Date Pinwheel Cookies

18 ounces ground dates
1 cup water
1 cup chopped nuts
1 cup shortening
2 cups brown sugar
3 eggs well beaten
4 cups whole wheat flour
½ teaspoon baking powder
½ teaspoon salt

Combine dates and water in double boiler and cook until well mixed. Add nuts and cool. Cream shortening and brown sugar, add eggs, and beat. Add remaining ingredients, mix well, and chill. Divide into 2 parts and roll separately into rectangle less than ¼ inch thick. Spread with date filling. Roll up and chill overnight. With sharp knife, cut ¼ inch thick. Bake at 400° F 10 to 15 minutes. Makes 5 dozen.

Lee Anderson's Covalda Date Company, P.O. Box 908, Coachella, California 92236. Free price list.

Anderson's dates are organically grown in a sun-filled valley at the foot of 10,000-foot mountain ranges. Several varieties are grown, the foremost being the Deglet Noor date, a medium-brown-colored fruit which ranges in texture from moist to very soft and accounts for over 90 percent of the American date crop. A distinctive nutlike flavor is characteristic of sugar-tip dates; it is caused by the natural phenomenon of moisture in the air at the time the dates are ripening.

Khadrawy dates, a softer textured fruit, and Calmyrna and Black Mission figs are also sold. During late June and July, Anderson's has organically grown Thompson seedless grapes (22-pound lug under $10, FOB Coachella). Each box comes with instructions for freezing. Available in season are Ranch Marsh white grapefruit in field runs, that is, packed in 30-pound cartons just as they were picked from the trees and not sorted into sizes, less than $3, plus shipping. The Andersons say that over the years they've learned a lot about the sex life of dates. Just ask. Dates run about $1 per pound for sugar tips and Deglet Noors, up to $3 per pound for extra-fancy Medjhools. There are quantity discounts for 15-pound flats.

The Barfield Groves, Polk City, Florida 33868. Free brochure.

The Barfields are growers and shippers of tree-ripened citrus. Their juice oranges are the seeding, the pineapple, and the Valencia, all with seeds. For out-of-hand eating they have the navel. Grapefruits include the seedless Marsh, the seedless pink, and the large, flavorful Duncan. Temples, tangelos, and tangerines are also available. All of the above can be ordered by the ½ ($9.50), the ¾ ($12.25), and the full bushel ($14.25), in various mixed packs and single-item packs. If the larger quantities are too much, they have prepared 2 different junior gift packs. One is all oranges and the other contains premium oranges and tropical marmalades. Prices include shipping east of the Mississippi and bordering states.

Jacob Ben-Ezer Ltd., U.S. Office: 4 Park Avenue, New York, New York 10016. Head Office: 2 Levontin Street, Tel Aviv, Israel. Free brochure.

The Jaffa orange is grown and packaged on the Mediterranean shore of Israel by some fifteen thousand farming families. It is Israel's number one export item. The Ben-Ezer family has been farming in Israel for over eighty years and has opened a New York office to facilitate the distribution of gift cartons to the United States and Canada. Each carton, weighing 20 pounds, contains about 45 individually wrapped Jaffas for about $15, including delivery.

Caledonia Cold Storage Company, 379 South Pine Street, Caledonia, Minnesota 55921. Prices on request.

Under the brand name "Sno Pac," this family-owned, organic farming operation processes and freezes organically grown produce. Products sold include peas, corn, buckwheat, millet, raspberries, strawberries, asparagus, green beans, and carrots. Prices are more than competitive, with many items close to half the retail price. Ginseng is raised on a commercial basis, and a color booklet on ginseng by Ramon Gengler, the owner of Caledonia, is available for $2.

Cartwright Groves, P.O. Box 372, Carrizo Springs, Texas 78834. Free price list.

Texas grapefruit and juice or eating oranges are available from Cartwright Groves, a small organic citrus operation, starting in early December. Assorted juice oranges, large eating oranges, tangelos, and tangerines, as well as red or white grapefruit, can be ordered by the bushel in individual varieties or mixed. All orders are shipped parcel post and with the exception of Texas, orders of 2 or more bushels being delivered to one address can be shipped via truck freight.

Grilled Grapefruit Cocktail

Sprinkle seeded, sectioned half grapefruits with brown sugar (or drizzle with honey), dot with butter, sprinkle with cinnamon and nutmeg (sprinkle with sherry or rum if desired), brown under the broiler.

John F. Cope Company, Inc., P.O. Box 56, Rheems, Pennsylvania 17570. Free price list.

Mr. Cope's specialty is the corn business. Extra-fancy, special dried sweet corn and fancy, regular-grade corn come packaged in 14-ounce canisters. John Cope's special grade is younger, sweeter, and more tender than the regular grade and comes cellophane-wrapped for gifts. Wet-pack dried corn can also be obtained.

Dried corn still retains its popularity in Pennsylvania Dutch cooking, because it is believed to be more flavorful than the nondried, vacuum-packed variety most of us are used to. Dried corn is prepared in much the same way as dried beans. The kernels are rinsed and left to stand in cold water overnight, rinsed, and then boiled until tender. Two 14-ounce cans of the special grade are $6.25 west of the Mississippi; $5.25, east.

Fourteenth-Century Pear and Grape Goose Stuffing

½ teaspoon whole leaf sage (broken up)
4 tablespoons parsley
½ teaspoon hyssop (broken up)
2 cups pears
2 teaspoons minced garlic
1 cup green grapes
½ teaspoon savory (broken up)
1 teaspoon salt
1 cup chopped celery
3 cups bread crumbs
1 egg

Mix all ingredients together and stuff goose (or duck, chicken, turkey, etc.).

Day and Young, Orchard Lane, Santa Clara, California 95052. Free catalog.

Crown comice pears from the Santa Clara Valley are the specialty of Day and Young. Developed in southern France in 1849, this variety of pear was introduced to California in the late 1800s and is considered by many to be the most flavorful pear variety. Gift boxes of individually wrapped fruit range from 8 to 10 giant-sized pears per box to about 2 dozen petite crowns to the box, both about $10 delivered. Pears are available for delivery only between November 10 and January 5. Day and Young offers gift plans and gift hampers containing other California fruits, nuts, and candies.

Ira D. Ebersole, 25295 Southwest 194th Avenue, Homestead, Florida 33030. Prices on request.

Avocados, mangoes, and limes are organically grown by Ira Ebersole without the use of poisonous insecticides. Avocados are available from mid-July through January, mangoes from mid-June through mid-September, and limes year round. Prices are FOB Homestead, Florida, and shipments can be made by parcel post, special handling, UPS, Greyhound bus, or air freight. Avocados and mangoes are about $4.00 per 13-pound lug; limes, $2.50 for 10 pounds.

GNL Shallot Distributors, 51 DeShibe Terrace, Vineland, New Jersey 08360. Free price list.

Most shallots grown in the United States come from southern New Jersey, and GNL will supply them in any quantity directly from the farmer to the consumer. It specializes in "shallots-by-the-month" plans which send ¼- or ½-pound quantities monthly for a 5- or 10-month period. No shallots are shipped in May or June when the shallots are of inferior quality. GNL features gift subscriptions and will enclose in the first box anything which the sender provides as long as it leaves enough room for the required shallots. Although shallots are often expensive in local, fancy greengroceries or difficult to find, subscription rates from GNL run from about $4 to $10, depending on the plan chosen. A sample ¼-pound package can be ordered for under $1.

Hadley Orchards, P.O. Box 495, Cabazon, California 92230. Free brochure.

Hadley's desert orchard, located just west of Palm Springs, is visited by a tremendous number of vacationing travelers. The inventory of native-grown products is impressive and includes an excellent selection of dates, nuts, and dried fruits, homemade preserves, honey, and sweets, as well as health and backpacking foods. Close to 300 items are stocked for mailing.

As well as a large assortment of regular sun-dried fruits such as Calimyrna ($1.49 per pound) and Black Mission figs (89¢ per pound), and banana chips ($1.59 per

---

COOKING DRIED FRUITS

Place fruit in saucepan, and add water to cover. Bring to a boil. Lower heat and simmer fruit until plump and tender. If more sweetening is needed, add sugar at the end of the cooking period. Adding sugar at the beginning makes the fruit less able to absorb moisture and become tender.

For extra flavor in cooked dried fruits, add:

A stick of cinnamon and a few cloves at the beginning of cooking.

One teaspoon of grated lemon or orange rind at the beginning of cooking.

One-half cup raisins to dried apples, apricots, or mixed fruits before cooking.

---

pound), Hadley's also processes unsulfured sun-dried apples, apricots, pears, peaches, figs, French prunes, cherries, and dates, ranging from 79¢ for a 1-pound bag of prunes to $3.09 for a 2-pound bag of peaches.

Fifteen varieties of nuts are available. They come raw, natural, roasted, and some are barbecue, cheese, onion, and ham flavored, and range from $1.59 per pound for shelled, natural almonds to $2.29 per pound for shelled, roasted, and salted cashews. Carob-coated soybeans, mixed nuts, and Hadley's blends of raisins, fresh-shredded coconut, seeds, and nuts are available as well.

Harwood Hill Orchard and Gift Shop, Route 7 North (Business), Bennington, Vermont 05201. Free brochure.

This is a family-owned orchard operated by the third generation of Harwoods. They grow 40 varieties of apples, including MacIntosh, Cortland, northern spy, and red delicious. All varieties can be ordered in boxes of 15, 30, or 45 apples, ranging from about $4.00 to $11.00. Varieties can be assorted. The Harwoods market nearly all their produce, along with other Vermont products, at the family's two-hundred-year-old, hand-hewn barn. During the fall season, when the cider presses go into operation, guests are invited to see the making of apple cider and apple syrup. Although the Harwoods do not ship apple cider, apple syrup can be ordered in quarts ($4.50), pints ($3.00), and half-pints ($2.00).

Hickin's Mountain Mowings Farm and Greenhouses, Black Mountain Road, Brattleboro, Vermont 05301. Free brochure.

Frank Hickin sells his products with the enthusiasm of a proud father. "He is the only person . . . who can work up a missionary zeal about a carrot" (*Brattleboro Reformer*). In an average season, Mountain Mowings Farm has more than 100 different varieties of vegetables and fruit. A visit to the farm is necessary in order to obtain most of the fresh produce, but Mr. Hickin will ship shallots (about $3.50 per pound) and Fancy Vermont apples—MacIntosh (30¢ each; a bushel—120 count—for about $10.00), Cortland, spy, delicious, and Macon. Typical of the care given to mail orders is the use of apples to fill the empty spaces in the gift hampers of its other products.

Ishigo, Inc., P.O. Box 8, Honomu, Hawaii 96728. Free catalog.

Fresh fruit is air-shipped from the Hawaiian Islands. There are field-ripened pineapples (about $6 each, including delivery) from Lanai, the pineapple island, and papayas (10 pounds for $11) grown on volcanic beds in Puma on the island of Hawaii. Jams and jellies come in exotic flavors such as poha berry, passion fruit, and guava. Tins of macadamia nuts, tropical fruit juices, and Kona coffee are among the other island specialties which can be ordered from Ishigo.

Jaffee Bros. Natural Foods, P.O. Box 636, Valley Center, California 92082. Free price list.

The Jaffees, national distributors of naturally grown and processed foods, have been operating a family-owned business from their Southern California ranch for almost thirty years. Primarily wholesalers, Jaffee Bros. will send minimum orders of 5 pounds of dried fruits and nuts to individuals at reasonable prices. Many varieties of unsweetened, unsulfured dried fruits are available, including whole, dried, red ripe bananas (less than $5 for ten 8-ounce packages), whole rings of pineapple, and sundried coconut (5 pounds under $5). Macadamias, walnuts, and filberts can be ordered with or without the shell, and whole cashews or pieces, Spanish peanuts, and almonds come shelled. Organic fresh fruit by the case include tree-ripened oranges and lemons, and avocados. Prices are low. Jaffee also has yellow and green organic soybeans, ready-to-eat toasted soybeans, and raw and toasted carob pods, all by the 5-pound bag, under $5.

Le Jardin du Gourmet, Les Echalottes, West Danville, Vermont 05873. Catalog 50¢.

Le Jardin du Gourmet, which started out dealing only in shallots, now offers a vast array of imported and difficult-to-find seeds, bulbs, and plants, as well as a nice selection of imported specialty foods. The shallot service is still available, and individual orders are accepted, as well as monthly or bimonthly subscription plans, about $18.00 for ¾-pound monthly. Another, but much more expensive, ingredient in French cookery is the truffle. Le Jardin has canned French truffles, ranging from whole, black, extra-brushed truffles to a 7-ounce tin of peelings. Fresh white truffles are occasionally available as well. (In 1974 they sold for $300.00 a pound.) Varieties of mushrooms available include chanterelles, morels and cèpes (tinned and dried). There is a selection of unusual imported vegetables such as salsify, snow peas, chestnuts, and sorrel.

Kaste's Morningside Orchards, Galesville, Wisconsin 54630. Free price list.

Kaste's Morningside Orchards features 12 varieties of organically grown apples. The apples, packaged in boxes weighing about 40 pounds and costing about $9 per box, are fertilized only with organic compost and grown without the use of residual sprays. Harvesting is from mid-September to late October. Well-known varieties include MacIntosh, Jonathan, Cortland, and red and golden delicious. Prairie Spy available in early October is recommended for its excellent flavor and storage qualities. Haralsons are tart winter apples and North Western Greenings are good for cooking and eating. A visitor to the orchards can buy fresh apple cider and cider vinegar, which are not available for mail order.

KEEPING APPLES AT THEIR BEST

To preserve the crisp, juicy quality of apples, they should be kept in the coldest part of the refrigerator, just under freezing. A general rule of thumb is to store apples close to the temperature of the climate in which they were grown. Commercial produce houses refrigerate apples at about 32 degrees up to nine months. Warm air destroys the flavor of apples and disintegrates the flesh to a mealy, soft texture.

In addition, the quality of apples can be further maintained by wrapping them individually in paper that has been previously soaked in mineral oil. (Even plain paper helps.)

Lynchburg Hardware and General Store, Box 239, Lynchburg, Tennessee 37352. Free catalog.

The General Store sells 16 varieties of canned garden vegetables which are popular in Tennessee and other parts of the South, such as black-eyed peas, crowder peas, turnip greens, and field peas. They are only sold by the case of 24 cans, but you can make any assortment you would like as long as it totals 24, 48, 96, 192, or however hungry you are. Prices run about $13 for a case of 24 cans.

"Mr. Artichoke," Boggiatto Packing Company, Inc., 11000 Blackie Road, Castroville, California 95012. Free brochure.

Castroville is the artichoke capital of the world, as is clearly stated by the long banner that stretches across its main street. Artichoke groves, bordered by farmers' roadside stands, neatly line both sides of the highway that runs southwest to the Monterey Peninsula. The moist, cool climate of this region is said to produce a crop close to the original Mediterranean variety. Artichokes can be bought all year, but early spring is the peak season. The Boggiatto Packing Company calls the fall and winter months of November through February the artichoke's "winter-kissed" time. Artichokes produced in this season have bronze-tipped outer leaves caused by a light frost. This condition causes the vegetable to mature slowly, and is thought by some to enhance the delicate flavor of the artichoke. Hours-old large artichokes come packaged 12 per carton; small, 24 per carton. Delivered prices are $9.00 a box west of the Mississippi; $12.50, east of the Mississippi.

Mueller's Organic Farm, 233 South Dade Avenue, Ferguson, Missouri 63135. Prices on request.

Al Mueller now runs the farm started by his grandfather in 1875. The land has always been farmed without chemicals, although it was not called "organic" until 1950 when Mr. Mueller became acquainted with Rodale's organic gardening magazine and began incorporating some of his new ideas into the farming operation. Although a wide variety of vegetables and fruits is grown, sweet potatoes are the main item offered for mail order. Available in bushels and half-bushels, they keep well for an extended period of time.

Plantation Acres, 515 Plantation Road, Merritt Island, Florida 32952. Prices on request.

Plantation Acres is not a company but rather a family enterprise built around a lychee grove. Popular for centuries in the Orient, lychees grow in clusters on large, subtropical evergreens. A fairly perishable fruit, the lychee does not ripen when picked prematurely, so air freight is the best method of shipping. In order to enjoy the lychee year round, the lychee nut was developed, which is not a nut at all but simply the dried fruit, dried in the skin without special treatment or additives. When properly dried, the product will remain preserved much the same

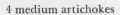

French-Fried Artichokes

 4 medium artichokes
 1 egg
 ½ cup milk
 ½ cup biscuit baking mix
 ¼ cup flour
 1½ teaspoons double-acting baking powder
 1 teaspoon salt
 ½ teaspoon garlic powder
 ¼ cup finely chopped onion
 1 tablespoon chopped parsley
 Salad oil for deep-fat frying

Wash and drain artichokes. Cut off top half of artichokes and trim stem. Snip off all outer leaves down to pale green leaves. Slice artichokes in halves lengthwise. Cut each half into quarters lengthwise; remove choke. Blend together egg and milk. Stir in baking mix, flour, baking powder, salt, and garlic powder until well mixed. Fold in onion and parsley. Dip artichoke slices in batter to coat thinly. Heat 2 inches of salad oil in 350° F. Fry artichokes, a few at a time, until golden brown, about 6 to 8 minutes. With slotted spoon remove artichokes and drain well on paper towels. Sprinkle with salt if desired. Serve hot.

as a raisin or a prune, except that the meat is protected by the hard shell of skin. The nuts need no refrigeration and can be shipped via parcel post or UPS. Plantation Acres offers the fruit in both dried and fresh form, the fresh lychee in the month of June and the dried at any time of the year. Prices vary from year to year, but the average price of the dried fruit is $4 per pound.

Savage's Citrus Barn, Inc., Route 1, Box 150, Raymondville, Texas 78580. Free brochure.

Growers of Texas fruits, the Savages sell their crops of ruby red grapefruit and oranges from their roadside barn. The ruby is a variety of pink grapefruit that, along with the Thompson or pink Marsh, was developed mainly in the Rio Grande Valley of Texas. It has seeds, but it is a juicy and sweet fruit. Both the oranges and grapefruit are available in cartons weighing 13 pounds or 40 pounds (delivered price, $10 and $15). The main shipping season runs from November 15 through March 15, and to assure Christmas deliveries, the Savages need orders early.

For an inedible flavor of Texas, they have a grow-your-own cactus garden, which consists of 10 miniature cactus plants for indoors or out.

Sugaripe Farms, P.O. Box 5879. San Jose, California 95150. Free brochure.

From the Santa Clara Valley, Sugaripe Farms will send dried fruits and nuts in bulk and in gift arrays. Jumbo peaches and pears (10 pounds, under $20, delivered), apricots (10 pounds, under $30), and prunes (10 pounds, a little over $10) come in 5- and 10-pound packs. All fruits, including raisins and dates, come in a number of boxed assortments. Although several varieties of nuts are available with mixed fruit assortments, California walnuts, in bulk burlap sacks of 5 and 10 pounds, are the only nut that can be ordered separately.

SWEET ORANGES AND THE BEST OF THE JUICE ORANGES

The name "sweet" refers to a group of oranges made up of many varieties. It's what most of us think of when considering an orange. By far the most popular in this group is the navel, California's main citrus crop and the most important commercial variety for eating out of hand. Florida grows more varieties than any other state and is known in particular for the Valencia, distinguished by its fine juice.

Sweet oranges grown in the West are especially bright in color with a sweet flavor and are notably easy to peel and segment. When compared to the thinner-skinned Florida varieties, Western oranges have a thick skin and firm flesh, but contain less juice.

The Valencia, grown largely in Florida and to a lesser extent in California, is rated by the Department of Agriculture as having the best-tasting juice. In addition, the Florida Valencia is said to produce a sweeter juice than its Western counterpart. Valencias grown in the West are available from late April through October, while those from Florida are marketed from late March through June.

Florida also produces several orange varieties with good juice aside from the prized Valencia. Each has a different growing season, making juice oranges available most of the year. There is the Temple marketed from January through March, the Hamlin from early October to December, and the pineapple from December through February.

In general, Florida oranges are thought to be the best for juice and California varieties the best for eating.

Sunray Orchards, Route 1, Box 299, Myrtle Creek, Oregon 97457. Free brochure.

Sunray Orchards ship 3 varieties of tree-ripened prunes. They say that different prune varieties are as distinctive as varieties of other fruits. Sunray grows the Colossal Moyer, a large, naturally tart prune that is thin-skinned and tender (76¢ per pound in bulk boxes) ; the Date (46¢ per pound in bulk 25-pound boxes), sweet and slightly smaller; and the Perfection, less sweet than the Date with a meaty flesh. Bulk prices are FOB Myrtle Creek. Smaller quantities are available at higher prices—about $1 per pound, delivered.

Sunshine Groves, Inc., Box 390119, Miami Beach, Florida 33139. Free brochure.

Avocados and mangoes are among the tropical fruits that can be shipped from Sunshine Groves. Avocados are in season from July to November, the summer variety being Pollocks, followed by Halls in early fall, and then Choquettes. Four mango varieties mature from June through August, the last being the large Keitt mango, considered by many to be the finest. Both fruits are sold by the lug or half lug which weigh approximately 14 to 17 pounds (about $15) or 7 to 9 pounds (about $10), delivered prices depending on the variety.

Sunshine Groves also sells several varieties of oranges, grapefruits, and tangelos by the bushel and ½ bushel (½ bushels of most varieties about $12), and offers a monthly fruit plan which can be purchased individually or in any combination. Perfect delivery of fruit is guaranteed. The competition won't allow avocados to be shipped into California.

Timber Crest Farms, Rancher Waltenspiel, 4791 Dry Creek Road, Healdsburg, California 95448. Free brochure.

On Timber Crest Farms, located in Northern California's inland valleys, Rancher Waltenspiel produces a large selection of organically grown dried fruits. In his literature he tells how some of his fruits are processed. Apricots, peaches, and pears, for instance, are washed in cold spring water, cut in half, pitted, and laid on trays to dry. Prunes and figs are washed and dried whole. Raisins are picked from the vine as grapes and laid on rolls of paper between the vines.

Papaya slices, pineapple, apples, and cherries, as well as the above-mentioned fruits, are dipped in honey once they have dried. Individual bagged varieties or packages of mixed assortments come boxed in several sizes. Because of numerous requests, Timber Crest's bulk-dried fruit in 5-pound bags is now part of its mail-order business. Representative prices which include shipping: cherries, pineapples, peaches, and apples, all about $10 for 5 pounds; prunes, dates, and raisins are less, as are figs (Calimyrna and Mission running between $7 and $8 for 5 pounds). Bulk fruits are not honey-dipped.

SIMMERING FRESH FRUITS

Use only enough sugar to bring out the flavor of the fruit; too much sugar masks delicate flavors. Sugar is generally added before cooking to help fruit keep its shape, and sugar makes the fruit less able to absorb moisture. For fruits that hold their shape, however, sugar can be added to water the last few minutes of the cooking period. Cook the fruit only until tender. This helps retain color, flavor, and nutrients.

To Cook Fresh Fruits

Mix sugar and water and bring to a boil. Add fruit to boiling syrup. Cover and return to boiling, then reduce heat until syrup just simmers. Cook until fruit is tender but not mushy. Stir as little as possible to avoid breaking fruit.

For extra flavor in simmered fruits, add:

A few cinnamon candies to syrup (good with apples and pears).

A few sprigs of fresh mint.

A teaspoon of fresh (grated) or dried orange or lemon peel during the last few minutes of cooking.

A stick of cinnamon and a few cloves to syrup.

Paul A. Urbani Truffles, P.O. Box 2054, 130 Graf Avenue, Trenton, New Jersey 08607. Free price list.

It has been said that Paul Urbani is a man who has set his heart on making America truffle-conscious, or as Mr. Urbani puts it, on "trufflizing America." Mr. Urbani inherited his business from a long line of Umbrian truffle producers who started back in 1750 with Paul the first (the present Paul is the fifth of that name). His realm includes an estate of thousands of acres run under his family's supervision in the Italian province of Umbria.

Mr. Urbani says "the truffle is truly an economical food, even if it has to be shipped in from Italy. Its properties as a flavoring agent are such that a thin slice can serve an entire tin of liver pâté, and a single small truffle, properly sliced and strategically distributed, can flavor an entire turkey. The high price of truffles," he claims, "is only an optical illusion."

Black truffles, available in "extra" and "first choice" grades, come whole, unpeeled and brushed, peeled, and in pieces or peelings. White truffles come whole in "extra selected" grade. For many years, Mr. Urbani has received requests from chefs for truffles in puree form to be used in various dishes, sauces, soups, and mixtures that are made by spoon or in small portions. Black or white truffle puree is now available; however, it is sold in case lots only. Truffles are sold both wholesale by the case lot or by the individual tin at about 35 percent above wholesale prices.

Valley Cove Ranch, P.O. Box 603, Springville, California 93265. Free price list.

Valley Cove Ranch says it is the largest purely organic citrus grower and packer in the country. Details of the organic cultural methods used at the ranch are described in its literature. The principal fruit varieties offered are navel and Valencia oranges, Marsh seedless grapefruits, Lisbon lemons, satsuma and kinnow mandarin oranges, and fancy tangerines, in season from mid-November through mid-July. All fruit is tree ripened and not washed, dyed, or subject to any type of processing prior to shipment. Fruit is sold in ½- and full-carton quantities, 18 and 38 pounds respectively, or by the pound. One variety of oranges is currently selling for 20¢ per pound and a 30- to 32-pound carton of grapefruits runs about $4.50. Prices do not include the shipping charges, and discounts of 15 percent are offered on orders of 100 pounds of fruit shipped to the same address.

Vita-Green Farms, Inc., P.O. Box 878, Vista, California 92083. Free brochure.

Will Kinney, owner of Vita-Green Farms, maintains an organic, ecology-oriented farm that stretches through an inland valley northeast of San Diego. Garden-fresh fruits and vegetables, nuts, seeds, and beans are available by the lug or the pound at very reasonable prices: yams ($15 for a 40-pound box), casaba melons (a 30-pound box is less than $10), asparagus, cherimoyas, citrus, papaya (about $10 for a 12-pound flat), and globe artichokes (around $6 a dozen) are among some 60 items grown at Vita-Green Farms. Dried fruits, a good selection of shelled and unshelled nuts, seeds for sprouting, hulled seeds, and beans are also available.

If you are of the mind to grow your own herbs and vegetables, a lengthy list of seeds accompanies the food brochure. From Vita-Green Farms you can also order 23 farm and garden, ecology-oriented products, including a food dehydrator that comes in five different sizes (said not to destroy vitamins or enzymes). Another item: a pet snake. "It's a wind driven snake that looks and acts like a very vicious and hungry reptile of great ambition and ability. It keeps the birds, squirrels, and the like from preying on the crops," says Mr. Kinney. The snake is, of course, harmless and is shipped along with instructions and suggested uses.

Vita-Green Farms must have all food orders by Saturday noon for shipment the following week, in order to allow for harvesting, and proper cleaning and packing of orders.

Walnut Acres, Penns Creek, Pennsylvania 17862. Free catalog.

Walnut Acres sells a vast variety of foods, many of them organically grown, all chosen for their healthful qualities. By the pound there are dried beans: garbanzos (89¢ per pound), red ($1.08 per pound) and green (94¢ per pound), lentils, black-eyed peas (54¢ per pound), split peas (54¢ per pound), yellow peas (64¢ per pound), and black turtle beans which Walnut Acres suggests be picked over before cooking (65¢ per pound). (There may be a few small organic stones among them.) Seeds include poppy seeds ($1.80 per pound), pumpkin ($2.65 per pound), and sunflower seeds ($1.21 per pound), freshly hulled, not vacuum packed. For sprouting there is a mix of alfalfa, mung beans, and whole green lentils ($1.25 per pound). Unblanched nuts include black walnut pieces ($2.88 per pound), filberts ($1.92 per pound), and pignolias ($4.30 per pound). There are also blanched raw peanuts from Virginia ($1.19 per pound) and unblanched raw Spanish peanuts (84¢ per pound).

Dozens of Walnut Acres' own brand of canned and condensed soups, with all ingredients listed, include varieties such as black bean (62¢), chicken-sunflower (72¢), and cream of chive soups (58¢). Save by ordering by the case. Also available are several dry soup mixes and vegetable patty mixes. A very big selection of canned fruits and vegetables includes tomato puree (49¢), succotash (58¢), pinto beans (50¢), blueberries sweetened with honey (95¢), and pure pumpkin (46¢). Canned juices include Walnut Acres' cranberry nectar ($1 per quart), vegetable juice cocktail, and apple juice (46-ounce tin, 90¢), as well as juices from other manufacturers. Walnut Acres offers several delivery methods, including inexpensive truck drop-off shipments to the East Coast.

Fruit Bonbons

1 cup dried figs
1 cup raisins
1 cup pitted dates
½ cup candied orange peel
1 cup chopped nuts
2 tablespoons frozen orange juice concentrate
    or
2 tablespoons sherry
⅔ cup confectioner's sugar, chopped coconut, or
    chopped nuts

Mix fruits and orange peel. Put through finest blade of food chopper. Add chopped nuts. Moisten with orange juice concentrate or sherry, as desired. Shape into small balls, using about 2 teaspoons of mixture per ball. Roll in confectioner's sugar, chopped coconut, or nuts. (About 35 calories each.) Yield about 7 dozen.

W. S. Wells and Son, 174 High Street, Wilton, Maine 04294. Prices on request.

W. S. Wells specializes in canned dandelion greens and claims that it is the only processor exclusively of such in the United States. The greens are sold in case lots of 24 cans for about $18.

Wileswood Country Store, P.O. Box 388, Huron, Ohio 44839. Free brochure.

Wileswood Country Store features old-fashioned food and gift items, but its specialty is hybrid yellow popcorn ($4.59 per pound, ppd) grown on its own farm. The popcorn is available in a cotton grain sack complete with mailing tag. The store also offers a special popping oil ($3.35 for 13½ ounces) blended from coconut oil and seasonings and a popcorn-seasoning salt for 89¢. Finally, there is the popper which can be used on any type of stove or outdoors on a grill.

Roy Wilkins, Route 1, Box 60, Newberg, Oregon 97132. Prices on request.

Oregon weather is unpredictable, and often cold temperatures will delay the maturing of crops, reducing a farmer's selling season to a short period in late spring and summer. Because of this, Roy Wilkins suggests that you inquire each spring as to the availability of his crops for shipment. Wilkins's orchards and vines produce English walnuts, filberts, and a variety of fruits such as pears, blueberries, and Brooks prunes. Figs are a part of his crop, but they can only be sent a short distance. He also grows Steuben grapes, delicious eating and fine for juice.

Williams-Sonoma, Mail Order Dept. 3086, P.O. Box 3792, San Francisco, California 94119. Prices on request.

Special giant shallots (about the size of a garlic bulb) are grown in California and packed for Williams-Sonoma. Developed for the restaurant trade to be less time-consuming to peel than the tiny ones, they are available by mail in 1-pound net sacks. The minimum order of 2 pounds runs about $7.50, which includes postage charges.

M. V. Wine Company, 576 Folsom Street, San Francisco, California 94105. Prices on request.

In the fall, the M. V. Wine Company can arrange to have fresh, whole black truffles air-shipped directly from Paris. These rare, aromatic fungi are difficult to obtain, so the supply is limited and orders are filled on a first-come, first-served basis. Whole truffles are sold in ¼-ounce units with a 1½-ounce minimum required. The cost is $12 per ounce, plus shipping charges. Recipes from a well-known Paris restaurant, including a Christmas menu for truffled turkey, are provided. Delivery time is 4 days from Paris, and the truffles will remain fresh for 2 weeks after delivery.

For additional sources, see:
Chapter 8. . . . to Nuts:
    Joseph Fry (fresh vegetables)
    Torn Ranch (dried fruits)
Chapter 14. Ethnic Foods: tinned and dried fruits and vegetables)
Chapter 17. Health Foods: (tinned and dried fruits and vegetables)

4. MEAT AND POULTRY

HERE you will find the finest cuts of beef usually seen only in top restaurants; the superbly cured hams and bacons of Virginia; and a great selection of salamis, sausages, and smoked meat. High-quality steaks and roasts such as hotel prime rib of roast, filet mignon steaks, crown roasts of lamb and suckling pigs are available from the large meat packinghouses of the Midwest, and Boston. This quality meat is, of course, expensive, but it is delicious! For the freezer, halves and quarters of naturally raised beef and veal can be obtained directly from farmers at fairly reasonable prices.

Sausage and all its cousins can be ordered in dozens of varieties from some of the country's best Old World sausagemakers. Although genuine sausagemakers are slowly disappearing, we have found those who still persist in keeping the art very much alive. There are delicacies such as yachtwurst, mettwurst, Lebanon bologna, Polish sausage and much more; many establishments make all of these items fresh daily from recipes generations old.

Delicious old-fashioned hams, cured, smoked, and aged according to prized recipes, are available from many fine producers throughout the South and the Northeast, including four processors of Virginia's famed Smithfield hams. Opinions vary widely from Jamestown to Vermont as to whether a ham should be pepper-coated before or after it is smoked; whether corncobs, plain hickory wood, or apples and hickory wood produce the best flavor in smoking; and whether the ham should be hot- or cool-smoked and for what period of time. All of these processes are represented here; the choice is yours.

All perishable meats are packed in dry ice and shipped air freight to your door; their safe arrival is guaranteed.

Bardstown Farms, Inc., 1468 North Third Street, Bardstown, Kentucky 40004. Free price list.

Bardstown Farms hams and bacon are dry-cured, cool-smoked, and aged slowly. Hams can be bought whole with the bone in (about $25.00); for an additional charge, the ham can be sliced uncooked (an extra $1.50), cooked ($4.00 additional) and sliced, or cooked with or without the bone. Center cuts of bacon are sold by the slab or sliced.

Bardstown Farms calls part of its smoking and aging process the "June sweat." "During the early days when farmers first cured pork, it was found that rather than eat a ham shortly after it was cured the flavor improved if the ham was left hanging in the smokehouse through part of the warm months. Soon it was commonly accepted that a ham was at its best after June. Old timers said it had been through the 'June sweat.' "

Baum's Bologna, Inc., P.O. Box 289, Route 3, Elizabethtown, Pennsylvania 17022. Free brochure.

Baum's makes Pennsylvania Dutch pure beef sausages. There are hickory-smoked sweet bologna, spiced Lebanon bologna, and sugar-cured dried beef. Hickory sticks are miniature sweet bolognas sold by the package or the pound (under $4 per pound). The regular bolognas come in 1½-pound midgets (about $6 ppd) up through giants of 9½ pounds (about $23 ppd) or more. Other regional specialties which can be ordered from Baum's include dried apple snitz and a selection of Pennsylvania Dutch condiments such as chowchow and spiced cantaloupe slices.

Bremen House, 200 East Eighty-sixth Street, New York, New York 10028. Free catalog.

European-style meat products can be ordered from Bremen House, a large German food emporium located in Manhattan's Yorkville area. Whole Westphalian hams run between 5 and 15 pounds. Among the smoked meats and wursts sold by the pound are touristenwurst ($3.60), kochmettwurst ($2.80), plockwurst ($3.60), cervelatwurst ($3.60), and lachsschinken ($5.00), that tender smoked pork with a delicate flavor reminiscent of smoked salmon. Tinned meat spreads from Germany include a calves liver sausage and a blutwurst spread (4-ounce tins, just over $1.00). A minimum order is $10.00 and shipping is additional.

PREPARING AND COOKING HAMS

ON SOAKING HAMS

Some hams need soaking and some do not. Those that have been long aged, that is, hung from six months to a year such as the Smithfields, need to be soaked for at least 12 hours to remove excess salt. Generally, the amount of time a ham is soaked depends on one's individual taste. The longer a ham is soaked the milder the flavor.

To soak: Wash the ham in hot water and scrub it thoroughly with a stiff brush to remove all signs of pepper and mold from the surface. Then soak the whole ham in cool water from 12 to 48 hours, changing water several times as necessary.

INITIAL COOKING

Top of the stove method: Place ham, skin side down, in broiler or kettle sufficiently large for ham to be completely immersed in cold water. Cover. Simmer (do not boil) for 20 to 25 minutes per pound or until meat thermometer inserted near the bone registers 160 degrees. Add hot water as necessary to keep covered. Ham is done when bone at large end leaves meat and when a meat skewer stuck into meaty portion comes out easily. Remove from water and cool slightly before browning.

Oven method: Preheat oven to 375° F. Place ham in large roasting pan. Fill halfway with water. Cover. Cook, turning occasionally and adding water if necessary until meat thermometer inserted at bone in thickest part reaches 160°. Shank bone will be loose.

Alternate oven method: Preheat oven to 170°. Place ham in large roasting pan and add 10 cups of water. Cover. Cook 45 to 50 minutes per pound.

Water in which ham is cooked may be seasoned with wine vinegar and bouquet garnis or apple cider and bouquet garnis to which cloves have been added (1 part vinegar or cider to 4 parts water).

BROWNING OR GLAZING

While still warm, remove skin carefully without tearing the fat. Start at butt end and pull toward hock. Trim excess fat. Score fat, dot with cloves, and cover with brown sugar and cracker or bread crumbs (optional). Bake in 450° F oven, basting frequently with natural juices until browned.

Broadbent B&B Food Products, Route 1, Cadiz, Kentucky 42211. Free catalog.

In the rolling hills of Kentucky's Trigg County, corn-fed hogs are raised, hickory-smoked, and aged to produce a number of pork meat products. Country hams are rubbed with salt, sugar, and other "secret" ingredients, and come short-trimmed; that is, the major section of the shank is removed. Broadbent says that, if thinly sliced, its smallest 7-pound cooked ham (a little over $30 postpaid, depending on destination) will serve 20 to 25 people, and that its uncooked ham can be stored unrefrigerated for up to a year.

Other meats available from Broadbent's hogs are dry-cured, smoked slabs of bacon and sausages. Broadbent's five recipes for sausage produce a smoked pork sausage, a beer sausage, the black knight summer sausage, an all-beef summer sausage, and a summer sausage made of beef and pork. A 1½- to 2-pound roll is about $6 ppd, depending again on destination. The summer sausage is fully cooked and can be kept without refrigeration.

Broadbent also ships Western boneless strip sirloins (six 11-ounce steaks about $34, delivered) and filet mignons (eight 6-ounce filets about $33 delivered). Two weeks until delivery is required on these.

Turkeys, cured with molasses and spices and hickory-smoked, are sold by the whole 10-pound bird; for enthusiasts of white meat, there is a 5-pound smoked turkey breast, about $20, which includes delivery.

The Bruss Company, Golden Trophy Steaks, 3548 North Kostner Avenue, Chicago, Illinois 60641. Free catalog.

The Bruss Company, purveyors of meat to restaurants and clubs, also ships in small quantities to individuals its hen and tom turkeys, U.S. prime beef, and several other items.

For about $35 one can choose six 10-ounce boneless sirloin strip steaks (often referred to as "New York Cut"), six 12-ounce bone-in sirloin strips ("Kansas City Cut"), eight 8-ounce filet mignons, four 16-ounce T-bone steaks, or sixteen 6-ounce top sirloin butt steaks. Roast cuts are the full or center loin and rib eye. Rib roasts can be ordered full, meaning 7 ribs, including backbone and short ribs (about $60 for an 11- to 13-pound roast), or in smaller quantities with 3 or 4 ribs.

Lamb is also part of the Bruss inventory. They have a 5-pound crown roast (about $45), boneless leg of lamb (6 to 8 pounds, $32), and loin chops (sixteen 6-ounce chops for $41).

All of the above can be bought on a 12-month plan or ordered individually. Bruss also carries prepared specialties such as chicken Kiev (twelve 7-ounce servings for around $32) and Rock Cornish hens stuffed with wild rice (nine 10-ounce birds, about $35). Telephone orders are accepted at (800) 621-6638. Illinois residents call collect (312) 282-2900.

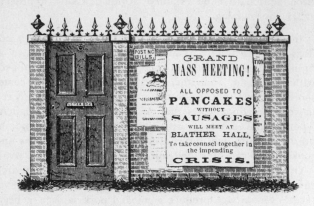

Burgers' Ozark, Country Cured Hams, Inc., Highway 87 South, California, Missouri 65018. Free catalog.

The Burgers cure and smoke hams, bacon, and poultry. Whole turkeys (about $20.00 for a 10-pound bird, plus postage), turkey breast (4 to 5 pounds, about $13.00, delivered), and chicken are sugar-cured and hickory-smoked. The Burgers say the chicken, their newest product, has much the same flavor as the smoked turkey. After smoking, the 2¼-pound birds weigh 1¼ to 1½ pounds and run about $12.00 (delivered), for 4 chickens.

Corn-fed porkers are used for cured and hickory-smoked bacon (in 4- to 10-pound slabs at about $2.00 per pound, plus postage), sausages, and hams. Slabs of bacon and hams are smoked with green hickory wood and sawdust. The Burgers process two country hams; one is aged for four to six months (12- to 20-pound hams, $1.65 per pound, plus postage) and the second for a year (only slightly more per pound). Both hams can be purchased whole or sliced, and in center-cut steaks.

The sausage selection consists of a summer sausage (which needs no refrigeration), an all-beef smoked sausage (about $7.00, delivered, for a 3-pound sausage), and a stick sausage made of mixed meats and spices.

Mel Cordes, Route 1, Box 16, Henning, Minnesota 56551. Prices on request.

Pure-bred Angus beef are fed naturally grown wheat from the pastures of the Cordes ranch. They are sold by quarter or the half and Mr. Cordes will cut according to customer's specifications. Cut and ready for freezing, quarters and halves range from about $1 to $1.70 per pound, depending upon the grade. (Whole live beef—10 percent discount.)

Mr. Cordes also produces large crops of hardspring wheat. He says that his wheat has always been farmed naturally and grown on the same crop-rotated land since his first planting. A minimum of 10 pounds can be ordered; however, he prefers to sell wheat by the 90-pound bag. The Cordes farm also has legume seeds for sprouting which can be sent in any amount. Prices for wheat range from about 9¢ to 12¢ per pound, depending upon quantity.

Early's Honey Stand, R.R. 2, Box 100, Spring Hill, Tennessee 37174. Free catalog.

Erskine Early came to the mail-order business in a roundabout way. A toll road ran past his daddy's house on which travelers paid tolls to the private owners at toll gates located every six miles. (A wagon was charged 15¢, a loaded wagon 25¢, a car was 20¢, horseback riders paid a dime, and pedestrians were free.) The Earlys set up a roadside stand and did a brisk business in home-style, Tennessee hill country foods. They never intended to get into the mail-order business, but people would write to them asking for another ham or such and they obliged.

Erskine Early prides himself on offering smoked meats made in exactly the same manner as his pioneer ancestors. The country sausage is made "just like we did in 1925 and that goes for the hams and bacon too. My old uncle, Charlie Ward who was a half Cherokee was a master at curing meats. His hams were a work of art. We still cure our meats without the use of any of the new fangled dopes, dips or chemicals. No pumping or needling. We use only hickory smoke, sugar, salt, natural spices and honey in our curing process." Whole hams, 12 to 16 pounds, run between $30.00 and $40.00, depending on size and destination.

Early's pure pork sausage (cost about $1.75 per pound, plus shipping), with no cereal or fillers, is available only from November 1 to March 20. Hams and bacon are available year round and come with cooking suggestions and directions for making redeye gravy. Early's will also send a 2-pound bag of green hickory chips ($2.00) so you can give your barbecued meats the same smoked flavor Early gives his (well, almost).

Honey, the original product, is still selling well, and there are other Tennessee specialties such as sorghum and a unique corncob jelly made from red corncobs (five 7½-ounce jars for about $7.00 ppd).

Euro-Veal Farms, Inc., P.O. Box 156, Provimi Road, Watertown, Wisconsin 53094. Free catalog.

Euro-Veal Farms is the mail-order division of Provimi, Inc., a major purveyor of milk-fed veal to fine restaurants throughout the country. Sliced veal, veal chops, ground veal-steaks, veal liver, and diced veal are packaged in reusable Styrofoam containers. About $50 will bring an assortment containing 2 pounds each of veal slices, chops, and either ground veal or liver. Each assortment of veal is packed in dry ice, and safe arrival is guaranteed within the continental United States.

Braised Veal Chops with Gremolata

¼ cup flour
½ teaspoon salt
⅛ teaspoon pepper
4 loin or rib veal chops, ¾ inch thick
2 tablespoons fat
1¼ cups water, tomato juice, or sauterne wine
2 tablespoons flour
3 tablespoons cold water
Salt
Pepper

Combine flour, salt, pepper; coat chops. Sauté chops in fat until well browned. Add liquid, cover, and simmer 45 to 50 minutes or until meat is tender. Remove chops to hot platter; remove pan from heat. Combine flour and cold water to make paste. Add ¼ cup liquid from pan to paste. Stir paste into liquid; return to heat; cook, stirring constantly until gravy bubbles. Add seasoning to taste and pour over chops.

GREMOLATA

Mix 1 clove finely chopped garlic with ¼ cup chopped parsley and grated rind of 1 lemon. Sprinkle over chops.

Greenberg Smoked Turkeys, Inc., P.O. Box 329, Tyler, Texas 75701. Prices on request.

Smoked turkey for the holiday season is Greenberg's specialty. The birds have their wings, neck, and skin removed before smoking and weigh from 6 to 15 pounds after shrinkage due to the smoking. The Greenbergs do not advertise. In mid-October each year, they send a letter to their customers advising them of prices for the coming holiday season. This year the turkeys are running a little over $2 per pound, plus postage. They point out that their mailing list is compiled from actual customers and is not sold or traded.

Harrington's, Richmond, Vermont 05477. Free catalog.

A Harrington pig starts out as a Midwesterner and is corncob-smoked in Vermont (a 16-pound ham, bone in, uncooked, runs about $45.00). Hams come uncooked and cooked, bone in and boneless. Corncob smoking is also used for Harrington's bacon, slab or sliced, pork loins, whole roast or rib chops (4 pounds, about $17.50), and the Canadian bacon (about $9.00 for 1½ pounds). Harrington's country pork sausage is a mixture of lean pork and spices with no fillers (2 pounds, about $7.00). It is not sent out in summer months. Also available are smoked poultry: duck (about $9.50 each), turkey (9 to 11 pounds, about $24.00), and ringneck pheasant (about $13.00 each) which has been praised by food writer Craig Claiborne of *The New York Times* as particularly juicy and delicate in flavor. Another specialty item is the smoked and sugar-cured dried beef (1 pound, $7.00). Harrington's has some thoughtfully assembled gift packages, such as a selection designed for a single person. A New England dinner can be rounded out with Harrington's canned baked beans, Indian pudding, fish chowder, and brown bread. The above prices include Eastern delivery.

ITT Gwaltney, Inc., Smithfield, Virginia 23430. Free price list.

Gwaltney, one of four producers of the genuine Smithfield ham, offers the dry-cured, long-smoked, whole Smithfield. Uncooked, a 12- to 15-pound ham costs about $35.00; cooked, about $40.00 (weighs 10 to 12 pounds); or cooked, boneless, and pressed, weighing 10 to 12 pounds, at $5.50 per pound. For a milder flavor, the company processes the Williamsburg ham, which differs from the former in that the aging and smoking time is shortened and it is a bit cheaper. For example, the whole 11- to 13-pound uncooked Williamsburg is $26.00. This ham is sold in the same forms as the Smithfield, as well as sliced. Bacon is produced in Williamsburg style, and can be ordered by the slab or sliced. (A 3-pound slab is about $7.00.) All prices include postage.

Hickory Valley Farm, Little Kunkletown, Stroudsburg, Pennsylvania 18360. Free catalog.

Hickory Valley Farm specializes in Pennsylvania Dutch–style smoked specialty meats. There are whole hams, cured with sherry and hickory-smoked (10- to 14-pound average,

Fried Ham with Redeye Gravy

Slices no thicker than ⅛ inch are best for frying. Wash, trim off skin, and score fat. Melt 1 tablespoon ham or bacon drippings in heavy skillet until sizzling; lay in ham slices. Serve with redeye gravy made in pan after ham is fried.

REDEYE GRAVY

Add an amount of water or black coffee equal to drippings in the pan. Stir while heating to reduce the volume of liquid and until the gravy turns a rich red.

for about $33.00), slab bacon (about $2.25 per pound for an 8-pound piece), Canadian bacon ($3.50 per pound in 7-pound rolls), and heat-and-serve sausage (4 pounds, under $10.00). There is also a hickory-smoked and champagne-cured turkey. Various gift assortments are offered. Hickory Farms sells a line of farm-style soups such as split pea, lima bean with ham, or lentil soup with chunks of kielbasa, about $1.00 for a 16-ounce can. For a hickory-smoked flavor at home, a 3-pound package of hickory chips can be ordered. All prices include delivery.

Joyner Smithfield Hams, P.O. Box 387, Smithfield, Virginia 23430. Free brochure.

Hams from peanut-fed pigs are dry-cured, pepper-coated, and smoked with hardwood. The Smithfield ham comes both cooked (fatted, baked, and glazed—$3.50 pound), or uncooked ($2.49 per pound)—both with the bone in. Boneless cooked Smithfields come square-shaped at $5.40 per pound or tied natural-shaped at $4.75 per pound. The red-eye country ham is $2.90 per pound, cooked with bone; $2.15 per pound uncooked with bone. Joyner recommends this cut for frying and broiling. Dry-cured Virginia smoked bacon is available by the slab with the rind on for $2.15 per pound.

Kite's Hams, Jim Kite, Jr., Wolftown, Virginia 22748. Prices on request.

Jim Kite was a pitcher for a professional baseball team in Denver until he heeded the unsolicited advice of a less-than-enthusiastic fan. It was a bad day, the team was losing, and an onlooker rose and shouted, "Pray tell, Kite, give us a break. Go out and earn an honest living." Kite did just that. His father had been curing some hams, but wasn't really interested in pursuing the business, so Jim took it over. Every year since, his business has increased.

Kite's hams have taken first place for the last two years under the judgment of the Virginia Association of Meat Packers, and in 1976 his ham won the Grand Champion Prize at the Virginia and North Carolina Meat Association Convention.

Craig Claiborne, in an article describing his favorite foods, mentions that this ham is conceivably the finest produced in America. It's a country ham, sugar-cured. The average ham weighs between 12 and 15 pounds and runs about $2.15 per pound. Mr. Kite, by the way, has never advertised, not even in the Yellow Pages.

Lawrence's Smoke House, Route 30, Newfane, Vermont 05345. Free brochure.

Beef salami and pork products are flavored from the smoke of dry-flint corncobs at Lawrence's Vermont Smoke House. Hams come cooked and uncooked, by the whole or the half, and both can be ordered boneless. Whole hams, averaging 10 pounds, are about $35. The bacon selection consists of country-style regular bacon (a 4½-pound slab

---

Country Ham and Biscuits

Country Ham and Biscuits, a Southern tradition, is a classic and delicious way to serve cured ham for luncheon and hors d'oeuvres. Place several thin slices of cooked ham between halves of small light biscuits and serve piping hot.

BISCUITS

2 cups flour
4 teaspoons baking powder
  Wee pinch of salt (as ham is salty)
½ cup ground ham
2 to 4 tablepsoons shortening
¾ cup milk

Sift flour and baking powder. Mix with salt and ham. Cut in shortening with knife until all has the consistency of meal. Add milk, handling as little as possible. Pat out with hands or roll on floured board. Cut out and place on ungreased baking sheet, 450° oven, 12–15 minutes.

---

about $15) and Canadian bacon (a 2- to 2½-pound piece, about $13). Smoked pork shoulder picnic is also available. (When smoked, this cut is usually boiled rather than baked.)

The Lawrences point out that their grain-fed pork is smoked only with the flavor the cobs produce and that nothing additional is added.

Irving Levitt Company, Inc., 34–36 New Market Square, Boston, Massachusetts 02118. Free catalog.

Irving Levitt claims to sell "the finest meat money can buy." There are filet mignons (twelve 8-ounce filets, $55), rib and loin lamb chops (ten 6-ounce chops $35), crown rib roasts, weighing about 15 pounds (around $65), and smoked pheasants by the brace ($36). Levitt's large, prime sirloin roasts weigh approximately 13 pounds, and a pair of jumbo veal sweetbreads tips the scales at about 5 pounds ($28). To ensure perfect cooking, all the roasts come with an inserted, disposable roasting gauge. Entrées such as 6 pounds of Alaskan king crab, or an 8- to 10 pound venison leg (either for about $50), and prepared items such as a dozen coquilles St. Jacques or 2 dozen clams casino (again, about $50), are offered only to those ordering a meat item as well.

McArthur's Smokehouse, Millerton, New York 12546. Free brochure.

This famous smokehouse has been run by the McArthur family for three generations, and they have earned a handsome reputation for their industry. The old, wood-slated, New England–style building, which until recently housed the curing vats and smokehouse, is now a shop with wooden meat cases and smoky walls, where the meats, together with cheddar, homemade mustard (an 8-ounce canning jar for $2.50), and dried, *whole* green peas ($1.50 per pound) are sold.

McArthur's selection of meats, poultry, and game birds is impressive. There is a smoked crown roast of pork to serve 10, which is accompanied by baking and stuffing suggestions (about $50.00 and weighing around 10 pounds), and a smoked leg of lamb, uncooked with the bone in (about 6½ pounds and under $30.00) or table-ready and boneless (2½ pounds and about $15.00).

The McArthur ham comes in three versions: unbaked, bone in (12-pound ham, about $37.00); fully baked, bone in (10 pounds, about $40.00); and fully baked boneless (about 5 pounds for $25.00). All three are bathed in molasses and brine for seven weeks, soaked for twenty-four hours to remove excess salt, and then smoked for three days over heavy hickory logs.

The McArthurs say that the curing and smoking of their capons and pheasants are designed to maintain the original identity of the bird. The capon, about $20.00, is a meaty bird and weighs about 5½ pounds after smoking. Smoked game hens weigh about 9 ounces ($3.50 per pound), and make an unusual hors d'oeuvre that goes especially well with Scotch and bourbon. Whole turkeys (10 pounds, under $25.00), and turkey breasts (about 5½ pounds and just over $20.00) are cured with molasses and spices before the smoking process.

An item called Canadian Roast is made by tying two Canadian-style bacons or boneless loins together. It is fully baked and costs about $6.00 per pound for a 3- to 5-pound roast. Canadian-style bacon can also be ordered ($5.50 per pound), as well as country-cured bacon, Banger's British-style breakfast sausage, and country sausage—all in the vicinity of $3.50 per pound.

The beef selection includes spiced corned beef brisket ($12.00 for about 4½ pounds) and smoked chipped beef (under $3.00 for a ½-pound package), which is advertised as "not overly endowed with subtlety . . . but it wasn't in the old days either."

Manukian's Basturma & Soujouk Company, 1720 South Orange Avenue, Fresno, California 93702. Free price list.

Manukian's mail-orders several Armenian specialties. Dried beef products include basturma, a dried, salted beef cured with a hot, spiced fenugreek paste (about $4.50 per pound), and soujouk, a spiced Armenian sausage (under $3.50 per pound), and a cooked beef salami (about $2.25).

Crown Roast of Smoked Loin

  3 pounds sauerkraut
  2 cups sauterne
  1 pound sausage meat
 12 ounces pitted prunes
  1 9 to 12 pound crown roast of smoked loin
    Salt and pepper
    Garlic

STUFFING

Wash sauerkraut to remove salt. Simmer 2 hours in own juice, plus sauterne. Add water if necessary. Fry sausage in small, thumbnail-sized pieces, till brown. Cut prunes in ¼-inch pieces. Add sausage and prunes to sauerkraut, after 2 hours of simmering.

Season roast with salt, pepper, and garlic. Place in shallow dish. Fill center of roast with stuffing. **Cover** center and bone tips with foil and roast at 360° F for about 2 hours.

Martin of Smithfield, 2400 Schuster Drive, Cheverly, Maryland 20781. Free brochure.

The Martins' hams from Virginia's peanut-fed hogs are cured, smoked, and processed in the tradition of Smithfield, Virginia, The "Smithfield" ham, the most expensive at a little over $40 for a 9- to 11-pound ham, is hickory-smoked, aged nine months, and cooked in wine sauce. Virginia hams come salt-cured, cooked, and glazed (about $40 for a 9- to 11-pound ham), or sugar-cured, uncooked (under $30 for an 11- to 13-pound one), The Martins also have "Smithfield" slab bacon (4 to 6 pounds, just under $20), Lebanon bologna (3½ pounds, just over $10), and Genoa and Pavone hard salamis (5 pounds for $16 and $17), All prices include mailing charges.

Nodine's Smokehouse, Goshen, Connecticut 06756. Free brochure.

Nitrite-free hardwood- and hickory-smoked bacon is just one of the specialties of this Connecticut smokehouse ($2.50 per pound). Sausage varieties include a spicy link breakfast sausage, kielbasa (both about $2.25 per pound), and even hot dogs ($2.00 a pound), also nitrite free. In addition there are hams ($2.50 per pound) and pheasants, ducks, and capons, smoked roast beef ($5.00 per pound), chipped beef ($5.40 per pound), beef jerky ($10.00 per pound), and smoked Vermont cheddar cheese ($2.90 per pound).

Old Mill Farm, Quakertown, Pennsylvania 18951. Free price list.

The Old Mill Farm is exclusively a mail-order business which keeps former residents of the Pennsylvania Dutch area supplied with one of their favorite foods—scrapple (six 15-ounce cans for $10 ppd). For the uninitiated, scrapple is a spiced pork and cornmeal mash mixture which is served sautéed. Other Pennsylvania Dutch specialties are sold—among them, Lebanon or beer bologna (under $3 per pound). The Old Mill invites inquiries for products not listed on its price sheet.

Omaha Steaks International, 4400 South Ninety-sixth Street, Omaha, Nebraska 68127. Free catalog.

This company is known primarily for its steaks, but it also offers a wide selection of other meats, poultry, and prepared items for dinners and cocktail parties. The selection of choice-cut roasts, steaks, and chops is complete, and most steaks can be ordered in various thicknesses.

Ready-to-bake poultry, such as pheasant (4 for about $40), quail (12 for about $45), and stuffed Cornish game hens (6 for just over $30) are available, as are a number of prepared dishes, among them chicken Wellington, which is breast of chicken coated with pâté (eight 5-ounce portions and two 10-ounce packages of Madeira wine sauce for $32), and chicken Cordon Bleu (breasts stuffed with Canadian bacon and Swiss cheese; ten 6-ounce portions about $35).

Omaha's line of cured and smoked products is made up of country-style ham steaks (six 8-ounce steaks about $20), turkey, chicken (two 2-pound birds about $13), and fully cooked corned beef (just over $20 for 4 to 4½ pounds). All prices include delivery.

In addition to a catalog, Omaha sends out eight mailings a year to mail-order customers, with such specials as a $10 saving on 20 boneless strip sirloins. The company also encourages savings through bulk orders that are sent to one address. For example, there is a discount of $1 per item on an order of 5 to 11 selections, and $3 per item on 12 or more selections. Credit cards are accepted, and telephone orders are taken at (800) 228-9055 and (402) 391-3660, collect (for Nebraska residents).

CONFEDERATE ARMY SOUP AS MADE AT GENERAL PICKETT'S HEAD QUARTERS

One ham bone, one beef bone, one pod red pepper, black-eyed peas. Boil in a mess pot. Splendid on a wet day.

Mrs. Owens' Cook Book, 1882, by Mrs. Frances E. Owens

Ozark Mountain Smoke House Inc., P.O. Box 37, Farmington, Arkansas 72730. Free brochure.

The Sharps' farm and smokehouse is located right behind the family's old stone cabin. They have several stores throughout the South where they sell their smoked poultry and meat products as well as their homemade preserves, relishes, sweets, and Ozark lye soap.

Hams are cured with salt and sugar for a briny flavor and hickory-smoked with a little sassafras. The Sharps say that their hams need no soaking or simmering. They can be ordered uncooked or cooked and boneless, all between $30 and $40, depending on size and style. The poultry selection includes whole turkeys with a choice of sizes, boneless turkey breast, and Rock Cornish cross bird, ready to eat. Dry sugar-cured smoked bacon and Canadian bacon are available in addition to smoked summer sausage, a blend of pork, beef, and spices. Meats are wrapped in a printed muslin calendar bag.

Pfaelzer Brothers, 4501 West District Boulevard, Chicago, Illinois 60632. Free brochure.

This company is mainly a purveyor of meats, poultry, and seafood to restaurants, hotels, and commercial transport, such as planes, trains, and steamship lines, but it also has what it calls a home delivery service which offers an inventory of over 100 items shipped by air.

Steaks, roasts, and other fine-quality cuts of beef, veal, and lamb are sold. Steaks come in varying thicknesses and are trimmed to retain a quarter-inch of marbled fat.

Pork products include spareribs and loin back ribs for barbecuing, hickory-smoked ham, and Canadian bacon.

In addition, Pfaelzer sends what it calls "Specialties." These are items originally introduced for the commercial trade. Some examples: Steak-A-Bobs (sirloin chunks alternated with red and green sweet peppers and Brandywine mushrooms on a stainless-steel skewer (6 pounds, about $40); fondue cubes; dried beef for stew; pepperoni and pizza sausage; and a shish kebob assortment (2 pounds each of pork tenderloin, lamb shoulder, and beef, about $35). Hors d'oeuvres, such as rumaki and French puff pastry in 6 different varieties, can also be ordered, a package of 25 pieces costing under $25.

Stuffed, boneless chicken breasts are prepared a la Kiev,

Cordon Bleu, and a la Piquant (twelve 8-ounce portions, about $37). Other poultry items are turkey, duck, Rock Cornish game hens, and pheasants. Telephone orders are accepted at (800) 621-0226. Illinois residents call (312) 927-7100.

The Prime Shoppe (M. Berenson Company, Inc.), 18–20 Faneuil Hall Market, Boston, Massachusetts 02109. Free brochure.

Prime meats from Boston's Faneuil Hall Market. Tenderloin steaks (plain or wrapped in U.S. prime bacon) and sirloin strip steaks are available in a box selection of 6 each (under $30.00) or in several combination packs. Hams, hickory-smoked and dry-cured by The Prime Shoppe, can also be ordered (14 pounds each and gold-wrapped), about $23.00. Prime will make up boxes of any combination of cuts, including chopped sirloin. Whole sirloins (11 to 15 pounds at $3.50 per pound) and whole tenderloins (6 pounds at $3.50 per pound) are cut to desired proportions.

Rose Packing Company, Inc., R.R. 3, South Barrington Road, Barrington, Illinois 60010. Free brochure.

This company is a large producer of Canadian-style bacon, which doesn't come from Canada and isn't really bacon. (This misnomer refers to smoked pork filets.) The center-cut loins are cured, smoked, and fully cooked. Regular country-style loins are recommended for breakfast or sandwiches, and the deluxe round loins for roasts. Both cost about $15 for a 5-pound piece, which includes delivery. Telephone orders are accepted (800) 323-7363 and (312) 381-5700 (for Illinois residents).

Seltzer's Lebanon Bologna, 230 North College Street, Palmyra, Pennsylvania 17078. Free brochure.

Seltzer's Lebanon bologna, a cured beef sausage with thirteen spices, is made from a highly guarded family recipe. Essential to the production of this Pennsylvania Dutch product is slow hickory smoking. The whole bolognas, some as long as 48 inches, are sold nationally, but the basic mail-order size is the 2-pound ($6.00) or 3-pound ($8.00) sausage chub in a special mailing carton. A 9-pound bologna is $17.50. Prices include postage, and a discount is given on orders of more than one of the same size sausage to the same address.

Signature Prime, 143 South Water Market, Chicago, Illinois 60608. Free catalog.

Throwing a luau? Signature Prime has whole suckling pigs that are great for spit roasting (averaging 21 pounds, about $60). Choice-cut beefsteaks and roasts make up the bulk of the Signature Prime line (various combination packages run about $50), but there are also other meat and poultry selections. A Frenched crown roast of lamb is made from 18 ribs, weighs about 8 pounds, and costs about $70.

Other lamb selections include double loin chops (twelve 8-ounce chops, about $50), and double rib-eye chops (about the same price). Veal comes in boneless rib slices, chops, and veal porterhouse steaks (all in about $50 packages). There is beef brisket, corned kosher style (6 to 8 pounds, about $32), cooked or fresh. Domestic fowl includes whole turkeys (hens or young toms), breasts, Rock Cornish hens, and prepared items such as stuffed chicken legs or breasts Cordon Bleu. Among the wildfowl there are pheasants, squabs, and partridge. Wild game prices are quoted on request. Due to the seasonal character of wild game, both the prices and availability change on a short term basis. Varieties include Canadian brown bear, venison from northern Wisconsin whitetail deer, imported New Zealand wild goat, and South American llama. For telephone orders and special requests call (312) 829-0900 (for Illinois residents) or (800) 621-0397.

The Smithfield Ham & Products Company, Inc., Smithfield, Virginia 23430. Free brochure.

Amber-brand Smithfield ham, cut from peanut-fed porkers, is cured, spiced, smoked with hickory wood, apple and oak, and aged from one to two years. Hams are canvas-wrapped and can be ordered baked (9 to 10 pounds) with or without the bone (7 to 8 pounds). Both run about $40, plus shipping. A milder-flavored ham is the cooked James River brand, which is cured, heavily hickory-smoked and mellowed by a shorter aging period of four to six months (about $33 for a 12- to 14-pound ham, plus shipping). Amber Smithfield bacon slabs come by the whole (about $20 for an 8- to 10-pound slab, plus mailing charges) or the half.

The company packages and mail-orders a number of Amber and James River food products in cans and jars. Deviled ham and sliced cooked ham are among the selection, which also includes Smithfield horseradish sauce, barbecue and meat sauce, and chili sauce with meat, to mention a few.

Smithfield Packing Company, Inc., Smithfield, Virginia 23430. Free brochure.

By statute of the Commonwealth of Virginia, only hams actually processed in the little village of Smithfield can legally be designated "genuine Smithfield Ham." Under the brand name of "Luter," the Smithfield Packing Company offers hams which have been packed in dry salt, covered with pepper, hickory-smoked, and aged for at least twelve months. Bone-in hams, 9 to 12 pounds, are about $3.50 per pound, delivered; boneless, 7 to 11 pounds, are also sold at about $4.70 per pound. Bone-in Jamestown country hams are a milder cure than the Smithfields (10 to 12 pounds, about $3.00 per pound), which are available boneless as well. Both varieties are fully cooked and come with carving and serving suggestions. Dry salt-cured smoked bacon comes packaged in a cloth bag and can be kept indefinitely without refrigeration (3 to 5 pounds and about $2.25 per pound, delivered).

TO CARVE A WHOLE HAM

Cut a wedge-shaped piece from fat side of the ham about 6 inches in from end of the hock.

Start slicing from the ham at an angle of 45 degrees and bring knife to the bone. Cut slices from the bone. As slicing progresses and slices become larger, the angle of the knife should be decreased.

A proper slicing technique is easy to acquire. However, remember to use a very sharp knife for thinnest possible slices.

The Standard Casing Company, Inc., 121 Spring Street, New York, New York 10012. Free catalog.

This company has available many types of casings made from the lining of various parts of beef, hog, and sheep inners. Although Standard Casing does not have its own catalog, it will send along a 10-page publication put out by the International Natural Sausage Casing Association which lists and explains casings for preparing every type of sausage including English Medium—the most common casing and the one used in making fresh Italian sausage. The only purpose of the catalog is to give you an idea of what exists; it does not list prices. Once you know what kind of sausage you want to make, Standard will be happy to recommend the right type of casing and will quote the minimum quantity for purchase along with the total price.

Some excerpts from the catalog:

Beef rounds are used for ring bologna, ring liver sausage, mettwurst, Polish sausage, blood sausage, kishka, and Holsteiner. These casings derive their name from their "ring" or "round" characteristic and are usually considered among the finest on the market because they are liberally measured, accurately calibrated, closely cleaned and fatted, all scored, tender, and waste material is removed.

Beef bungs are used for capacolla, veal sausage, large bologna, Lebanon, and cooked salami. Almost every sausage-maker uses beef bungs caps, among the most popular items in the entire beef casing line.

Beef bladders are used for round mortadella and round, square, and flat minced specialties. The largest casings from cattle, beef bladders are oval and will stuff from 5 to 14 pounds of sausage.

Beef middles are used for Leona-style sausage, all other types of bologna, dry and semidry cervelats, dry and cooked salami, and veal sausage.

Hog casings are used for country-style sausage, linked hog sausage, large frankfurters, kishka, kielbasa, and pepperoni.

Sheep casings, as the name implies, come from lambs and sheep. They are used principally for pork sausage and frankfurters. They are strong, yet extremely tender eating.

Hog bungs: Regular are used chiefly for liver sausage and braunschweiger. *Sewed* are produced in double-walled and single-walled varieties. Both are made by sewing two pieces of the smaller sizes of regular hog bungs to obtain a larger, more uniform, finished product. Being "tailor made," so to speak, sewed hog bungs can be obtained in almost any shape or size. The double-walled type is used almost exclusively for liver sausage, braunschweiger, and Genoa; the single-walled, for Thuringer and hard cervelats.

Hog middles are easily recognizable by their curly appearance, which also distinguishes the products for which they are used. These are: certain types of Italian salami, such as frisses; liver sausage; and braunschweiger. The same care that distinguishes handling of other casing items is exercised in the processing of hog middles.

Hog stomachs are used principally for headcheese, souse, and blood sausage. They are carefully cleaned, gauged, and cured to ensure top quality.

Teel Mountain Farm, Stanardsville, Virginia 22973. Free brochure.

The Pruesses raise their milk-fed baby beef and veal organically and naturally on 350 acres of pastures and wooded country in the Blue Ridge Mountains. Baby beef, the red-meat stage between veal and older, larger beef, are seven to eight months old and weigh 450 to 500 pounds before processing. Both the veal and beef are flash-frozen and come packaged in a 28-pound box with dry ice, cut into family-sized portions, and wrapped in heavy, laminated freezer paper. A baby beef box contains individually wrapped sirloin, porterhouse, T-bone, and rib steaks cut about 1 inch thick; 3- to 4½-pound eye round, sirloin tip, bottom round and chuck roasts; and 1-pound packages of ground beef and stew meat. Baby beef is also sold by the quarter animal in 56-pound packages containing half a hind quarter and half a front quarter.

Veal is sold by the quarter animal in 28-pound packages. Each box is made up of evenly divided cuts from the half, which include veal cutlets, scallopini, roasts, chops, stew meat, and ground veal. A 56-pound taster-sampler combination package made up of half veal and half baby beef and an assortment of all cuts is about $245.

In addition to air shipping throughout the United States, the Teel Mountain Farm refrigerated trucks, which hold the frozen meat near zero degrees, delivers its meats from Illinois to Texas and from Maine to Florida several times a year.

United American Food Processors, Gourmet Fare Division, 15 Spinning Wheel Road, Hinsdale, Illinois 60521. Free catalog.

Item #999 in the catalog is Montie, a grand champion steer purchased by United American and currently residing in Chicago's Lincoln Park Zoo. He may be purchased for $5000 plus delivery. Other meat and gourmet specialties are available and are listed in the catalog.

Fred Usinger, Inc., 1030 North Third Street, Milwaukee, Wisconsin 53203. Free catalog.

Frederick Usinger came to this country in 1880 with a pocketful of sausage recipes which he turned into a million-dollar business. His grandson, also called Frederick, carries on this well-known family-owned enterprise. Usinger's carries close to 100 sausages and luncheon meats which are shipped all over the world and flown directly to restaurants as far away as Honolulu.

Usinger's makes blood sausages, liver sausage, sausages to be cooked, such as Holsteiner and Saucisschen, cervelat or summer sausages, and lunch meats. Bratwurst, a white link sausage made of ground veal and pork, smoked bratwurst, and spiced bratwurst are a few of its many link sausages for cooking or grilling. Ready-to-eat sausages include hard, garlic-flavored German salami; all-pork Genoa salami; smoked beef sausage; country-style, soft garlic salami; and spreads, such as teawurst and smoke-flavored mettwurst. Among the selection of liver sausages and luncheon meats are goose liver–style sausage, a pâté spread called Hessesche Lindleberwurst, a baked meat loaf, yachtwurst, and cooked beef tongue. Headcheese (seasoned diced cuts of pork), heavier smoked, German-style headcheese and smoked pepper beef pastroma are a few more of Usinger's varied list of lunch meats. Close to 100 meat products are featured in the catalog, all running about $2 and $3 per pound. Packing and delivery charges are additional, as is the dry ice used (15¢ per pound).

Weaver's Famous Lebanon Bologna, Inc., P.O. Box 525, Lebanon, Pennsylvania 17042. Free catalog.

The making of the sausage-like food called bologna has been a Pennsylvania Dutch tradition in the Lebanon Valley since the 1800s. Weaver's makes its bologna by curing beef and aging it in wooden barrels. The beef is then coarsely ground, flavored with spices, and forced into casings which are hung to cold-smoke. A 3½-pound sausage costs under $10.00. Dried beef comes by the 4- to 6-pound piece (at about $3.75 per pound) or sliced. Pork products in slabs or slices include wood-smoked bacon and skinless, wood-smoked ham. Various combo packs of meats, cheeses, and pretzels are also available.

5. GAME

ZEBRA steak, anyone? or fillet of rattlesnake? They are available by mail, along with almost every other game meat in the world. For a change of pace, you can order Canadian goose, mallard duck, antelope shoulder chops, or a leg of bear. To take the exotic a step further, why not try an oven-ready peacock or, perhaps, wild boar? For those big occasions, a hippopotamus roast may be just what you are looking for.

While the prices for these items are sometimes high, the quality and uniqueness easily justify the expense. And many items are quite reasonably priced. Ground buffalo steak, for example, can be ordered for as little as $1.50 a pound. Whatever your choice, have fun.

Bison Pete, Box 96, Wheatland, Wyoming 82201.

Pete's buffalo ranch is just outside the town of Wheatland. He is a delightful character and a devoted buffalo entrepreneur. Aside from buffalo meat (his major interest) Bison Pete sells robes ($220.00) made from the animals' fur as well as the skulls ($25.00) and horns ($10.00 a pair). These items are listed at the bottom of his meat brochure with sizes and prices.

Buffalo meat is sold by the half ($1.20 per pound) and the quarter carcass ($1.70 per pound hinds; $1.05 per pound fronts) and in individual cuts. Steaks, roasts, and other cuts can be ordered through the year, but halves and quarters are obtainable only in midwinter when the bison are slaughtered. (Pete says this is when the bison's fur is prime.)

Cuts on hand regularly include tenderloin ($10.00 a pound, come two 8-ounce steaks in a package) and rib steaks ($3.25 per pound), bisonburger ($1.40 per pound), and steamboats, the last coming from the thigh, the same cut as the ham from a pig ($2.25 per pound, average weight 55 pounds).

Special cuts and sizes can be ordered, as long as you let Pete know ahead of slaughter time. He invites visitors: "As always, fusspots are welcome, but you must be punctual." A minimum order is $50.00. Telephone orders are accepted at (307) 322-9497 or messages can be left at (307) 332-9680.

Great Humpedback Buffalo Barbecued in Salt Jacket

10 pounds prime rib roast
12 cups flour
12 cups rock salt
   Pepper
   Garlic, if desired

Mix flour and salt together thoroughly. Add water to this mixture until it makes a firm dough. Rub buffalo with pepper and garlic. Roll dough about 1½ inches thick and mold over roast. Place in 350° F oven 3½ hours for medium rare, about 4½ hours for well done. Break jacket with hammer and remove before serving roast.

Czimer Foods, Inc., Route 1, Box 285, Lockport, Illinois 60441. Free price list.

Game animals and birds are the specialties of Czimer Foods. There are oven-ready Canada geese ($4.95 per pound), peacocks ($6.95 per pound), partridge ($3.50 for a 12-ounce bird), pheasants ($2.69 per pound), wild turkeys ($2.59 per pound), bobwhite quail (a box of a dozen, about $23.00), squabs (a 15-ounce bird about $3.00), and Muscovy ($1.89 per pound) and mallard ducks ($2.69 per pound). Buffalo, venison, bear, moose, elk, antelope, and reindeer come in standard cuts such as rump roasts or chops or ground meat. A moose roast is $2.95 per pound and ground elk is $2.50 per pound. Liver can be chosen from such animals as wild pig or mountain sheep (both $2.25 per pound). Even more unusual taste treats are lion steak ($5.95 per pound) and llama roast ($3.75 per pound). Smoked specialties include ham of reindeer ($4.25 per pound) and mallard ducks ($4.50 per pound). Prepared chicken delicacies include leg meat with almond and apple dressing and boned breast with mushrooms enclosed in pastry crust. Czimer's price list ends with "ask us for the unusual." It's hard to think of anything more unusual than rattlesnake meat, which runs about $7.00 per pound, or beaver steak which is under $2.00 per pound. Shipping and dry-ice packing are additional. Czimer also sells teeth of all varieties (feathers and bear claws, too).

Durham Meat Company, P.O. Box 4230, San Jose, California 95126. Free brochure.

Buffalo, the mainstay of the Plains Indians diet, is once again becoming available. Durham Ranch raises its own buffalo for marketing without hormones or growth stimulants. Buffalo cuts (steaks, $4.25 to $7.50 per pound, roasts, about $3.00 per pound, ground meat, $1.50 per pound) are

> **Wild Duck with Sauerkraut**
>
> ¼ cup bacon fat
> ¼ to ½ cup chopped onion
> 1 unpeeled and diced apple
> 1 quart canned sauerkraut, drained
> 1 wild duck, dressed and split in half
>
> Heat fat in deep, heavy frying pan over low heat. Add onions and simmer until golden. Add apple, stir, and add sauerkraut. When hot, place duck—cavity side down—on sauerkraut. Cover and cook slowly about 1½ hours or until tender. Season to taste. Makes 2 to 3 servings, depending on the size of the duck.

Jugtown Mountain Smokehouse, 77 Park Avenue, Flemington, New Jersey 08822. Free catalog.

Jugtown processes the meats of local Hunterdon County farmers and runs a number of gourmet shops throughout New Jersey. The catalog contains the most-asked-for items carried in the stores, which are numerous in themselves, and mentions that 10,000 specialty food items from all over the world can be shipped, as can over 200 imported cheeses and the Jugtown line of hickory-smoked game, poultry, meats, sausage, and bolognas. Pheasant ($7.50 each, 2 to 3 pounds), capon ($15.50 each, 5 to 6 pounds), and duck ($12.50 each, 3 to 4 pounds), are among the selection of smoked poultry and game. Featured breakfast items are smoked link sausage (2 pounds, $4.50), fresh country sausage meat (2 pounds, $4.00), and Irish (1½ pounds, $5.50) or Canadian bacon (2-pound package, $5.75), as well as beef bacon (2-pound package, $4.50). Other meat specialties are smoked pork chops (2-pound package, $5.75), beef chips, and last but not least, the country ham—about $3.00 per pound.

Madison Farms, Box 902, Camden, South Carolina 29020. Prices upon request.

This is a family operation in the business of distributing quail for local farmers to many Southern restaurants and by UPS or air to individuals. Quail weigh from 4 to 5 ounces each and are individually packaged, 16 birds to a box for about $33 plus handling.

Manchester Farms, P.O. Box 97, Dalzell, South Carolina 29040. Prices on request.

Quail? A brace for dinner, one on toast for breakfast? The birds, averaging 3 to 4 ounces each, are available all year round. They are packed in dry ice in a Styrofoam container, frozen and individually wrapped. Sixteen birds cost a little over $30, 48 birds around $75. Major credit cards are accepted.

Pel-Freez Rabbit Meat, Inc., P.O. Box 68, Rogers, Arkansas 72756. Free price list.

New Zealand white rabbits from the Ozark Mountains of Arkansas and Missouri can be ordered from Pel-Freez. Rab-

similar to beef and can be cooked in much the same way. A minimum order from Durham is 10 pounds. The meat is frozen and shipped packed in dry ice. Air freight is recommended for shipments outside of California. A bull or heifer yearling (live animal) is $500 in September but $560 in April. A mature bull is $1000 to $2000 but a mature cow only $750. Prices FOB the ranch.

Iron Gate Products Company, Inc., 424 West Fifty-fourth Street, New York, New York 10019. Free price list.

An offshoot of and sole distributor for the "21" Club, Iron Gate offers an interesting selection of game in season. The selection ranges from snow grouse ($9.00 each), mallard duck ($4.00 per pound), pheasant ($4.50 per pound), and chukar partridge ($7.00 each) to buffalo (rump roast, $5.50 per pound, prime ribs, $6.50 per pound, or rounds, $4.60 per pound and averaging 35 pounds) and boar (hams, $6.00 per pound, or the whole animal—80 to 120 pounds, at $5.50 per pound). A crock of "21" Club Sauce Maison ($3.25) and "21" Club hard candy ($4.00 for a 1-pound box) are other specialties of the house, as are gourmet treats ranging from filleted mahimahi (a Hawaiian delicacy) to oysters imported from Prince Edward Island.

Jackson Cold Storage & Distributors, Box A, Jackson Hole, Wyoming 83001. Free brochure.

This outfit makes salami and jerky from the meat of the mighty buffalo. They offer Jackson Hole Buffalo Salami, which is moist and heavily spiced; Teton Wilderness Salami, a milder salami with a sage flavor; Pioneer Buffalo Salami, a heavily smoked salami with a mellow blend of spices; and Saloon Salami made with white wine flavoring, cheddar cheese, and spices; and buffalo jerky, the old trail standby, all for about $6.25 for a 1-pound roll, including delivery. A number of gift packs are available containing a combination of the above-mentioned items, together with smoked salmon steaks, smoked trout, and cheeses.

Marinade for Game

UNCOOKED MARINADE FOR GAME

(For 4 to 6 pounds of meat)
2 onions, quartered
2 carrots, sliced
2 stalks celery including leaves, chopped
8 parsley sprigs, chopped
2 bay leaves
½ teaspoon thyme
2 teaspoons salt or to taste
10 peppercorns
6 cloves
2 cups Burgundy or claret wine
½ cup wine vinegar or lemon juice
½ cup oil

Mix all ingredients in a large bowl and let sit for a while, stirring occasionally. Add meat and refrigerate for about 12 hours, turning several times.

COOKED MARINADE

Using the same ingredients and proportions as above, heat oil and add vegetables, stirring until onions begin to turn translucent. Add the remaining ingredients and bring to a boil. Reduce heat immediately and simmer for 30 minutes. Add meat after marinade is thoroughly cooled.

Juniper Berry Sauce for Game

2 tablespoons butter or drippings
2 tablespoons arrowroot
2 cups water
1 tablespoon soy sauce
½ cup Madeira or sherry
2 teaspoons crushed juniper berries
Salt and pepper to taste

Melt butter; stir in arrowroot; gradually add water, soy sauce, wine, and juniper berries. Cook over low heat, stirring constantly until smooth and slightly thickened. Add salt and pepper to taste.

Roast Leg of Venison

1 (4-pound) leg of venison
6 thin slices of salt pork
2 cups of port wine
10 peppercorns
2 bay leaves
2 carrots, sliced
2 onions, peeled and sliced
½ teaspoon dried thyme
Salt
¼ cup light cream

TO MARINATE

Cut 6 slashes in meat and insert slices of salt pork. Mix wine, vegetables, and seasonings in a deep pot. Add roast and refrigerate for 2 days, turning meat several times a day.

TO COOK

Remove meat and vegetables from marinade. Dry and let stand (covered) until room temperature. (Leave marinade in pot and set aside.) Preheat oven to 300° F. Place meat and vegetables in open pan and roast for 1 hour. Raise temperature to 450° F and roast for 15 minutes longer. Remove roast to hot platter.

SAUCE

Strain pan juices into marinade. Skim fat. Simmer until liquid is reduced to ¾ cup. Remove from heat. Add cream, stirring constantly, and season to taste. Reheat cream, taking care not to boil.

Serves 4.

bit meat is all white meat and extremely low in cholesterol and calories. The rabbits, which are sometimes available in supermarkets, come whole or cut up. Four rabbits (9 pounds, $32) or six rabbits (16 pounds, $43) come in individual, frozen, vacuum-sealed packages. Each order is accompanied by a recipe booklet and Pel-Freez guarantees that every shipment will arrive frozen, even in the hottest weather. Pel-Freez will ship out of the continental United States at additional charges. Ask for specific details. Credit cards are accepted; price includes delivery.

Prairie Pride Farms, Box 517, Grand Island, Nebraska 68801. Prices on request.

Prairie Pride Farms is a family operation in the business of raising and selling quail. An average 4- to 5-ounce quail is about $1.30. The best time to buy is from November through March, when the largest selection of sizes is on hand. Each quail is individually packed, accompanied by recipes, and shipped air freight, collect.

Zeldner's Wild Game Center, 638 Clinton Street, Buffalo, New York 14210. Free catalog.

Moose roast instead of McDonald's? Wild boar for your next barbecue? For those whose tastes run to the exotic, Zeldner's offers a wide range of unusual meats and poultry. Game birds include pheasant (smoked or fresh, $3.75 per pound), mallard duck ($7.50 each), partridge, woodcock, quail ($1.80 each), wild turkey ($3.39 per pound), squab, guinea hen, and Canadian geese. All come oven or pan ready, and the wild turkey is also available in feather. Large game such as venison (steaks, $3.95 per pound), elk ($5.49 per pound), bear, reindeer ($5.49 per pound), buffalo (steaks and roasts, $3.49 per pound), moose, and antelope can be had in hindquarters, forequarters, or butchered to cuts such as rib steaks, rump roasts, and ground meat. Many items are available smoked, such as whale steaks and mallard ducks. Several varieties of rabbits and hares, both domestic and imported, are sold, as well as small game animals such as beaver, raccoon ($2.89 and up), and native Southern possum ($2.89 and up).

If this isn't enough for the jaded appetite, other possibilities are alligator steaks and elephant roasts. Seafood when available includes seal flippers and sea turtle. On a high cholesterol diet? Zeldner's sells bear fat. All game meats and game birds are offered for sale in accordance with Federal and New York State laws and regulations.

For additional sources, see:
Chapter 4. Meat and Poultry:
    McArthur's Smokehouse
    Signature Prime

6. FISH AND SEAFOOD

LANDLOCKED? Pining away for pickerel? Here are sources that guarantee fresh orders of fish and seafood delivered to your door wherever you live. The range is great—from regional specialties seldom marketed outside local areas to retail fish markets, commercial fisheries, and wholesalers who handle domestic varieties as well as imports from many countries. There are bluepoint oysters from Chesapeake Bay, prized for eating raw on the half shell; crayfish meat from the Louisiana bayous; and the revered dungeness crab of San Francisco's famous Fisherman's Wharf. Many fine shops famous for caviar will scoop your order directly from large refrigerated tubs containing pounds and pounds of little black gems. A pot of live Maine lobsters, tiny bay scallops, or a bushel of long-necked steamers can be air-shipped directly from New England.

If freshly shucked shellfish strike your fancy, they are available. Gallon tubs of juicy chopped clams (great for white sauce over pasta, clam cakes, or chowder); and shucked oysters (often used by professional cooks for such delicious dishes as oysters Rockefeller, oysters casino, oyster fritters, or just for enjoying in their natural state). While these items are especially prepared for the restaurant trade, several companies included here offer 5- and 8-pound containers of shucked oysters and clams among many other special items at very reasonable prices.

Cured fish comes smoked, dried, salted, pickled, and marinated. There are herring marinated in wine and cream, dried salt cod, and smoked whitefish and brook trout. A choice of smoked salmon ranges from the most expensive, gently cured, pale-pink Atlantic varieties from Nova Scotia, Scotland, and Ireland to the less expensive, more kippered or hot-smoked Pacific salmon. Freshly caught ling cod and abalone from the Pacific, red snapper and pompano from the Gulf, and flounder, bluefish, and shad from the Atlantic are among many varieties of fish that can be ordered from the teeming metropolitan markets of Boston, New York, and Seattle, as well as seaports such as Nantucket, Baltimore, and New Orleans.

Fish and shellfish are shipped either fresh and well-iced or flash-frozen with dry ice. Don't balk at the frozen products. Flash freezing is done by commercial fisheries shortly after the catch. This process is so effective that products are solidly frozen within twelve minutes, leaving no time for deterioration. These frozen products bear little resemblance to the frozen fish and shellfish common to the supermarket.

From shrimp to swordfish. Whatever your pleasure, you will find the great variety of fish and shellfish included here a real treat.

N. Alioto's Pacific Fair Restaurants, Fisherman's Wharf, 155 Jefferson Street, San Francisco, California 94133. Prices on request.

Adding to the charm of San Francisco's wharf is Alioto's wooden sidewalk stand heaped with steaming dungeness crab and sourdough bread, both of which Frank Alioto will air-ship anywhere in the country. Crab, averaging about 2½ pounds each, are available from the second Tuesday of November until the end of July. A minimum order of 6 is required for shipment. Six crabs ($32) and 6 loaves of bread ($7) can be ordered by telephone (415) 776-7300. Air freight is additional.

Battistella's Sea Food, Inc., 910 Touro Street, New Orleans, Louisiana 70116. Free brochure.

Battistella's is a large New Orleans fish house with an extensive selection of seafood. It sends a surprising variety of fresh local products, as well as other domestic and imported fish and shellfish.

Local Gulf species that can be ordered year round include speckled trout from Mexico (fillets, $2.25 per pound), pompano (fillets, $5.50 per pound; whole, $3.25 per pound), and shark (95¢ per pound), all of which are seldom found in most markets. Pompano is considered by some to be one of the finest fish caught in domestic water. It is shipped North to some expensive restaurants, but for the most part pompano is consumed locally. Shark meat is also difficult to obtain, even from wholesale markets of major cities, since so much shark is punched out with cookie cutters and sold as sea scallops or shredded and used in place of crabmeat in many restaurants. It's a tasty fish, with a firm white flesh, and makes for delicious and rich eating.

Fresh local shellfish include crayfish meat, shrimp (from $3.50 to $6.50 per pound), and oysters. Oysters can be bought in the shell, packed 100 or 200 to the box. or shucked in 1-gallon tubs with their natural juice ($18.00). The latter are terrific, not just for cooked appetizers and entrées, but for eating on the half shell (assuming empty shells are on hand).

Palombo alla Teglia (*Shark Fillets with Anchovies*)

1 medium onion finely chopped
1 to 2 cloves minced garlic
½ cup olive oil
6 anchovy fillets (washed, dried, and mashed)
½ cup dry white wine
3 tablespoons chopped parsley
4 medium fillets or 6 small fillets
Flour
Salt and pepper

SAUCE

Sauté onions and garlic in 2 tablespoons oil until golden brown. Add anchovies, wine, and parsley, and cook over medium heat until wine has evaporated. Turn off heat.

FILLETS

Dredge fillets in seasoned flour and sauté in left-over oil over very high heat for several minutes on each side. Remove to platter and top with sauce.

Note: Shark meat is similar in taste to swordfish and can be substituted for swordfish in recipes.

Briggs-Way Company, Ugashik, Alaska 99683. Free price list.

In a remote Alaskan village, the Briggs family has for fifteen years been putting up freshly caught Alaskan salmon in glass canning jars. The jarred salmon (king, sockeye, medium red, and red) has received rave reviews from many sources including *The Whole Earth Catalog*. The fish is skinned, boned, filleted, and hand-packed within hours of being caught and is said to bear little resemblance to tinned salmon. It is available salted or unsalted, packed in 5-ounce jars, 12 to the case (about $18). A newer product of the Briggs-Way Company is smoked salmon caviar spread, a salt-preserved, lightly smoked and seasoned pasteurized product made from salmon roe. The spread comes in 2½-ounce jars, 4 (about $10) or 6 (about $15) to the case. Prices include postage and insurance.

Burdines, P.O. Box 2350, Miami, Florida 33101. Free catalog.

Florida seafood specialties from the Atlantic and Caribbean waters are shipped by Burdines packed in dry ice in a reusable cooler. Stone crab claws, a unique Florida specialty, come precooked and can be enjoyed hot or cold (10 pounds, about $57.00). Fresh Florida lobster ($40.00 for 4 lobsters) comes ready to heat and serve and, if desired, stuffed with crabmeat dressing ($3.00 additional). Rock shrimp (26 to 30 to the pound) a rare deepwater seafood, can also be ordered (6 pounds about $45.00). Burdines offers complete seafood dinners with a choice of appetizers such as blue crab claws or shrimp ring with cocktail sauce, entrée of lobsters, stone crab claws, rock shrimp, or red snapper, and a tangy key lime pie for dessert. Dinners for 6 run between $40.00 and $50.00. Prompt and perfect delivery is guaranteed and all prices include delivery east of the Mississippi; $2.50 per pack additional for other states. (Of course, Burdines is duly famous for its citrus fruits, avocados, and coconuts, which are also listed in the catalog.)

Caviarteria, Inc., 870 Madison Avenue, New York, New York 10021. Free price list.

Beluga to go! "Would you send three pounds of fresh beluga to Laredo (or Los Angeles, Philadelphia, my New York hotel)?" So go the calls to Caviarteria. The owners import directly and sell to stores at the same prices they say they charge their retail customers. Thus their caviar, ice-packed and air-shipped anywhere in the United States, is not only fresh, but low in price. Low in price for caviar, that is. The fresh caviars offered include the king of caviars, Malossol beluga, large, shiny, gray pearls, from both Russia and Iran; medium-grain Iranian Sevruga; broken-grain Russian Kamchatka; golden-grain Iranian; fresh red salmon caviar, huge, unctuous orange-red beads not at all like the more familiar red-processed roes; and pressed Iranian, broken eggs of a jamlike consistency, a favorite of many caviar devotees for its intense flavor.

All fresh caviars will retain their flavor for about one month if properly refrigerated. Vacuum-packed caviars will keep longer, but all preserved caviars are saltier than the fresh. Varieties of preserved caviars offered are Russian Kamchatka, Iranian Sevruga, and Iranian and Russian beluga.

Caviarteria offers several gift plans. The "El Magnifico" at $500 is a gourmet's extravaganza with monthly arrivals of caviar, smoked salmon, pâtés, cheeses, and other delicacies. More modest plans are also available.

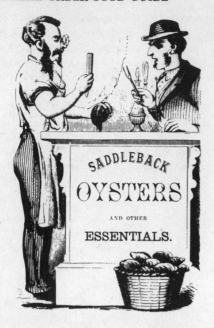

SADDLEBACK OYSTERS AND OTHER ESSENTIALS.

Cotuit Oyster Company, P.O. Box 563, Little River Road, Cotuit, Massachusetts 02635. Prices on request.

"Cross country oysters" are the specialty of the Cotuit Company. Harvested to order from the waters of Cape Cod, the oysters are shipped fresh in their shells anywhere in the continental United States. They come in packages of 60 or 120 oysters, with the larger order running about $28, plus UPS charges. Recipes, storage hints, and opening instructions are included. A professional oyster knife can be ordered to help in opening the little fellows.

Don's Seafood and Steak House, 301 East Vermilion Street, Lafayette, Louisiana 70501. Free price list.

Until recently, Don's shipped its Louisiana seafood specialties all over the world. Unfortunately, due to local express carriers' inability to guarantee undamaged delivery, the Steak House was forced to discontinue this service. However, the frozen products are still being mail-ordered, providing that shipping arrangements are made by the customer. Many are using air-freight delivery and seem quite satisfied, according to Don's general manager. Currently available are 15-ounce frozen packages of shrimp and okra gumbo ($3.25), seafood gumbo ($3.25), crayfish bisque ($3.95), and crayfish etougee ($7.95). Case prices are also offered.

Embassy Seafoods, Inc., P.O. Box 268, 3 Cottage Park Road, Winthrop, Massachusetts 02152. Free brochure.

Embassy's salted and smoked fresh fish come from the North Atlantic fishing boats that moor in Gloucester harbor. Mackerel and cod, both common in these cold, Northern waters, are cured by Embassy in brine and pure white table salt. Twelve salt mackerel fillets, each weighing al-

most a pound, come in a reusable wooden bucket (12-pound bucket, $24). Salt codfish can be ordered in a 5-($15) or 10-pound pail or a 2-pound box. Embassy cures another plentiful North Atlantic fish, the herring. It is smoked instead of salted and is sold by the 2-pound box.

Embassy Seafoods' tinned seafood items are lobster meat (three 5-ounce cans about $17), king crab, steamed clams in the shell (about $3 a dozen), salmon, and shad roe (three 7½-ounce cans around $18). Also, fish and shellfish are combined with foods, wine, and spices in a line of seafood dips and spreads. The lobster dip, for instance, is a mixture of lobster meat, lobster butter, cream cheese, sherry, and other ingredients (about $1 per 6-ounce tin), while the salmon spread is a combination of smoked salmon and aged cheddar cheese (three 2½-ounce cans for just over $2). All prices include postage.

Stephen Faller Ltd., Industrial Estate, Mervue, Galway, Ireland. Free price list.

Stephen Faller, purveyor of Irish smoked salmon, will airmail full sides of salmon weighing between 2 and 2¾ pounds. A side of the Galway Bay smoked red salmon runs about $25, including delivery charges.

Feby's Fishery, 1111 New Road, Elsmere, Delaware 19805. Prices on request.

Maryland blue crabs are the specialty of this Atlantic Coast fishery. Available by the dozen, the crabs are priced by size. Jumbo blues run between $10 and $16 a dozen, smaller number 1 crabs are about $7, and still smaller number 2s average $5 for 12. Shucked oysters come by the pint with prices again varying by size.

Gourmet Appetizers, Inc., 203 East Houston Street, New York, New York 10002. Prices on request.

Fresh caviar and cured fish are the specialties of Gourmet Appetizers. In fifty years of operating this colorful little shop in the heart of Manhattan's Lower East Side, owner Joe Haber has created a thriving business attracting customers from Houston Street uptown to RCA, south to Miami and west to the Palm Springs Raquet Club and the Beverly Hills Hotel. What is everyone ordering? Caviar—beluga (giant grain, $90.00, 14 ounces), Sevruga (small grain, $60.00, 14 ounces), and cod roe caviar paste ($1.00 a tube). Other popular specialties are smoked brook trout ($4.50 a pound) and whitefish ($4.00 a pound); pickled herring in wine (75¢ for an extra-large fillet), cream, or clear sauce; and salmon—pickled lox ($10.00 a pound), kippered salmon ($6.00 a pound), and belly lox ($10.00 per pound) or Nova Scotia ($7.95 per pound for western, $12.00 per pound eastern Gaspé).

Hegg & Hegg Smoked Salmon, Inc., 801 Marine Drive, Port Angeles, Washington 98362. Free brochure.

Hegg & Hegg offers a unique service to those lucky enough to catch a salmon in Washington. They can have their fish smoked or canned by the company, a small wooden spoon being inserted in the fish's mouth to identify it during the process. For others, less effort is required to order a whole (4 pounds, about $15) or half (about $9) alder-smoked Puget Sound salmon. Prices include delivery.

Other specialties from the Pacific Northwest sold by Hegg & Hegg include red sockeye salmon—smoked or regular—dungeness crab meat, white albacore tuna, smoked butter clams, smoked sturgeon, smoked Pacific oysters, and north Pacific shrimp meat. These come in assorted gift packages or by the individual case of 6 or 12 tins (six 7½-ounce tins of red sockeye, about $10; of dungeness crab, 6½-ounce cans, about $25; of smoked sturgeon, 6½-ounce cans, $10). Delivery is guaranteed within the United States on all gift packs, cased goods, and smoked salmon.

The House of Kilfenora, East Kingston, New Hampshire 03827. Free catalog.

Peter Kiely, an expatriate Dubliner, was so bombarded with requests from his friends to bring back smoked salmon from his frequent trips to Ireland that he decided to make it a business. The 2¼- to 2½-pound sides of salmon are flown in fresh from the Republic of Ireland and air-shipped directly to the customer at about $30 per side. Those who are familiar with Irish smoked salmon recognize it as being distinctly different from Scotch salmon. Irish is described as having a stronger, more robust flavor than the Scotch, which is referred to as either more "bland" or "subtle," depending on whether one prefers it or not. Both Irish and Scotch salmon are dry-cured, while other salmons or lox may be cured by marination. This is one of the reasons why the dry-smoked is more expensive: it loses weight by dehydration rather than gaining it by marination. The Kielys are purveyors to the restaurant trade as well as a mail-order concern, so they have fresh supplies of salmon on hand at all times.

Island Seafoods, Steamboat Wharf, P.O. Box 178, Nantucket, Massachusetts 02554. Prices on request.

The Gliddens, owners of Island Seafoods for four generations, are wholesalers of specialty seafood items located on Nantucket's famous wharf. They have bay ($5.00 per

Clam Cakes

    1 cup minced clams with juice
    ⅔ cup whole wheat pastry flour
    1 small green onion chopped fine
    ½ cup cottage cheese
    ½ teaspoon salt
    1 tablespoon oil
    2 eggs
    ¼ cup yogurt

Stir all of the above ingredients in a bowl until completely mixed. (Add more flour if batter is too thin.) Pour dollar-sized patties on a griddle as you would regular pancakes and cook on each side until light brown. Serve as a finger food—hot or cold with a spoonful of yogurt on top of each cake. Makes about 36 dollar-sized cakes.

pound) and sea scallops ($3.50 per pound) and swordfish ($4.00 per pound), all flash-frozen and packed in 5- and 10-pound containers. Clams are also available by the peck. Cherrystones come 150 to the peck ($10.00), and littlenecks about 250 to the peck ($20.00). Occasionally, bluefish, flounder, and cod can be ordered; you will have to inquire.

Anton Josephson Company, P.O. Box 412, Astoria, Oregon 97103. Free price list. Color catalog with recipes $1 credited to first order.

Smoked and pickled salmon made from locally caught fish (four 9-ounce jars, just over $15) are the specialties of the Josephson Company. The Scandinavian-style smoked salmon is available in 3 types: moist, medium, and dry, in 2- to 10-pound pieces. Moist, medium, and dry refer to the combined amount of oil and water in the salmon. The moist and medium come from Chinook salmon, the dry from chum salmon. It takes 3 pounds of fresh salmon to produce 1 pound of smoked salmon. Although the salt content is about the same in each of the types, the drier type generally tastes saltier. Smoked salmon Scandinavian-style refers to the process of salt curing and dry smoking. The drier the salmon, the longer the smoking. No artificial coloring or flavoring is used in any of the Josephson products. Ten pounds of salmon cost about $50; 3 pounds, about $20. Salmon are shipped by regular mail in winter and by air in summer months (additional $2 charge).

Smoked Salmon and Potato Kugel

4 tablespoons butter
2 onions, chopped
5 potatoes, peeled and sliced
  Pepper
6 slices smoked salmon
2 eggs
1 teaspoon salt
1 cup light cream
½ cup milk

Melt the butter in a skillet. Sauté the onions in it for 10 minutes, stirring frequently. Preheat oven to 325° F. Slice the potatoes as thin as possible. In a buttered casserole, arrange successive layers of potatoes, sprinkled with pepper, and the smoked salmon and sautéed onions. Start and end with the potatoes. Beat the eggs, salt, cream, and milk together. Pour over the potatoes. Bake for 50 minutes, or until set and lightly browned on top. Serve as a luncheon or supper dish.

Larkin's Seafood, 110 North Eutaw Street, Baltimore, Maryland 21201. Free brochure.

Captain Jack Larkin owns one of Baltimore's well-known seafood restaurants and is also a major packer, importer, wholesaler, and distributor of fish and shellfish, many varieties of which come from local Chesapeake waters. All fish and shellfish available by mail order are the same as are sold to the restaurant trade and come in institutional packaging. For example, marinated herring in wine or cream sauce is sold by the gallon tub (about $13.00), chopped clams by the ½ gallon (weighs about 4 pounds and cost is about $1.65 per pound), various-sized shad roe by the set (around $4.00 per pound), and crabmeat by the pound carton. In general, a great variety of imported and domestic shellfish is available, such as hotel prime soft crabs, local bay scallops ($3.25 per pound), backfin crabmeat, crab cakes (just over $5.00 a dozen), and a choice of lobster tails from either warm or cold water (approximately $7.50 per pound). The latter commands a higher price.

Chesapeake Bay is, of course, famous for its bluepoint oysters, and Larkin's oysters can be bought shucked by the gallon in 4 grades, machine- or hand-breaded by the dozen, or in the shell in boxes of 100.

The fish selection is also worthy of note. Larkin's has fancy steelhead salmon (a 12- to 15-pound fish at about $2.85 per pound), and rainbow trout gutted or boned, as well as local fresh bay rock and shad (dressed in a 5-pound box at about $2.60 per pound) and flash-frozen varieties of fillet with or without the skin, breaded or in squares.

Other Larkin's specialty items are New England and Manhattan clam chowder (about $11.00) and clam juice packed in 50-ounce containers and sold in case lots of a dozen.

Legal Seafoods Market, 237 Hampshire Street, Cambridge, Massachusetts 02139. Prices on request.

This is a very busy market. Perhaps the boom is due to Julia Child, a faithful patron. Legal Seafoods does not have a brochure or list; however, the market does air-ship fish and shellfish. Live lobsters are available on a daily basis ($5.29 to $5.49 per pound, depending on size); although Legal has a great selection of seafood, the availability of items other than lobster cannot be guaranteed. If you are interested in a particular fish or shellfish and it is in season, Legal probably has it. Arrangements at the arrival end of air shipment must be made by the buyer.

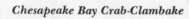

Chesapeake Bay Crab-Clambake

50 live, hard-shell blue crabs
25 dozen soft-shell clams
50 small onions (2 ounces each)
50 small potatoes (2 ounces each)
25 ears of corn
 6 lemons cut in wedges
 4 to 4½ pounds butter or margarine, melted

Wash clamshells thoroughly.

Peel onions. Wash potatoes. Husk corn, remove silk, and break corn in half.

Cut pieces of cheesecloth and heavy-duty aluminum foil, 18 inches by 24 inches each, making 2 of each for each serving.

For each serving, place 2 pieces of cheesecloth on top of 2 pieces of foil. Place 2 crabs, 1 dozen clams, 2 onions, 2 potatoes, and 2 pieces of corn on cheesecloth.

Tie opposite corners of cheesecloth together. Pour 1 cup of water over package. Bring foil up over food and close edges with tight double folds.

Place packages on grills about 4 inches from hot coals. Cover with aluminum foil.

Cook 45 to 60 minutes or until onions and potatoes are cooked.

Serve with lemon wedges and melted butter or margarine. Serves 25.

DELECTABLES OF THE LOBSTER

The "tomalley" or liver of the lobster which turns green when cooked is highly seasoned and delicious and considered by many persons to be the best eating of all. Also worth saving is the red or coral, the undeveloped spawn of the female lobster. It makes a fine sauce.

Long Island Oyster Farms, P.O. Box AD, Greenport, New York 11944. Free price list.

Long Island Oyster Farms, a well-known name in the New York area, is a major supplier of farm-bred oysters to purveyors, restaurants, and retail fish markets and also ships boxes containing from 100 ($9.50) to 250 ($19.50) oysters to individuals via UPS (charges additional). Unfortunately, the Farms shipping radius extends only as far west as Illinois and as far south as Georgia.

Long Island oysters have a tangy flavor and a higher salt content than most; and because of the preservative qualities of salt, these oysters will keep up to two weeks refrigerated between 35 and 40° F.

Murray's Sturgeon Shop, 2429 Broadway, New York, New York 10024. Free price list.

Schmaltz herring in Peoria! Bialys in Biloxi! Thanks to Murray's Sturgeon Shop the entire country can enjoy "appetizing" delights long relished by New Yorkers. Lox and bagels (15¢ each), kippered salmon ($2.19 per ¼ pound), homemade pickled herring fillets (99¢ each) or pickled salmon ($2.49 per ¼ pound) in cream or clear sauce, smoked sable ($1.59 per ¼ pound), whitefish ($5.59 per pound for a large fish)—all can be shipped Tuesdays through Fridays via express mail or air freight, packed in ice with delivery guaranteed the following day throughout most of the United States. Of course there is also sturgeon, genuine lake sturgeon, at $4.50 for ¼ pound, and for lox one can choose from Nova Gaspé ($16.00 per pound) or the salty-type belly lox at $11.55 per pound. Murray's also sells a complete line of domestic and imported canned fish and caviar, fresh and vacuum packed. Buy your cream cheese and get ready.

Pure Food Fish Market, 1511 Pike Place, Seattle, Washington 98101. Prices and orders by phone only.

Pure Food Fish Market ships any type of seafood anywhere in the world. During the summer of 1976, for example, it air-shipped 100 pounds of Pacific salmon to a customer in Texas for an old-fashioned cookout. Whole king salmon (about 3.00 per pound), dungeness crab (just over $1.00 per pound), and whole tuna (around $1.29 per pound), are among a fine selection of fresh seafood available from this market. Just call and ask for Sol Amon. He will tell you what is in season and quote prices. Orders are air-shipped with dry ice the same day they are taken. Telephone orders are accepted at (206) 622-5765.

Ritchie Bros., 37 Watergate, Rothesay, Isle-of-Bute, PA20 9AD, Scotland. Prices on request.

Smoked salmon from the pure rivers of the Scottish Highlands. This firm, situated on the River Clyde on the west coast of Scotland, has been in the business of smoking Scottish salmon for the past fifteen years. It uses the "authentic bland cure," smoking the fish over oak shavings,

---

Salmon Seattle Style with Mustard Dill Sauce

    4 center-cut salmon chunks (2 pounds each)
    ¾ cup salt
    ¾ cup sugar
    ¼ cup crushed peppercorns
    2 bunches fresh dill

Cut salmon chunks in half lengthwise and remove back and rib bones. Combine and mix salt, sugar, and peppercorns. Prepare one chunk (2 halves) of fish at a time. Rub about 3 tablespoons of spice mixture into 1 piece of fish. Place, skin side down, in 8- or 9-inch-square glass, enamel, or stainless-steel container 2 inches deep. Top fish with ¼ bunch of dill. Repeat process with second half of fish, placing skin side up on first half. Cover with double thickness of heavy-duty foil. Place a plate on top of fish and put a weight on top of the plate. Refrigerate 48 hours, turning fish every 12 hours, separating halves slightly and basting with accumulated liquid in dish. Serves 25.

MUSTARD DILL SAUCE

    1 cup Dijon-style mustard
    ¾ cup sugar
    ½ cup vinegar
    1 tablespoon powdered dry mustard
    1⅓ cups salad oil
    ¾ cup chopped fresh dill

Beat all ingredients together except oil and dill. Add oil slowly, beating constantly, until a thick emulsion is formed. Fold in dill; cover and chill.

which it is believed brings out the natural flavor of the salmon. Smoked 2-pound sides of salmon are available for dispatch by insured airmail to most countries of the world direct from the Ritchie Bros.' salmon kilns for about $26.

Russ & Daughters, 179 East Houston Street, New York, New York 10002. Prices on request.

Predating the modern feminist movement by more than half a century, Mr. Russ, noting that daughters are just as important as sons, named his establishment "Russ & Daughters." Located on Manhattan's Lower East Side, Russ & Daughters also provides some of New York's famed "appetizing." Prices are available upon request for such specialties as schmaltz and matjes herrings (between $1.25 and $2.00 each), smoked whitefish ($4.99 per pound for a large fish), salmon trout (89¢ per ¼ pound), brook trout ($4.99 per pound), butterfish ($4.99 per pound—extra-large fish), sable ($3.59 per pound), pickled salmon ($2.19 per ¼ pound), either plain or with cream sauce), chopping herring ($2.29 per pound, lake sturgeon ($3.50 per ¼ pound), and real Gaspé peninsula Nova Scotia salmon ($2.99 per ¼ pound). Russ also sells reasonably priced fresh and pasteurized sturgeon caviar and fresh and jarred salmon caviar.

Dried strings of imported mushrooms, so pungent that just two or three will flavor a whole pot of soup, and a complete line of dried fruits—Blenheim apricots, pears, peaches, apples, cherries, and figs (Turkish, and Greek when available)—can also be ordered. Call (212) GR 5-4880 any day but Tuesday, or write for prices and shipping arrangements. Russ claims that its "prices are the lowest in the country but the quality is the best."

Sabella's of Marin in Tiburon, 9 Main Street, Tiburon, California 94920. Prices on request.

Sabella's seafood restaurant and fish market are located on the shore of San Francisco Bay in Tiburon. It will send almost all varieties of West Coast fish and shellfish, as well as live Maine lobsters and Eastern cherrystone clams.

The famous West Coast abalone can be ordered all year in frozen 5-pound blocks between $7.00 and $9.00. Pacific oysters come shucked in quarts or gallon containers. These oysters, plump and distinctive in taste, are often preferred for such cooked dishes as brochette, creamed oysters, and fritters.

Pacific hard-shell clams come in packs of mixed sizes, from small to large, and are best steamed (9¢ to 85¢ per pound, depending on the kind). Special quality Monterey squid are cleaned and available by the 5-pound box ($1.59 per pound), and West Coast whole fish, such as ling cod, kingfish, and whitefish, are sent fresh in iced containers. Sabella's has plentiful supplies of fresh Pacific salmon (from $3.50 to $4.50 per pound), especially during season from May through November. Telephone orders are accepted. Telephone (415) 435-2814.

Saltwater Farm, York Harbor, Maine 03911. Free catalog.

Maine lobsters and New England steamers have been the business of Saltwater Farm for twenty-seven years. Live lobsters can be bought in three sizes from 1⅛-pound regulars to 1½-pound selects all year; limited supplies of jumbo lobsters (2¾ pounds) are usually available in late spring through early summer. Prices depend upon the number of lobsters ordered and the size. For example, a half-dozen regulars are under $40.00, while a dozen run about $70.00. If jumbos were chosen instead, they would be about $80.00 and somewhat over $150.00. Tails from 1¼-pound or larger lobsters can be had flash-frozen, 12 for $35.50 or 20 for $55.50. Soft-shell, long-necked New England steamers are shipped in minimum orders of half a peck (serving 8) for about $5.50.

Saltwater Farm's Southern shellfish varieties are fresh Florida lobster (about $45.00 for 4), cooked stone crab claws (10 pounds about $60.00), the lobster-flavored rock shrimp (8 pounds just over $55.00), and crabmeat-stuffed red snapper (4 pounds for $40.00), which will serve 6 to 8.

There is also an extensive line of Saltwater Farm's own brand tinned fish and shellfish meats, dips, chowders, and sauces. Smoky fish dip, sherried tuna spread, lobster morsels, lobster sauce, and clam and fish chowders are among the selections. Complete full-course dinners are also described in the catalog.

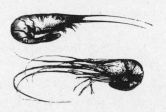

Wilbur-Ellis Company, P.O. Box 81246, San Diego, California 92138. Prices on request.

Wilbur-Ellis originally pioneered the distribution of canned abalone some forty years ago throughout the Far East, where the bulk of this product was shipped. (Abalone is regarded as a great delicacy among the Chinese and has a certain religious significance.) Since the availability of abalone in California is in an acute decline, much is now imported from Mexico. Enthusiastic divers have practically depleted California's supply.

The canned abalone is packed in 1-pound, tall tins and is sold by the case lot of 48 tins. Calsea brand contains from 1 to 3 whole abalones per tin ($238 per case of 48 tins). Marmex Pieces brand contains chunks ($160 per 48 tins). Case lots cannot be bought with a mixed assortment. Price FOB San Diego.

ABALONE

The deliciously rich flesh of the abalone can be baked in sauce, broiled, sautéed in butter with herbs, breaded and sautéed, deep-fried, stir-fried in peanut oil with fresh vegetables (for which there are many Chinese recipes), or stuffed with crabmeat and shrimp.

Stuffed Abalone

```
4 tablespoons crabmeat
4 to 6 medium-sized shrimp
  Butter
1 abalone steak
  Sauce béchamel (flavored with sherry)
  Parsley (finely chopped)
```

Sauté crabmeat and shrimp in butter for several minutes. Remove from pan with slotted spoon. Sauté abalone in the same butter for a minute or less. Dip shellfish in sherry-flavored béchamel sauce and spread on abalone. Sprinkle with parsley. Roll steak and fasten firmly with toothpick. Brush rolled abalone with sauce and run under preheated broiler until lightly browned.

Wisconsin Fishing Company, P.O. Box 965, Green Bay, Wisconsin 54305. Free brochure.

Wisconsin Fishing Company is a commercial fishery and supplier to restaurants and retail markets and claims to be the largest fish business serving the individual by mail order. Their fresh and saltwater fish come from the lakes of northwest Canada, the Arctic waters of Iceland, Newfoundland, Greenland, and Alaska, while shellfish are imported from various overseas sources.

Because Wisconsin Fishing Company caters to restaurants, it carries interesting items that are seldom found at the retail level. For example, you can order octopus ($1.10 per pound) and squid by the 5-pound carton, clam strips by the pound, Alaskan crab legs, jumbo lobster tails ($5.50 per pound in a 10-pound carton) and lobster tail

ON THAWING FROZEN FISH AND SHELLFISH

To avoid soggy fish, do *not* thaw fish or shellfish at room temperature. Instead, partially thaw in the refrigerator, allowing 8 hours per pound for most fish, 9 hours for lobster tails, and about 7 hours or less for oysters, scallops, and shellfish. If in a hurry, fish may be thawed under cold running water in watertight wrappings. Shrimp should be thawed *only* under cold running water. Defrost all fish and shellfish only until portions separate easily. Breaded items should *not* be thawed, but cooked frozen so that bread crumbs remain crisp. Fish may be cooked frozen, but at much lower temperature and 1¼ times as long as the recipe calls for.

meat ($5.25 per pound in a 5-pound carton), large shrimp pieces ($2.25 per pound in 3-pound poly bags), all sizes of shrimp, including jumbo (raw, peeled, and deveined, and breaded), jumbo frogs' legs ($2.50 per pound in a 5-pound carton), cooked Chilean langouste ($2.75 per pound in a 5-pound carton), breaded haddock squares, and turtle meat (5 pounds at $1.50 per pound).

Most saltwater varieties of fish are sold filleted in 10- or 15-pound weights; salmon and halibut come whole (averaging 15 pounds; $1.55 per pound) and steaked (under $2.00 per pound in 15-pound cartons). Other fish varieties include lake and rainbow trout ($1.40 per pound in 10-pound cartons), whitefish, and lake herring.

Supplies are available all year, and are shipped by Greyhound bus. Prices are reasonable and substantial discounts are given on large orders.

For additional sources, see:
Chapter 7. From Soup . . .: (chowders)
Chapter 14. Ethnic Foods: (tinned specialties)
Chapter 16. Meals by Mail:
    Captn's Pick
    Clambake International
    Meatique
    Wickford Shellfish Company
    William Poll

ОБѢДЪ.
—.—

Батвинья.

Консоме Жардиньерѣ.

Пирожки.

Филе де Бёфъ а ла Тулузъ.

Филе де Канетонъ а л'Оранжъ.

Пуншъ Рояль.

Жар. Молодыя Пулярды.

Саладѣ.

Спаржа ан браншъ.

Свѣж. Ананасъ

гарни де Глясъ.

7. FROM SOUP . . .

NOW you have a chance to taste all the soups you have heard about yet never tasted, and also to reexperience the memorable soups you have tasted but can't seem to find. For example, have you ever tried a good she-crab soup made the Southern way? a hearty, old-fashioned New England fish chowder? or a light, delicious bing cherry soup? These can be ordered along with other interesting concoctions. We have found several restaurants that will ship the soups that made them famous—special vegetable soups such as chive or watercress, and interesting varieties of fish and seafood soups and chowders. From one company you can order mixes for making your own soup by the gallon. If you can find someone who loves the same kind of soup you do, it is often profitable to order soups by the case at a considerable saving. If you are interested, write and ask.

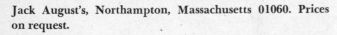

Jack August's, Northampton, Massachusetts 01060. Prices on request.

Jack August, an old-time restaurant owner and food merchant, has canned one of the most popular items on the restaurant's menu—his homemade chowders. He has available Manhattan and New England clam chowder and fish chowder by the 15-ounce can, all about 85¢ a can, plus delivery.

Catelli-Habitant Inc., Commercial Street, Manchester, New Hampshire 03105. Prices on request.

This is the manufacturer and distributor of French-Canadian soups which are sold mainly in the New England area. Thirteen varieties include French-Canadian–style yellow pea soup, bean soup with bacon and onion. Catelli-Habitant sells by the case lot of 24 cans only. Price runs about 50¢ a can, depending upon shipping charges.

Chalet Suzanne Foods, Inc., P.O. Drawer AC, Lake Wales, Florida 33853. Free brochure.

"Chalet Suzanne, an inn and restaurant near the geographical center of Florida, is the kind of place a traveler might come upon accidentally if he got lost after a wrong turn off the Sunshine State Parkway a few miles north of Lake Wales. Or, conceivably, he might come upon it intentionally if he had spotted Chalet Suzanne soups on a gourmet food counter and decided to trace them to the source." So says *The New York Times*.

In 1956 the Hinshaw family, owners of Chalet Suzanne, began canning their famous soups, prompted by the requests of many customers. Thirteen varieties are now available and include romaine (which went to the moon aboard Apollo flights), chive, mushroom, and watercress, along with seafood and chicken soups. The Hinshaws also make two sauces—curry and Newburg. Soups and sauces are put up in 13-ounce cans, and romaine and New England clam chowder are available condensed in 50-

ounce cans. Arrangements can be made for one gift box of 6 hot or cold soups in varieties indicative of the season to be mailed every other month throughout the year, a year's subscription costing about $50. Six cans of your choice are $8, including postage.

Harold's Cabin, 445 Meeting Street, Charleston, South Carolina 29403. Free catalog.

Harold's Cabin is a fancy-food store which offers some of the specialty foods of historic Charleston. It is believed that she-crab soup originated in Charleston in the 1800s and Rhett Butler may have dined on catfish stew (about 70¢ a 16-ounce tin) or shrimp bisque. These and other southern fish delicacies, such as crab roe (7½-ounce tin, less than $1.50) and crab roe pâté (3½-ounce tin for about 80¢), are available by mail. Harold's also sells a line of Southern relishes and jams such as fig preserves and green pepper jelly, and has an interesting line of cheese spreads, most noteworthy of which is Savoure (about $5.00 per pound), which is made from a recipe said to be brought from Tripoli by an old sea captain.

Mayacamas Foods, Ltd., 19275 Arnold Drive, Sonoma, California 95476. Free brochure.

When turtles became an endangered species, Mayacamas mocked up a soup mix blend that earned the undying gratitude of all turtles. This is one variety in the line of 10 dried mixes each of which comes in a 7½-ounce jar capable of making one gallon of soup. Exotic choices include Senegalese, a chicken, lemon, curry blend; Greek avgolemono; borscht; and crème of almond soup. The more traditional varieties are cream of mushroom and cream of chicken. The mixes need no refrigeration, even after opening, and may be ordered separately, in gift samplers, or in a mixed case of 12 jars (about $30). Mayacamas seasoning blends include herb mix, savory salt, and lemon pepper. The soup mixes and blends can be added to sour cream, yogurt, or cream cheese to create dips, or mixed with buttermilk and mayonnaise for an unusual salad dressing.

Moore and Co. Soups, Inc., 166 Abington Avenue, Newark, New Jersey 07107. Free price list.

Green turtle soups, shellfish soups, and a variety of other seafood products are available from the manufacturer of Moore Soups. The tinned turtle selection is made up of turtle consommé and turtle soup, both flavored with sherry wine; turtle chowder; turtle and pea (boula); and turtle meat with broth.

Moore also makes shrimp and lobster chowder, Manhattan and New England chowder, clam madrilene, and crab soup Maryland. The selection of seafood products includes lobster, shrimp, and crab bisques, along with lobster sauce and Newburg sauce with sherry wine. Moore products are sold by the case lot of 12 cans and range between $5.50 and $11.00 a case.

Pea Soup Andersen's Restaurant, Buellton, California 93427. Free price list.

Pea soup by post? Some of Pea Soup Andersen's Restaurant's customers have become so enamored by the special soup that the Andersens now can and ship it. In the 1920s, a Danish chef and his French wife opened a small café in which they served simple fare, including a French pea soup. The soup became so popular that three years after the first plate was served, the Andersens realized they needed to order peas by the ton. The problem of what to do with a ton of peas was solved when Anton Andersen dumped them in the window of his restaurant. Though a ton of peas seemed a staggering amount then, Andersen's today "splits" many tons of peas every month. In recognition of the restaurant's preeminence as probably the world's foremost pea purchaser, the pea growers of Idaho have named Andersen's the location of the start of the annual "National Split Pea Soup Week." The soup is available in a carton of 6 cans currently retailing for $2.50, plus additional charges for shipping. A "dietetic" version of the soup may also be ordered.

Pepperidge Farm Mail Order Company Inc., P.O. Box 119, Clinton, Connecticut 06413. Free catalog.

Some of the most interesting products in this mail-order catalog with its wide assortment of food items are the fruit soups under Pepperidge Farm's own label. These unique soups come in flavors from Bing cherry with Burgundy, to strawberry with sauterne, prune with orange, orange with apricot, and peach apple. They are ready to serve either hot or cold, as a first course or as a dessert. Recipes for using the soups as a cooking ingredient are included with each order. An assortment of 10 cans costs about $10. Other available soups include semicondensed vichyssoise, gazpacho, cream of watercress, Shii-ta-ke mushroom, and consommé madrilene.

Sid & Roxie's Cannery, P.O. Box 828, Islamorada, Florida 33036. Free brochure.

Florida specialty soups are canned in pint containers and offered by mail from Sid & Roxie's Cannery. From the Florida Keys comes conch chowder and from Caribbean waters there are turtle chowder and turtle soup. The minimum order is 6 cans, which can be in assorted varieties ($8.50 including shipping).

For additional sources, see:

Chapter 6. Fish and Seafood:
    Larkin's Seafood
    Saltwater Farm

Chapter 14. Ethnic Foods (tinned and dried soups and soup mixes)

Chapter 16. Meals by Mail:
    William Poll

Chapter 17. Health Foods (tinned and dried soups and soup mixes)

8. . . . . to NUTS

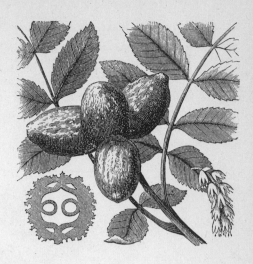

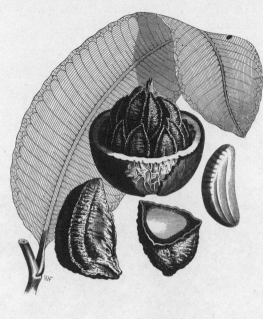

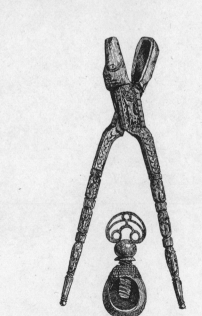

FRESH chestnuts, macadamias from Hawaii, pecans from the deep South, and almonds and filberts from California are among a wide selection available from family-owned orchards and major processors. Nuts come roasted, salted, plain, shelled and unshelled. There are nuts coated with tasty seasonings such as garlic, spicy barbecue sauce, or tangy cheese, as well as a tremendous selection of nuts in loose bulk in boxes and in sacks. You can order, for instance, the whole nut or halves and pieces in sizes ranging from 1 to 25 pounds. The many varieties offered in bulk are particularly exciting, especially if you tend to use nuts frequently in baking or in cooking.

W. W. Bolton and Son, Mobile Plantation Pecans, Route 2, Box 190-A, Theodore, Alabama 36582. Free price list.

Mobile Plantations is a young business devoted exclusively to pecans. Large Stuarts, gift-boxed, come unshelled (5 pounds for $7.50; 10 pounds for $12.75), or in extra large shelled halves (2 pounds for $7.50; 5 pounds for $14.75). Prices are postpaid east of the Rockies. A 5-pound box of broken pieces, excellent for cooking or baking is $10.75 and comes packaged for freezing. The main objective in storing nuts is to keep the nut oils from becoming rancid. In the freezer at 0° F, pecans should be able to be kept for about 2 years.

California Almond Growers Exchange, P.O. Box 1768, Sacramento, California 95808. Free catalog.

In addition to cocktail nibbles such as barbecued, hickory-smoked, or cheese-flavored almonds, and confections such as almonds that are honey-cinnamon- or mint-flavored, or candy- or sugarcoated, the Almond Growers Exchange has several offerings that will please cooks. One of these is ground, blanched almonds (six 6-ounce bags, about $6.00) and another is a 7-pound tin of almond paste (a little over $10.00). There is also a do-it-yourself marzipan kit containing a tin of marzipan paste, food coloring, shaping tool, and twelve recipe cards for marzipan-based items such as macaroon cookies and Danish pastry (about $6.00). Beside the many gift packages of selections of sweet, snack, and cooking nuts, custom packing is available in any combination of 4 ($5.45), 6 ($7.00), 12 ($11.75), or 18 ($16.25) tins.

T. M. Duché Nut Company, Inc., P.O. Box 845, Orland, California 95963. Free brochure.

The Duché Nut Company dates back to the time of Louis Napoleon Bonaparte, when Tristan-Mathieu Duché was forced to start a new career after he and forty other members of the French Parliament were exiled. After opening a food products plant in Belgium, he set up Duché Nuts in the United States. This generation of the Duchés are California almond growers, and they supply their crops to the confectionery, ice-cream, and salted nut industries as well as to individual mail-order customers.

Almonds come with cheese, onion/garlic, and barbecue flavors, just to mention a few. Natural ($42.00 for 25 pounds) and blanched almonds ($50.00 for 25 pounds) can be purchased unsalted in 3- to 25-pound cartons, and sliced, unsalted almonds come in packs of 3 pounds ($6.50) or more.

Joseph R. Fry, Route 2 Mehaffey Road, Powell, Tennessee 37849. Free price list; send self-addressed, stamped envelope.

Mr. Fry had trouble with indigestion for years, until he started growing and eating his own food. He is now seventy-eight and has been naturally farming nuts and vegetables on his Tennessee land for the last twenty-one years. Via UPS, he will ship chestnuts, hickory nuts, and walnuts by the 5-pound bag (all between 25¢ and 39¢ per pound), Jerusalem artichokes by the 5-pound container (about $2), and sweet potatoes by the 30-pound sack, at about 20¢ per pound. Delivery charges are additional.

Happy Dragon Chestnuts, Star Route Ettersburg, Whitethorn, California 95489. Free price list.

Thirteen chestnut trees thrive on the Etcheverry ranch in Whitehorn, California. The owner thought it would be a simple process to market the prolific crop of nuts, but not so in her vicinity. "Everyone hates them," she says. Chestnut trees still flourish in California, even though blight wiped out the trees east of the Rockies where the chestnut, harder to come by, is considered a delicacy.

Each fall, the chestnuts, organically grown and fertilized by the sheep grazing on the ranch, fall to the ground in large spiny burrs. Harvesting involves opening a burr with one's boots and plucking out the nuts. It is a tedious job, for it is all hand-and-foot labor. "The Dragon Lady" remembers wearing out three pairs of "city shoes" and two pairs of gloves during her first harvest. The chestnuts are packaged in a cloth bag (5 pounds $8; 3 pounds $5) and are accompanied by an interesting recipe booklet with directions for making dishes such as chestnut bread, cream of chestnut soup, main courses, vegetable combinations, and various confections.

Chestnut Bread

2 cups chestnut puree (about 1 pound)
1 boiled potato, mashed

In large bowl, mix chestnuts, potato puree with 2 cups warm water. Add ¼ cup sugar, 1 tablespoon yeast, 3 cups flour. Stir well and let rise, covered, until doubled. Then add:

1 cup skim milk powder
½ teaspoon ginger
1 cup warm water
2 tablespoons salt
¼ cup sugar
¼ cup oil
4 cups flour

Mix thoroughly, turn onto board, and knead well. Return to bowl, cover, and let rise until double in bulk. Punch down, shape into leaves or rolls. Let rise until double. Bake 50 to 60 minutes in a 350° F oven for loaves and 30 minutes in 400° F oven for rolls.

Hawaiian Holiday Macadamia Nut Company, P.O. Box 707, Honokaa, Hawaii 96727. Free catalog.

Macadamia nuts are grown, processed, and shipped by the Hawaiian Holiday Nut Company. The macadamias are available regular roasted and salted or flavored (hickory smoke, barbecue, or onion). Also sold are chocolate-covered macadamias, nut brittle, and unsalted macadamia nut pieces for the home cook. Dry-roasted coconut chips from Hawaii come plain and flavored.

The House of Almonds, P.O. Box 5125, Bakersfield, California 93308. Free catalog.

Whatever can be done to an almond, The House of Almonds seems to have done it. Almonds can be salted, roasted, barbecued, chocolate-coated, hickory-smoked, candied, stuffed into dates, mixed with raisins, baked into cakes, brittled, caramelized, and flavored with cheese, garlic, onion, banana, coconut, and orange ($10 for six 7-ounce tins of assorted flavors). For the purist there is a burlap sack full of 5 pounds of in-shell almonds (about $8) or the "gourmet" assortment which contains whole blanched, whole natural, diced natural, blanched slivered, and blanched sliced almonds—a total of 3½ pounds of nuts for about $12. All prices include delivery.

Kakawateez Limited, 130 Olive Street, Findlay, Ohio 45840. Free brochure.

After eighteen years in the poultry business, the Schiebers chickened out and went to nuts. While living in Mexico, where they operated a baby chick hatchery, the Schiebers tasted some nuts that had been processed by a Japanese-born man in his Mexico home. Enthused about the unique flavor this process produced, they bought the rights to process and distribute Totem-Kakawateez nuts anywhere in the world outside of Mexico. (Kakawateez is the Mexican-Indian name for nuts.) Peanuts were the first nuts they processed, but their line has now been expanded to cashews from India and East Africa, macadamias from Hawaii, filberts from Turkey, Brazil nuts from Brazil, pistachios from Afghanistan and almonds, Spanish peanuts, and Virginia peanuts from the United States. All of the nuts are coated, dry-roasted, and one of a kind is vacuum-packed in glass jars or various-sized plastic bags. There is also a jar of mixed nuts containing all the various types with the exception of peanuts. A minimum order is 4 jars in any combination desired. Peanuts are under $1.00, pistachios and macadamias close to $3.00, and all other varieties, about $1.50.

Koinonia Partners, Route 2, Americus, Georgia 31709. Free catalog.

This business in Americus, about ten miles down the road from Plains, proves that peanuts aren't the only thing in Georgia.

Koinonia (a Greek word meaning fellowship) was started by a theologian-farmer in 1942 as an experiment in Christian living. Koinonia withstood mounting hostility in the mid-fifties because of its tangible witness against racial prejudice, but an economic boycott forced it to sacrifice its chicken and egg business and begin a mail-order business in pecans. The partnership industries now include farming, sewing, handicrafts, pottery, a pecan-shelling plant, fruitcake bakery, and candy kitchen.

Pecans in the shell (5 pounds, a little over $7; 28 pounds, $35) are available in mid-November, all others in the early fall. Shelled pecan halves and less expensive pecan pieces come in various-sized containers (1-pound bags, just over $3) and in bulk (28 pounds, about $72). Sweet pecan products include apricot-glazed fruitcakes (3-pound cake, about $6), spiced halves coated with sugar, cinnamon, and butter (just over $3 per pound); Medjhool dates stuffed with pecans; and assorted flavors of pecan candy. A dietetic variety of candy is offered as well as a "health food" variety made from carob powder, molasses, wheat germ, and rose hips. Koinonia Partners offers substantial discounts on large orders for fund-raising projects. Ask for the quantity discount price list. Prices include delivery. Minimum order, $6.

SHELLING NUTS AND REMOVING NUT SKINS

Hard shells are easier to crack, and nutmeats break less often if nuts are first soaked in warm water several hours or overnight. Spread nutmeats and let them stand a few hours to dry before storing.

Removing skins from some shelled nuts gives them a delicate flavor and can easily be done by placing the nuts in boiling water or by roasting.

Almonds and peanuts: To blanch, put them into boiling water and let stand 3 minutes. Drain. Slide skins off with fingers. Spread nuts on absorbent paper to dry.

Filberts: Spread nuts in a single layer in a shallow baking pan. Bake at 300° F for 10 to 15 minutes or until heated through. Cool slightly and slip off skins.

Chestnuts: Blanch by dropping the chestnuts into boiling water. Let stand for 2 minutes. Remove a few at a time, cool slightly, and remove skins with a paring knife.

Remove shells and skins while nuts are still warm.

Northwestern Coffee Mills, 217 North Broadway, Milwaukee, Wisconsin 53202. Free catalog; 25¢ donations accepted.

Tucked away in the back of its handsome catalog is a very interesting line of nut butters prepared by the Northwestern Coffee Mills. They are all 100 percent nuts with no salt, sugar, or preservatives. Roasted varieties include almond, cashew, and peanut butters and "cream city blend," which is a combination of almonds, brazils, cashews, filberts, peanuts, sunflower seeds, and walnuts. The blend is available raw (unroasted), as is walnut butter. Prices range from about $2 for 2 pounds of peanut butter to just over $5 for the same amount of almond butter.

The Nut Factory, 3670 Mt. Diablo Boulevard, Lafayette, California 94549. Free brochure.

Ready-to-mail burlap sacks of California almonds can be ordered from The Nut Factory. Bagged varieties include salted, butter-roasted (2 pounds, $4.50 ppd), and barbecued ($6.50, 2 pounds, ppd). Other nuts, including candied Jordan almonds ($2.75 per pound) and a fancy nut mix ($4.00 per pound), are available either in standard packaging or, for 50¢ extra, in a red and white checkered box.

Nut Tree Pecan Company, P.O. Box 3890, Albany, Georgia 31706. Free brochure.

The Nut Tree Pecan Company is a Georgia cooperative founded to provide a service for growers who mechanically harvest pecans. Their services include cleaning, drying, and marketing in-shell pecans and shelling and marketing pecan meats. Pecan halves are available in 2-pound gift boxes ($7.50) and in-shell nuts come in 5- and 10-pound bags ($7.00 and $13.00). On shipments west of the Mississippi, add 15¢ per pound.

Roos Qualite' Pecan Company, P.O. Box 8023, Savannah, Georgia 31402. Free brochure.

The pecan had its origin along the swampy riverbanks of the Gulf Coast, and is now one of the nation's most important agricultural commodities. According to Roos, General George Washington was fond of pecan nuts and often kept them in his pocket, although how he managed to crack the shells with his fabled wooden teeth is not known. Roos has a clever nutcracker, which can be ordered along with Schley pecans in the shell. Shelled, mammoth pecan halves come in 1- to 5-pound ($7.00 to $22.00) transparent gift boxes, or, for a lower price, in decorated cartons (2 pounds $8.50 rather than $11.00). Pecan pieces are slightly lower in price than the halves ($4.00 per pound). The minimum shipping order is 2 pounds.

Texas Waxey Cake

½ cup plus 2 tablespoons butter
1 pound brown sugar
6 egg whites
2¼ cups flour
2 teaspoons baking powder
¼ teaspoon salt
1 teaspoon vanilla or rum extract
3 cups chopped pecans dredged in a little flour

Preheat oven to 225° F. Place pan of water in bottom of oven. Line bottom of ungreased tube pan with brown paper. Cream butter and sugar thoroughly. Add egg whites one at a time to sugar, beating well after each addition. Sift flour 3 times with baking powder and salt. Add slowly to egg and sugar mixture, beating until thoroughly blended. Add flavoring extract. Fold in chopped pecans. Bake in ungreased tube pan 1½ hours or until cake tester comes clean. Turn out on wire rack and cool. Wrap the cooled cake in Saran or foil and store in covered tin. Wait at least one day before slicing.

Note: The top of the cake will have a crackled, meringue-type crust which will soften as it ages.

Sternberg Pecan Company, P.O. Box 193, Jackson, Mississippi 39205. Free brochure.

The Sternberg groves are in the heart of the Deep South's pecan-growing region. Only one item is cultivated—the native nut. They come shelled, mammoth whole halves, fancy grade, and are packaged in gift boxes from 2 ($7.50) to 10 pounds ($30.00). The pecan season runs from November 1, when the new crops come in, to February or March.

Sunnyland Farms Inc., Route 1, Albany, Georgia 31702. Free catalog.

Sunnyland Farms offers a large array of nuts and nut products. Natural nuts include two varieties of pecans in the shell: Stuarts (5 pounds, $8.75), the large, common Georgia nut, and Schleys (5-pounds, $9.60), thin-shelled and smaller. Shelled halves (about $12.00 for 3 pounds of mammoth halves) and pieces (4 pounds, a little over $13.00) are available, as well as shelled California English walnut pieces (5-pound, 4-ounce economy box, $12.00), Ozark black walnut pieces (7-pound box, $20.00), slivered almonds (4-pound, 4-ounce "home box," about $11.00), cashews, hazelnuts, and Brazil nuts (all three in 2-pound,

Indian Cashew Nut and Pea Stew

        3 tablespoons cooking oil
        2 medium onions peeled and sliced
        1 teaspoon minced garlic
        1 teaspoon ground ginger
        ½ teaspoon freshly ground black pepper
        3 teaspoons garam marsala
        1 teaspoon arrowroot
    1¼ cups water
        ¼ cup shredded coconut soaked in the water
        1 green pepper chopped
        1 pound green peas, shelled
        ½ pound raw cashew nuts

Heat oil in saucepan. Sauté onions until golden brown. Add garlic, spices, and arrowroot. Fry for 2 minutes. Add water and coconut. Cook until it forms a pastelike consistency.

Add green pepper, peas, and nuts. Simmer gently until peas are tender, but not overcooked.

12-ounce boxes, between $7.00 and $8.50). Some of these come roasted and salted as well. A wide choice of nut confections includes spiced or orange-frosted pecan halves (3 pounds, about $11.00), chocolate-covered pecans and peanuts, pecan logs (three 6-ounce logs, $5.50), brittle (3 pounds, about $10.50), pralines, bark, and fruitcake.

These items can be ordered individually or in an enormous variety of combination gift packages. "Nuts for the Cook" is a combination box of 1-pound each of pecan halves, pecan pieces, walnut pieces (black or English), and Georgia peanuts (about $12.00). A unique items is pecan meal, finely powdered pecans which can be added to flour in baking or sprinkled over hot cereals; a 3-pound box is $15.75. Prices include delivery, except to those west of Denver (an additional 15¢ per pound).

Torn Ranch, 1122 Fourth Street, San Rafael, California 94901. Free brochure.

Torn Ranch prides itself on stocking the largest and best quality dried fruit and nuts, except where Brazil nuts

are concerned, in which case smaller is better and "tiny grade" is sold (about $2.50 per pound.) Nuts are roasted daily in the shop, and if requested the ranch will gladly omit the salt. Raw nuts are also offered and include most standard varieties, as well as whole macadamias (about $6.50 per pound), and hulled sunflower seeds ($1.30 per pound) and pepitas ($3.20 per pound). The large selection of dried fruits (all about $1.25 for 8 ounces) includes tropical fruits such as pineapple rings, papaya, and banana chips. There are three kinds of figs: Black Mission ($1.75 per pound), Calimyrna ($2.75 per pound), and Greek figs on strings (14 ounces, $1.25). Raisins, too, come in several varieties: giant black Monukka, golden seedless, Thompson seedless, and dried currants (all between $1.50 and $2.00 per pound). Confections made with its own nuts include a variety of chocolate-covered nuts and nut brittles. Light or dark chocolate-coated fruits are available in such choices as banana chip bark, grapefruit peel, apricots, and pitted dates and prunes, all from $2.50 to $4.50 per pound. Imported Australian dessert fruits ($2.75 to $3.75 for 12 ounces) include candied orange slices and glacé pears. For decorating pastries, there are bags of crystallized violets, roses, lilacs, and mint leaves imported from France.

There is an interesting selection of gift packages combining various Torn Ranch specialties. Gift #17 is 2 pounds of "Glorious Gorp," ($3.85), sometimes called trail or snack mix, which contains raisins plus ten different nuts and seeds. Gift #18 is "Seedy Stuff," which is just that (20 ounces, $2.99).

9. CHEESE

THERE are two basic types of sources for mail-ordering cheese. The first is the cheese-producing factory. Many are family-run businesses which offer just one or a few varieties. The second is the well-stocked cheese shop experienced in handling mail orders for a great variety of cheese, imported as well as domestic. Included here is a source for a farmhouse Stilton cheese in England; a place that mails cup cheese, a Pennsylvania Dutch specialty; and some shops that specialize in their own spreads and cheese balls. Supplies for home cheesemaking can also be mail-ordered, along with various cultures for yogurt making.

The French, Italians, Germans, Dutch, Swiss, and Scandinavians all contributed to the development of American cheeses, bringing to this country family secrets of the art of cheesemaking. Varieties of natural cheeses which are readily available by mail include Limburger, brick, blue, colby, Muenster, jack, Swiss, and cheddar. The preponderance of cheddar is an indication of how well this cheese can be shipped and stored. Cheddars run from about $7 for a whole 3-pound wheel to $104 for a 40-pound wheel, including shipping charges anywhere in the United States. Some sources will send just one type of cheese; many offer several varieties in gift packages.

For an excellent and comprehensive guide to cheese, *The Cheese Book* by Vivienne Marquis and Patricia Haskell is highly recommended. They tell the story of a man who walked into a cheese store in a large city. He was overwhelmed by the hundreds of cheeses—on counters, in open refrigerator cases, inside giant iceboxes; cheeses rising one upon another from the floor, huge wheels and millstones piled as high as the ceiling, each pierced with a marker bearing its name. He saw a round Pipo Crem', an orange Leicester, a fluffy, white Welsh Caerphilly. There were cheeses studded with cloves, streaked with sage leaves, wrapped in laurel; coarse-grained, crumbly, honey-soft cheese. Then the clerk asked him what he wanted. Desperately he took in the panorama—and fixed upon a safe and familiar object. With all the authority he could summon, he said, "Half a pound of Swiss, please." For those who do not have access to a cheese shop offering varieties of imported cheeses in particular, this chapter includes several sources which are experienced in mailing all sorts of cheeses. Included are fine Bries, a Spanish ewe's milk cheese, and even a cheese-of-the-month club.

Cheeselovers International, Cheeselovers International Building, Freeport, New York 11520. Free brochure.

A cheese club for cheese lovers. With a new membership of $9 (immediately refunded in the form of $9 worth of cheeses of your choice), Cheeselovers International will send a free cheese encyclopedia, recipe guides, information on how to give a wine- and cheese-tasting party, how to give a fondue party, along with an informative pamphlet on "love and care of cheeses." Each month members receive an Arrivals Option List offering a choice of between 15 and 20 imported and domestic cheeses. An announcement of cheese-related social events accompanies each monthly option list. In addition the club publishes a free gourmet guide resulting from questions asked by members on subjects ranging from cheeses to the correct wines to serve with a particular food. Prices on some varieties of cheese are said to be just above wholesale.

Cheese of All Nations, 153 Chambers Street, New York, New York 10007. Catalog $1.

Cheese of All Nations is much more than a cheese shop. It is an institution. In its home in Lower Manhattan, over 1000 cheeses are displayed. Cheese of All Nations is a direct importer from many individual cheesemakers throughout the world and can offer by mail an incredible variety. The 68-page catalog lists over 50 varieties of cheese from Denmark, almost 400 from France, and more than 100 from Italy. In addition there are cheeses from less prolific cheese-producing countries: 2 choices from Albania, 2 from the Azores, a sheep's milk cheese from Cyprus ($2.98 per pound), 5 from Iraq, and a dozen from Israel. There is a special listing of low-fat and low-salt cheeses, skim milk spreads, and domestic and imported kosher varieties. Each cheese listed in the catalog is described: Touareg from Africa is "made by Berber Tribes from Barbary States to Lake Chad. When cheese is made it is placed outside in sunlight to cure and turned occasionally until it becomes hard, dry and sweet"; Kajmak, from Turkey, is "sometimes known as Serbian butter, soft creamy, delicate, buttery flavor." There are special gift assortments such as kosher assortments for Passover and do-it-yourself selections in various price ranges. There is a minimum order of 1 pound of each cut cheese, which is individually freshly cut from bulk.

Crowley Cheese Factory, Healdville, Vermont 05147. Free brochure.

The Crowley Cheese Factory produces a colby-type cheese, similar in taste to cheddar but slightly softer and less pungent. The difference in texture comes from the colby process which prevents the curds from matting together, thus yielding a more open-textured cheese. Handmade by a century-old process from fresh, whole Vermont milk, the cheese is naturally aged in a wrapping of cheesecloth to mild, medium, or sharp flavor. The Crowley Factory prides itself on producing a unique American product in an age-old manner, and welcomes visitors to view the cheesemaking. Mail orders are accepted for 3- ($8.50 to $9.25) and 5-pound ($12.75 to $13.75) cheeses, prices varying with destination.

Dairyland Food Laboratories, Inc., 620 Progress Avenue, P.O. Box 406, Waukesha, Wisconsin 53186. Prices on request.

For cheesemaking, blue cheese mold can be ordered from the Dairyland Food Laboratories. It comes by the pound, about $9.50 plus postage, in powdered form and is a purified *Penicillium roqueforti* spore culture, which will keep about a year if properly refrigerated in a tightly sealed container.

Daisyfresh Yogurt Company, P.O. Box 36, Santa Cruz, California 95063. Free brochure.

A wholesaler of yogurt culture, Daisyfresh supplies fourteen hundred health-food stores and will also sell its dry Bulgarian yogurt starter directly to individuals. The culture is said to make a mild, full-flavored yogurt resembling sour cream. Each packet ($2.25) contains recipes and helpful hints on yogurt making. Also available by mail is Daisyfresh's yogurt-making equipment, which includes a culturizer heating pad, four 1-quart containers, and a yogurt manual.

Danny's Cheese Shops, 31 South Moger Avenue, Mount Kisco, New York 10549. Free catalog.

While many cheese purveyors do their ordering over the phone, Danny Lieberman goes to the market and personally selects all the cheeses he sells. His two shops carry over 300 varieties, representing the produce of numerous countries, including Switzerland, France, Austria, Denmark, Italy, Greece, and the United States, as well as his own secret recipe cheese balls, pistachio logs, spreads, and what he believes to be the finest Brie available. None of these contains preservatives, additives, or chemicals. Having started with gift packages mailed for his customers,

---

Yogurt Cheesecake

⅔ cup fine graham cracker crumbs
2 tablespoons softened butter or margarine
Sugar or honey
8 ounces yogurt cream cheese
2 tablespoons flour
½ teaspoon salt
3 eggs
2½ cups yogurt
½ cup evaporated milk
Juice and grated rind of 1 lemon
Cinnamon
Nutmeg

Mix crumbs, butter, and 2 tablespoons sugar. Press on bottom of 9-inch springform pan. Beat ¾ cup sugar, cheese, flour, and salt together. Add eggs one at a time, beating well after each addition. Blend in 2 cups yogurt and next 2 ingredients. Pour into lined pan and sprinkle with spices. Bake in slow oven (300° F) 50 minutes, or until firm. Spread remaining yogurt on top of cake and sprinkle with sugar. Bake 8 minutes longer. Cool before serving.

YOGURT CREAM CHEESE

Place a doubled dish towel over a pan. Take a quart of plain yogurt, stir if thick, and pour into the center of the cloth. Tie up the corners of the cloth to form a bag. Hang the bag over the pan. Allow to drain for 2 to 24 hours. Time determines whether the cheese is wet or dry.

Danny now sends cheese all over the United States and Canada. He believes that the key is to mail cheese in an underripe state in anticipation of its ripening on the way to its destination. Prices range from Jarlsberg at $1.29 per pound to Canadian cheddar at $4.50 per pound.

The Don Edwardses, Box 123, Townshend Road, Grafton, Vermont 05146. Prices on request.

The Don Edwardses devote their business exclusively to two fine Vermont products: cheddar cheese and maple syrup. The cheddar is made from raw whole milk from local farms, and is aged at least one year with no additives. The cheese comes in blocks ranging in weight from a 40-pound block currently selling for $104 down to a 2-pound block for $7. Prices are reasonable and include shipping and insurance charges within the United States. The syrup, available in containers from 1 pint ($5) to 1 gallon ($20), is 100 percent pure Vermont syrup with no preservatives.

THE GRATING CHEESES

FROM ITALY

Parmigiano-Reggiano, a delicious sharp cheese made from skimmed cow's milk, is prized as the greatest of the hard cheeses. It is often referred to as Parmesan outside the city of Parma where it was first made and from which it derives its name. Parmesan is the foremost of a group of Italian grating cheeses called Grana (grain) that are made up of millions of tiny crystals suspended throughout the curd. This gives the cheese its terrific grainy quality.

While the cheese is considered the best for grating, it is also an excellent table cheese when young and soft. In Italy, Parmigiano-Reggiano is traditionally eaten in this fashion as an after-dinner cheese.

Romano, when aged five to eight months, is enjoyed as a table cheese, and when aged a year or more is one of the most popular cheeses for grating, second only to Parmesan. Romano is less granular and not as fine in flavor as Parmesan and is usually much saltier. It was first made from ewe's milk in the grazing area of Latium, near Rome, but it is now made also from cow's and goat's milk. When made from ewe's milk, it is called Pecorino Romano; from cow's milk, Vacchino Romano; and from goat's milk, Caprino Romano. (It takes 100 pounds of milk to make 8 pounds of Romano.)

Pecorino Pepato, made from ewe's milk, is a Romano-type spiced cheese produced in Sicily and southern Italy. Sometimes the curd is packed and cured in layers, with whole black peppercorns placed between each layer, and sometimes the pepper is mixed with the curd in the vat.

Sardo or Sardo Romano is a salty, sharply flavored, extremely hard cheese. It is usually broken from the wheel with the aid of a cleaver and a hammer. At one time Sardo was made only from the ewe's milk, but now it is made from a mixture of cow's and ewe's milk. Authentic Sardo comes only from the island of Sardinia in Italy. Unfortunately, very little is being made there any more, but a close approximation of the cheese is now produced in Argentina.

Asiago cheese is made from cow's milk and is a sweet-curd, semicooked, Grana-type cheese with a pungent aroma. It originated in the commune of the same name in the province of Vicenza, Italy. As is the case with other grating cheeses, Asiago is often enjoyed as a table cheese when not aged. Table cheese of this kind that can be sliced is called Asiago di taglio (slicing cheese).

FROM SWITZERLAND

Sapsago, also called stockli, has been made in the canton of Glarus, Switzerland, for over five hundred years. It is a small, cone-shaped, very hard cured cheese made from slightly sour skim milk. A powder prepared from clover leaves is added to the curd, which gives this cheese a sharp, pungent flavor, an earthy aroma, and a sage-green color. It is often grated, mixed with butter, and used as a spread.

Saanen and Spalen or Sprinz, similar to both Swiss and Gruyère, are sometimes referred to as grating forms of Swiss. These cheeses are very hard cow's milk varieties with a sharp, nutty flavor, a deep yellow color, and a brittle texture. It is only in the last few years that Saanen and Spalen have been exported from Switzerland. Very strict controls require that the cheese be aged three years before export.

FROM THE UNITED STATES

Monterey or Jack cheese was first made on farms in Monterey, California, about 1892, and manufacture on a factory scale began about 1916. This cheese is known best as a soft-type cheese made from whole cow's milk, with a mild flavor and a high moisture content. "Dry Jack," a grating cheese, is made from partially skimmed milk or skimmed cow's milk, and aged for a minimum of six months. It's a delicious cheese with a yellow color and a well-oiled brown crust. While cured Jack is more pungent in flavor than young Jack, it is still considered to be one of the mildest of the grating cheeses.

Frigo Cheese Corporation, Box 158, Lena, Wisconsin 54139. Free price list.

Asiago, a cheese which originated in the Italian province of Vicenza, is the specialty of the Frigo Cheese Corporation. It comes in several varieties, ranging from the longest aged Asiago vecchio to Asiago fresco. Like other grating cheeses, this light yellow, piquant cheese may be used as a table cheese when not aged. Medium Asiago (18-pound loaf about $28) and *due usi* Asiago are suitable for either grating or table use. Frigo offers other Italian-style cheeses, among them yellow Parmesan and white Romano (20-pound loaf, $32) for grating and provolone, a smoked-flavor cheese for table use.

Gibbsville Cheese Company, Inc., Box 152, Route 3, Sheboygan Falls, Wisconsin 53085. Free price list.

Gibbsville Cheese is a small family business that handles and produces a wide variety of cheeses. The family's most popular products are those cheeses produced at their own Wisconsin factory and include cheddar (2-pound loaf, aged, under $4.00), colby, Monterey Jack, and Caraway cheese. (A midget longhorn is about $4.25.) Rindless cheddars aged (three years, $16.00), medium-aged (one year, $15.50), and mild-aged (three months, $15.00), colby, and caraway, are available in 10-pound economy boxes, which at a small additional charge can contain a mixed assortment. Cheeses are also sold by the pound or in assorted gift selections.

Grafton Village Cheese Company, Inc., Grafton, Vermont 05146. Free brochure.

Covered Bridge Cheddar is the name given to the product made by the Grafton Village Cheese Company. "We go about making our cheese the same way the old-time workmen went about making a bridge—using the best materials, the finest workmanship." Down the stream a bit there is, of course, an old covered bridge. Grafton's cheddar, made from whole raw milk, is sold in 8-ounce bars and 1- through 40-pound blocks. A 1-pound junior is $3.20; 5 pounds are $11.05. It is guaranteed aged for over one year.

Christian Hansen's Laboratory, Inc., 9015 West Maple Street, Milwaukee, Wisconsin 53214. Free brochures.

If you are into home yogurt and cheesemaking and cannot find a druggist to supply you, Christian Hansen's will mail its lactic cultures which include yogurt culture, acidophilus-yogurt culture, buttermilk culture, and acidophilus-milk culture ($1.25 each; minimum order is 1 dozen). Also sold are Hansen's cheese rennet, and cheese color tablets, vegetable rennet, and dandelion butter color, a bottled vegetable coloring for butters as well as cakes and pastries.

Yogurt Cucumber Soup

> 1 quart chicken broth
> 1 quart plain yogurt
> 2 cloves crushed garlic
> 2 cups coarsely diced cucumber
> ½ cup walnut pieces
> ¼ cup minced chives
> Salt and pepper to taste

Slowly mix cold chicken broth into yogurt until smooth. Add remaining ingredients, season to taste. Refrigerate until well chilled. Before serving, garnish with additional minced chives.

John Harman's Country Store, Sugar Hill, New Hampshire 03585. Free brochure.

John Harman left the rat race of Madison Avenue for rural retirement in a small New Hampshire village. His quiet country store sells New England specialties such as maple syrup and maple sugar and what he boasts is the "world's greatest cheddar cheese." Mr. Harman chuckles when he receives orders for the cheese from upper New York State, since the cheese originates in the upper New York area which has long been one of the finest cheese-producing sections in this country. Unpasteurized, uncolored, and unprocessed, the blocks of cheddar are aged at least two full years (5-pound block, about $13.00; 2 pounds, about $6.00). The Country Store offers 2 spreads of cheddar cheese combined with port wine in 7-ounce jars. One is flavored with cognac and the other spiked with rum. They cost about $6.50 for 2 jars. Shipping charges are additional to some states.

Welsh Rarebit

　1 tablespoon butter
　½ pound sharp cheddar, cut in small cubes
　1 slice crumbled bread
　¼ teaspoon salt
　　Dash cayenne
　½ teaspoon dry mustard
　½ cup beer or ale
　1 egg slightly beaten

Melt butter, add cut cheese, bread, and seasonings. As cheese melts (be sure to use low heat), add beer slowly, stirring constantly. Then add egg. Serve on crackers or crisp toast. Serves 4.

Honey Hollow Farms, P.O. Box 54, Bedford Village, New York 10506. Free price list.

Honey Hollow Farms offers just one item: aged, white Vermont cheddar cheese. The cheese comes in 3-pound wheels ($9), and discounts are given on case orders of 8 or more wheels.

Ideal Cheese Shop, 1205 Second Avenue, New York, New York 10021. Prices on request.

The same Brie served at some of New York's finest restaurants—Lutece, La Cote Basque, The Palace, Le Cygne, and Maxwell's Plum, among others—can be ordered from the Ideal Cheese Shop, which serves retail customers as well as the hotel and restaurant trade. The special Brie weighs 1 kilo and comes in a gift box, $11 plus postage. Another specialty is Explorateur, a French triple crème cheese available in limited quantities. Ideal has sold out on every shipment of this cheese since it started selling it a year ago and has a list of customers who will purchase the cheese whenever it arrives. The owner, Jerry Edelman, buys his cheeses from numerous importers, shopping for price as well as quality, and offers a very large selection of domestic and imported cheeses. A popular shop in New York, Ideal regularly ships orders to former retail customers who have moved from the city but still retain their loyalty.

Popular as a New Year's gift in fifteenth-century France, Brie was described in "An Ode to Brie" by St. Amant in the seventeenth century as "this gentle jam of Bacchus."

International Yogurt Company, 628 North Doheny Drive, Los Angeles, California 90069. Free price list.

Home yogurt making can save more than half the cost of commercial products. International Yogurt Company distributes dry Bulgarian yogurt culture produced by Rosell Institute of Quebec, Canada, in easy-to-handle powdered form which does not spoil and requires no refrigeration. Also offered are Kefir culture, acidophilus-milk culture, and cheese culture which is used for making fresh cheeses (Neufchâtel, cream cheese, and cottage cheese), buttermilk, and sour cream ($2.50 each). The International Yogurt Company offers a culture supply service which ships cultures monthly for 6 months or a year at a savings over individual prices. A yearly subscription runs a little over $20, which includes mailing. Further batches of cultured products are made by using "starter" from the first batch. This practice can be continued for about one month, when a new culture should be used to eliminate contamination.

Kolb-Lena Cheese Company, 301 West Railroad Street, Lena, Illinois 61048. Free catalog.

Originally manufacturers of just cheddar and colby, the Kolb-Lena Company now produces a wide variety of cheeses. Marketed under the Delico brand is Rexoli, a small, round, sour, and yeasty Italian-style cheese and Old Heidelberg, a soft cheese with a light Limburger flavor. Also available are domestic types of French Camembert, Brie, Greek feta, and Swiss Gruyère. Soft ripened cheeses range from $2.10 to $3.00 per pound; hard cheeses, from $1.50 to $2.25 per pound. Kolb-Lena will sell these cheeses individually or as a part of gift packages which contain, surprisingly enough, just Kolb-Lena cheese.

Kutter's Cheese Factory, 857 Main Road, Route 5, Corfu, New York 14036. Free leaflet.

This New York State cheese factory produces a mild, unsalted cheddar, aged about sixty days. Unsalted cheddar (about $1.50 per pound) is available only as a mild cheese, because without salt it cannot be aged more than sixty days and still develop a good flavor. Salt and longer aging produce the more familiar sharp cheddar (about $2.00 per pound). Muenster cheese, mild, with a softer texture and a touch of brick cheese flavor, is also sold. Both cheeses come in bulk blocks.

Kutter's uses a fermentation-derived coagulant instead of animal rennet in the manufacturing of its cheeses. There are no animal products used in the process, which complies, according to Kutter's, with the requirements of the strictest vegetarian.

Marin French Cheese Company, P.O. Box 99, 7500 Red Hill Road, Petaluma, California 94952. Free brochure.

Halfway around the world from its place of invention in France, Camembert is produced by the Marin French

Cheese Company under the label Rouge et Noir (three 8-ounce wheels cost a little over $7). Also made by the fourth generation in this family-run factory is breakfast cheese, a soft, butter-flavored cheese (six 3-ounce cheeses about $6), an 8-inch round of Brie (24 ounces, about $7), and Schloss cheese, which originated in Austria, and has a tangy flavor with a soft texture (six 3-ounce cheeses, about $6). Its sexist description in the brochure: "It is a man's cheese, replete with delicate naughtiness, ideal with black pumpernickel and a stein of beer." All Rouge et Noir cheeses are available individually or in gift assortments and prices include delivery in any of the states.

Nauvoo Cheese Company, Nauvoo, Illinois 62354. Free catalog.

The story of blue cheese has a legendary beginning. Some historians credit a shepherd boy who left his lunch of bread and curds in a limestone cave in southwestern France and later retrieved it, with the discovery of blue cheese. In this country a blue cheese, made from cow's milk, is aged in limestone caves in Illinois. It is available by mail from the manufacturer, the Nauvoo Cheese Company, along with a blue cheese recipe book. A whole 6-pound wheel costs $12.95, a half wheel $7.75, delivered. If tightly wrapped, the cheese can be frozen without impairing its quality.

Nichols Garden Nursery, 1190 North Pacific Highway, Albany, Oregon 97321. Free catalog.

Cheeses from Oregon's Rogue River Valley are available by mail from Nichols. Raw-milk sharp cheddar, a natural product with no color added that is not heat-pasteurized, is available plain or smoked ($4.00 per pound). Oregon blue cheese comes in a whole 5-pound wheel, about $14.00 (no shipping during the summer months). Salt-free cheddar ($4.00 per pound) is also sold, along with a special "Yeast n' Cheese," a blend of natural Italian cheese and yeast (2 pounds, $6.50). It is recommended for cooking and as a meat stretcher in casseroles and salads. Containing 50 percent yeast and 50 percent cheese, it has a high nutritional content of 44 percent protein. Nichols also offers some supplies for home cheesemaking.

THE BLUE-VEINED CHEESES

Roquefort is one of the finest cheeses in the world and is considered to be the best of the blue-veined varieties. It has a sharp, peppery, piquant flavor, with deeply mottled blue-green veins offset by a strikingly white curd. A French regulation limits use of the word "Roquefort" to cheese made in the Roquefort area from ewe's milk. The natural caves of Mount Combalou, unique to the Roquefort area, are used to age the cheese. Brisk movements of cool, moist air pass through the caves, keeping a favorable temperature for the mold growth and the ripening of Roquefort.

Bleu cheese is the French name for a group of Roquefort-type cheeses made in France from milk other than ewe's milk and for those made outside the Roquefort area regardless of the kind of milk used. The most well-known of these cheeses is Bleu de Bresse, a rich cheese, with dark blue veins made from unskimmed cow's milk; and Pipo Crem', called Griéges in France, a delicate bleu cheese with a higher cream content than most other varieties.

Blue, blue-mold, or *blue-veined* cheese is the name for cheese of the Roquefort type that is made in the United States and Canada. It is made from cow's or goat's milk, rather than ewe's milk.

Danish blue, made from homogenized milk, is rich in cream, with an almost buttery texture and strong in flavor, with heavy swirls of deep blue veins. Of all the blue or mold cheeses, Danish blue has the highest fat content, making it a richer cheese than most other veined cheeses.

Gorgonzola, the principal blue-green-veined cheese of Italy, is considered one of the world's great marbled cheeses along with Stilton and Roquefort. It is a rich, creamy cheese, often referred to as "the butter cheese" of the blues, with deep greenish veins rather than blue. The veins of the true Gorgonzola are jagged lines rather than swirling.

Stilton, favored as England's finest cheese, is a blue-veined cow's milk cheese drier and milder than French Roquefort and Italian Gorgonzola. Stilton is distinguished by narrow, blue-green veins of mold throughout the curd and the wrinkled, melon-like rind that results from the drying of molds and bacteria that grow on the surface. The open and flaky texture of the curd in Stilton provides conditions suitable for mild growth, so holes are not usually punched in the cheese as in Roquefort and Gorgonzola. At one time the desirable open, flaky texture was obtained by preparing curd in the evening and in the morning and mixing the two curds together. Some dairies still make the cheese twice a day, but the curds are not mixed.

J. M. Nuttall & Co., Dove Dairy, Hartington, Buxton, Derbyshire SK17 0AH, England. Prices on request.

The Stilton Cheesemakers Association's brochure traces the history of this famous cheese, which was first produced in the early nineteenth century and sold at the Bell Inn, Stilton, Huntingtonshire. The landlord of the inn, catering to the coach and carriage trade, obtained his supplies "from the wife's sister who was married to a farmer named Paulet near Melton Mowbray. She had learned to make the cheese from their mother who was housekeeper to a Lady Baumont at Quenby Hall."

The recommended method of serving the cylindrical Stilton is to cut the round end into pie-type wedges, an inch or so down with a sharp knife. The knife is then drawn around beneath the cuts to release the wedges. This fine, crumbly, blue-veined cheese is manufactured in farmhouses and small factories under strict controls, and the registered name can be used only on the genuine article. A large, whole Stilton weighing approximately 16 pounds can be ordered directly from the Dove Dairy, shipped either by air or surface for about $34. Whole blue Wensleydales are also available.

Original Herkimer County Treasure House, Upper Otsego Street, Ilion, New York 13357. Free price list.

Herkimer County, New York, was once the center of the cheddar industry in the United States. Wisconsin is now the leading producer, but Herkimer County cheddar, noted for its dry, crumbly texture and sharp flavor, is still available in whole wheels from the Treasure House (3-pound wheel about $10). The company also sells its own coldpack cheese food balls in various flavors such as a cheddar-and-blue-cheese blend with nuts (three 12-ounce balls about $9). Cheese spreads include blue, wine, onion, and sharp varieties. Assortment packages are offered, and mailing is recommended only between October 1 and May 15. Prices include delivery east of the Mississippi; there is a small additional charge for Western shipments.

Paxton & Whitfield Ltd., 93 Jermyn Street, London SW1Y 6JE, England. Free price list.

These well-known cheese merchants in Jermyn Street can supply several varieties by post. Among them are blue-veined Stiltons in whole (18 pounds), half, and baby (5 pounds, under $20) sizes. Stilton is also available in the traditional brown stoneware crocks. Other English cheeses include Truckle Cheddar (4 pounds, about $16) and a whole Walton Cheese (6 pounds, under $20), which is described as containing cheddar, Stilton, and walnut cheese. Prices are for United States and Canada delivery.

The Plymouth Cheese Corp., Box 1, Plymouth, Vermont 05056. Free price list.

The Plymouth Cheese factory was started in 1890 by a Colonel John Calvin Coolidge and four other local farmers.

It is run today by his grandson, John Coolidge. The intervening generation went to Washington. Plymouth cheese, a granular-curd, whole-milk American cheese, is made today by the same process used as when the factory opened. Naturally curded and aged, the cheese comes mild or medium-sharp in whole wheels of 3 ($7.50) or 5 pounds ($11.25) — slightly higher (less than $1.00 extra) west of the Mississippi. Sage, pimento, and caraway flavors are also offered. There are several gift packages which include wedges of Plymouth cheese, along with other New England specialties such as Indian pudding, baked beans, brown bread, and country relishes like watermelon pickle and mustard pickle.

Radloff's Cheese, Hustisford, Wisconsin 53034. Free price list.

Radloff's offers a large selection of Wisconsin cheeses. There are gift boxes of 3-pound cuts of such cheeses as cheddar, brick, colby, and Swiss, all between $6.00 and $7.00. Another gift selection is three 1-pound packages of cheddar curds ($6.10). In cheese country curds are munched on much the same way folks eat popcorn. Radloff's specialty is a medium-colored, lager brick cheese (approximately 2¾ pounds for $6.00). All cheeses also come in 5-pound bulk loaves at about $2.00 a pound. Prices are postpaid to Midwestern states, 50¢ additional elsewhere.

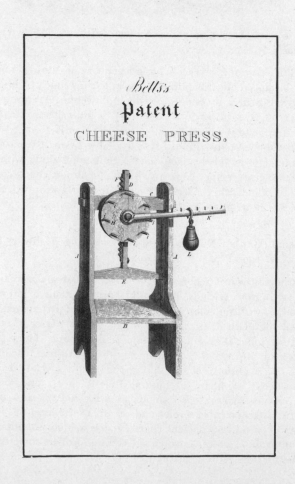

Bell's Patent CHEESE PRESS.

Fried Jack

¾ pound Jack
½ cup flour
 2 eggs, lightly beaten with
¼ teaspoon salt
 1 cup bread crumbs
 1 cup olive oil

Cut Jack into 2-inch squares, 2 inches thick. Roll in flour, dip into egg. Roll in bread crumbs, again into egg, and again in bread crumbs. Fry in hot oil just long enough for the bread crumbs to turn golden in color. Serve immediately. Serves 4.

The Seward Family, East Wallingford, Vermont 05742. Free price list.

The Seward Family produces a Vermont cheddar cheese, sharp yet mellow, aged approximately eleven months. No synthetic aging or flavoring is used. The most popular size is the 2½-pound block ($7 ppd), but whole wheels of 5 pounds ($12 ppd) and assorted gift packages with smoked, sage, and caraway cheddar cheese varieties are also sold.

Shenk Cheese Company, R.D. 6, Lancaster, Pennsylvania 17603. Prices on request.

Cup cheese; also known in this country as Pennsylvania pot cheese or cooked cheese, is made in many countries in the home as well as in factories. It has a smooth, buttery consistency and is available mild, medium, or sharp from the Shenk Cheese Company, about 70¢ for an 8-ounce cup. Also offered are 4-ounce packages of ball cheese (less than 50¢). Shenk also offers a selection of Pennsylvania Dutch condiments such as spiced cantaloupe, pickled watermelon rind, and corn relish, put up in pint jars and all $1 or under. Prices are less than $1 for 6½-ounce jars of jams and jellies, with such flavors as dandelion, red tomato, and ginger apple, and pint jars of apple or pear butter, including a special diabetic apple butter made without sugar or substitute. There is a 75¢ packing charge for an order, and postage is additional.

The Sonoma Cheese Factory, P.O. Box 215, Sonoma, California 95476. Free catalog.

The third generation of Vivianis now carries on the cheesemaking traditions brought to California by their family from Tuscany in Italy. Their specialty is a mellow, high-moisture-content cheese called Sonoma Jack. It comes in 3- ($6.95) and 11-pound ($17.95) whole wheels or in blocks by the pound ($1.65). Also offered in bulk cuts are mild ($2.00 per pound), sharp ($2.20 per pound), and raw-milk cheddars ($2.25 per pound), dry Jack for grating ($2.45 per pound), teleme ($2.30 per pound), caraway Jack ($1.85 per pound), and onion Jack ($1.85 per pound). The Factory mails a Bay-area, dry Italian salami (2 pounds, about $7.50) and a selection of California wines. The latter may only be shipped within California.

The Stallmans at Mapleton, 35990 Mapleton Road, Oconomowoc, Wisconsin 53066. Free catalog.

The Stallman family manufactures Bon Bree, a creamy port salut–type cheese. Among the other bulk cheeses offered directly from their Wisconsin factories are Gerber's brick and Limburger cheeses as well as several cheddars, longhorns, and a cellar-cured domestic Swiss. All are between $1.50 and $2.00 per pound. The minimum order on bulk cheese is 5 pounds, and there are also several gift combination packages to choose from.

Sugarbush Farm, Woodstock, Vermont 05091. Free brochure.

Sugarbush Farm is a mail-order concern that three times a year sends out a folksy newsletter full of cheese information and recipes to its customers. Its Vermont cheddars are "not processed, not colored, not pasteurized, not fussed with." *Gourmet* magazine has called Sugarbush "one of the most dependable places in America in which to find assertive yet richly mellow cheddar." In the manner of a French wine dealer, the owner, Jack Ayres, buys his cheddar all over New England, sampling and tasting as he goes. He then ages, cuts, and wraps his selections himself. (The prime cheddar is aged for two years.) Jack Ayres claims that there is no such thing as true farmhouse cheeses anymore. "It's all made in factories. Of course some of the factories look like farmhouses." Sugarbush cheddars are available in whole, 6-pound wheels ($14.00), blocks (2 pounds, $6.55), and foot-long bars ($3.65), sharp and medium sharp in flavor. Variations include maple-hickory–smoked cheddar and sage cheese, a supposed favorite of Henry VIII. Two new additions to the Sugarbush offerings are creamy Green Mountain blue and mild Green Mountain Jack. An introductory cheese package ($6.50) includes a bar of each of 4 varieties: smoked, cheddar, Jack, and sage. Prices do not include postage.

Trinacria Importing Company, 415 Third Avenue, New York, New York 10016. Prices on request.

This incredible emporium of gourmet delicacies and specialty cooking ingredients is a source for queso manchego, a Spanish ewe's milk cheese. It sells for about $3 per pound and is best ordered whole (4 pounds). Trinacria is the place to write to when there is a specialty food you can't find anywhere else. Although the only printed price list available is for Indian food, the chances are pretty good that whatever you want, the store has.

Cheese Bread

> 2 cups flour
> 2 teaspoons baking powder
> 1 tablespoon sugar
> ½ teaspoon salt
> ¼ cup butter in 4 parts
> 1 cup grated sharp cheddar
> 1 tablespoon grated onion
> 1½ teaspoons dill
> ¾ cup milk
> 1 egg, beaten

Grease a large bread pan. Preheat oven to 350° F. Sift flour, baking powder, and sugar and salt. Cut in the butter. Stir in the cheese, onion, and dill. Combine the milk and beaten egg in a separate bowl. Pour into the mixture and stir with a fork to moisten. Bake 45 to 50 minutes. Let cool in the pan for 10 minutes.

Wine and Cheese Center, 205 Jackson Street, San Francisco, California 94111. Free brochure.

A complete selection of domestic and imported cheeses is available from the Wine and Cheese Center. Because the shop is near a major wine-making area, it enjoys a close relationship with many small premium producers who do not have sophisticated distribution systems. Thus it is in a position to discover and ship a wide selection of California wines along with the cheeses. Unfortunately, only intrastate shipping of wines is possible. Thoughtfully selected gift selections come in boxes or handwrought Italian baskets. There is a black-waxed cheddar in its own mailer box (3 pounds, about $10.00), a local specialty of a 3-pound wheel of Monterey Jack with a round of sourdough bread ($10.50), a 1-kilo, boxed, whole wheel of Brie ($12.50) a sampler of 5 European cheeses, a selection of dessert cheeses, and a package of wedges cut from large country cheeses ($9.50). Telephone orders are accepted at (415) 956-2518.

For additional sources, see:
Chapter 5. Game:
 Jugtown Mountain Smokehouse
Chapter 7. From Soups . . .:
 Harold's Cabin
Chapter 14. Ethnic Foods:
 Dutch-Indonesian; Mrs. De Wildt
 British; R. W. Forsyth, Ltd., Fortnum & Mason
 Eastern European; Paprikas Weiss
 Italian;
 Scandinavian;
 Middle Eastern; Skenderis Greek Imports
Chapter 17. Health Foods:
 Cayol Natural Foods
 Deer Valley Farm and Farm Store
 David Hodas

10. CAKES, COOKIES, AND CONFECTIONS

THERE is only one compelling reason for mail-ordering candies, cakes, and confections—it's fun! The varieties of sweets offered by mail are enough to sate even the most jaded sweet tooth. People tend to become addicted to one particular chocolate or a special fruitcake, and mail order is a convenient way to keep a supply of a favorite goody on hand. Easy-to-purchase gifts might include a giant chocolate bar, a gingerbread house, a box of chocolate chip cookies, or an elegant assortment of chocolates. A very special occasion may call for a cheesecake shipped air freight from New York or a sachertorte flown in from Vienna. There are regional and foreign specialties such as butter cookies from Solvang, California, shortbread from Scotland, and saltwater taffy from the Boardwalk in Atlantic City.

Anna's Danish Cookies, 3560 Eighteenth Street, San Francisco, California 94110. Free price list.

In the history of the Danish people, the spirit of hospitality has been a distinguishing characteristic. Outstanding in this hospitality was rivalry in serving "Danske Smaakager," small, sweet cakes. The recipe for Anna's Danish Cookies was brought to the United States in 1937. The 5 varieties of cookies—butter, vanilla, egg, oatmeal, and coconut—come in assorted cartons up to 5 pounds (about $11.50) or in lithographed tin gift boxes (2 pounds, about $6.50). Prices include postage throughout the United States.

Astor Chocolate Corporation, 48–25 Metropolitan Avenue, Brooklyn, New York 11237. Free price list.

Three sizes of bittersweet chocolate cups are made by Astor. The smallest, in a gold foil holder, can hold ½-ounce of liqueur; without the foil it can be filled with cream or liqueur and floated in a cup of hot coffee. The larger shells are designed to be edible dessert casings and may be filled with such things as fruits, ice cream, or mousse. Minimum order is 3 boxes at $9.50 for the large cups, $8.50 for the smaller ones.

Bailey's, 26 Temple Place, Boston, Massachusetts 02111. Free brochure.

Established in 1873, Bailey's has a reputation for luscious ice-cream sundaes and handmade confections. The store doesn't mail-order its ice cream, but chocolates, dark or milk, are available by the pound or in assorted gift boxes (from $2.00 to $7.50). The "Bailey Sampler" is a single-layer box of 62 varieties of dark chocolates, milk chocolates, and caramels (about $5.00). A chart is enclosed so that you may note favorites and then specify your choice of favorites like pistachio truffle creams, checkerberry creams, chocolate

mint chips, coconut caramels, and pineapple cordials when reordering a personal mixture. Your special assortment will be kept on file and can be sent out at your whim or at periodic intervals.

For those with a single passion, a choice can be made from other goodies, such as fudge ($2.25 per pound) of several varieties; Bailey kisses ($2.95 per pound), which are caramel-covered marshmallows; crème mints ($3.25 per pound) in exotic flavors such as clove, wintergreen, and lime; peanut brittle ($1.95 per pound); barley pops (30¢) made in special molds; horehound drops ($2.40 per pound); and "Chicken Bones—Assorted" ($2.00 per pound). Bailey's guarantees safe delivery of its products and will replace without charge any shipment which is received in poor condition. The brochure notes that chocolates do not travel well in summer months. Postage is additional.

Bissinger's, 205 West Fourth Street, Cincinnati, Ohio 45202. Free leaflets.

The original Bissinger started business in Cincinnati in 1863. Bissinger nut balls, supposedly created for Louis Napoleon, contain freshly ground almond paste packed between pecans and walnuts and then dipped in fondant and chocolate (16 balls about $6). In addition to chocolate assortments and personal mixtures which Bissinger's will keep on file for its customers, the company features unique packaging of its confections. There is a muslin bag filled with taffy that can be dropped as is in the mailbox (under $3), a berry basket decorated with gingham and filled with mints (about $5), and modest to elaborate Easter baskets. Do-it-yourselfers might like to try a candy wreath kit with Christmas Starlight Mints and assembly instructions (about $4), or the imported Knusperhaus kit containing directions and everything needed to construct a cookie house—decorative and nibblable (about $13). Postage charge additional.

Butterfield Farms, Inc., 8500 Wilshire Boulevard, Suite 1005, Beverly Hills, California 90211. Free price list.

The address and the ingredients are consistent with the claim that the Butterfield Farms fruitcake is "the most expensively made fruitcake in the world." Made from French cherries, Spanish almonds, Malaysian pineapples, and French walnuts, aged in bourbon, rum, and brandy, it is baked with "just enough cake" to hold this international grouping together. Not just at Christmastime, but throughout the year, the cakes arrive in decorative tins (3-pound cake, about $12) or red leatherette boxes (2-pound cake about $10).

Byrd Cookie Company, P.O. Box 13086, 2233 Norwood Avenue, Savannah, Georgia 31406. Free brochure.

The Confederate Cannon Ball, a cocktail bit with onion- and garlic-flavored poppy and sesame seeds is one of the newer items produced by the Byrd Cookie Company. Benne Wafers, the original cookie, a round, nutmeg-flavored sugar cookie, are still baked (8-ounce tin about $4), along with a line of various cocktail nibbles, including Benne Bits, a cheese-flavored cracker; Railroad Trax, made with wheat germ; and Benne Straws, a spicy cheese, poppy seed, and sesame seed cracker—all about $4. Benne seeds are the spicy, honey-colored seeds (*Sesamum indicum*) brought to Georgia and South Carolina by African Blacks during the slave trade. They believed that the seeds bore the secrets of health and good luck. A brief history of the seeds accompanies the Byrd products, which come packaged in attractive tins.

Catherine's Chocolate Shoppe, Stockbridge Road, Great Barrington, Massachusetts 01230. Free leaflet.

Catherine's chocolates are hand dipped by New England confectioners. You can fool yourself into thinking that you are eating less by ordering the bite-size miniatures which average 60 to 70 pieces per pound. Boxed assortments are available, as well as old-fashioned specialties such as pecan roll, nut bark, rum balls, peanut brittle, and orange peel covered with bittersweet chocolate—all at about $3.75 per pound.

Charbonnel et Walker Ltd., 28 Old Bond Street, London W1X 4BT, England. Free price list.

Purveyor to Her Majesty, the Queen of England, Charbonnel et Walker offers a selection of its fine chocolates to mail-order customers. There are exquisite handmade boxes and presentation assortments (from $5 to $25) of chocolates, as well as chocolate specialties by the pound such as chocolate violet creams topped with crystallized petals (about $5 per pound) and chocolate ginger sticks. At Christmastime there are specially designed red and gold gift boxes.

Le Cheesecake Elegant, 150 East Seventieth Street, New York, New York, 10021. Free price list.

Delicious cheesecake made with a butter-cookie crust can be ordered in sizes of 6 ($5.15), 8 ($8.60), or 10 ($11.50) inches from Le Cheesecake Elegant. Tarts are 80¢. The other specialty of the house—pecan pie—is made with pure Vermont maple syrup and a crust of cream cheese pastry. An 8-inch pie is $4.35, 9-inch, $5.75. Shipping is additional.

Chocolaterie "Dauphine" Peter Reynhoudt, 24, Prof. Oranjestraat, Amsterdam, Netherlands. Free catalog.

This chocolate gift shop, with several branches in Amsterdam, will dispatch parcels all over the world. Its biggest specialty is an attractive wooden crate of Ringers choco-

lates filled with liqueurs (1¼ pounds, about $12). Also popular are the Rademaker's coffee candies, Droste assortments, and Driessen's chocolate delft tiles (1 pound, about $16). Ringers also makes an assortment of chocolates for diabetics. Prices are given in U.S. dollars and include shipping charges.

Colette French Pastries, 1136 Third Avenue, New York, New York 10021. Free list, prices on request.

If you crave a flaky croissant for breakfast and can't hop a plane to Paris or face several hours in the kitchen, you can order it from Colette French Pastries in New York (50¢ each). Colette's will ship some of its less perishable French baked goods. The "Trianon" is a rich chocolate cake, "Pain de Genes" is a cake made of fresh ground almonds, and "Brioche Mousseline" is described as a French and Danish coffee cake. Available by air shipment only are "Carmen," a cake of hazelnuts with fine layers of chocolate and mocha cream, "Manon," of almonds and mocha cream, and the "Chocolate Beret," an all-chocolate cake with chocolate butter cream filling. Plain, raisin, and fruitcakes may also be mail-ordered. Cakes range from $4 to $6.

Only fresh eggs and butter are used in all of Colette's preparations. In true French fashion, Colette is closed during July and August.

Conditorei Kreutzkamm, Postfach 50, 8000 Munich 1, Germany. Free brochure.

This family-run bakery, formerly of Dresden, offers some of the most famous German baked goods. There are several varieties of Christmas stollen (about $14 for a 3-pound cake, including shipping to the United States), lebkuchen (the German honey cakes), marzipan, assorted gift packages, and best of all—torten, including a sachertorte, a walnut cake, and some of Fritz Kreutzkamm's own special creations—all about $12, but shipping is additional.

Charles Demel and Sons, Kohlmarkt 14, 1010 Vienna, Austria. Prices on request.

For years this famous Viennese pastry establishment has been fighting legal battles with the Hotel Sacher to determine which one owns the original recipe for what Demel terms the "Sachertorte" (in quotes, of course). The cake, about $26, is named for its creator, Franz Sacher, once chef to Prince von Metternich. A rich but delicate combination of chocolate cake, apricot filling, and dark chocolate icing, the torte will arrive by air mail, attractively packaged and in excellent condition. It will remain fresh for several weeks.

Dutch Farm Kandies, 636 Markley Street, Norristown, Pennsylvania 19401. Free price list.

For those who must restrict their sugar intake, Dutch Farm provides a mail-order source for candies which contain no sugar, saccharin, or cyclamates. Boxed varieties include chocolates (two 8-ounce boxes, $4.50), fruit and nut jells (two 10-ounce boxes, $4.00), hard candies in assorted flavors, and solid blocks of milk or semisweet chocolate (four 6-ounce blocks, $6.00). Postage is an additional $1.25 for each item ordered.

Dutch Haven, P.O. Box 100, Soudersburg, Pennsylvania 17577. Prices on request.

Dutch Haven calls itself "the place that made Shoo-Fly Pie famous" and will mail its specialty anywhere in the United States. The 10-inch pie ($2.25), known as a "wet bottom" pie, is a famous Pennsylvania Dutch dessert made from a sweet molasses mixture.

The Famous Amos Chocolate Chip Cookie, 7181 Sunset Boulevard, Hollywood, California 90046. Free information.

The Famous Amos Chocolate Chip Cookie is the only cookie managed by the William Morris Agency. Promoted with a style generally reserved for an up-and-coming rock group, the Amos cookie seems to have become the darling of Hollywood, or so its press kit would lead one to believe. Billed as "The Cookie of the Year" by Cookie Monster and "This Cookie's Cookin'" by Sarahleigh, the "Winner of the 1975 Golden Brown Chippy Award," was "born at a very young age, on a preteflon cookie sheet in Los Angeles, California, during the great crumb famine of 1970," according to its official biography. The father of the cookie, Wally Amos, uses skills he acquired as a theatrical agent. The first Black hired by the William Morris Agency, "I was the Jackie Robinson of the theatrical agency business," he recalls. "You see, I manage the cookie."

The Amos Cookie is not just a PR job, though. It is a first-rate chocolate chip cookie, heavy on the chips and pecans. Costarring are chocolate chip with peanut butter and butterscotch chip with pecans. Minimum order is 2 pounds—$7.50 or $8.00 for a 1½-pound tin. Prices include mailing.

Ferrara Foods and Confections, Inc., 195 Grand Street, New York, New York 10013. Free brochure.

Opened in 1892, Caffe A. Ferrara was for many years not only the first but the only pasticceria in the United States. The pastry shop is still there, greatly enlarged, in the heart of New York's "Little Italy," but the confectionary company has grown to a nationwide business. Many of its specialties can be ordered directly by mail, among them petite babas (a 16-ounce jar about $2.50), rum and brandy cakes (14 ounces, $1.50), pandoro, panettone ($12.00 for a 3-pound, 3-ounce cake), and panforte dessert cakes (about $2.50 for a 14-ounce cake), and its own brand of amaretti, an Italian almond cookie (6½ ounces about $1.50). Ferrara has a complete line of brandied fruits and sweet syrups, and will also send assortments of Italian and French pastries by the dozen ($6.00). Pastry orders are shipped special delivery. All shipping charges are additional.

The Flying Bear, 356 North Main Street, Fort Bragg, California 95437. Free brochure.

The Flying Bear Building was one of the few in Fort Bragg, a lumber and fishing town 150 miles north of San Francisco, to survive what is known locally as the Fort Bragg earthquake of 1906 (which also happened to destroy San Francisco). The old-fashioned candy shop is one where everything is made entirely by hand. Initials trickled in chocolate on the tops indicate the filling in the dipped chocolates. English toffee candy, coated in chocolate and crushed almonds, comes in irregularly shaped chunks, and fudge is available in several flavors.

The process involved in preparing one of the Flying Bear specialties, "Rocky Road," is described in the brochure: To begin with, we make our own marshmallows . . . We cut the marshmallow in squares with a glorified ravioli cutter, smoosh it around in a copper pot full of melted chocolate, add chopped locally-grown walnuts, and scoop it by hand (a great sensual experience!) into baking pans to cool." "Rocky Road" is sold in large slabs, and, like all the candies, it leaves Fort Bragg in perfect condition. All candies range from about $4.20 for a 1-pound box up to $21.00 for 5 pounds. Shipping charges are additional and vary with destination. The Flying Bear notes that mail orders that are run over by trucks, trampled by buffaloes, or floated across the Mississippi will be promptly replaced.

Hadley Orchards, P.O. Box 495, Cabazon, California 92230. Free brochure.

Hadley is best known as a fruit and nut outlet in Southern California's desert region, but its extensive line of sweets is imaginative and deserves noting. Dates, nuts, coconuts, and other fruits serve as the basic ingredients for some 63 sweet treats. The fruit rolls include apricot, or pecan, walnut, and coconut date, all about $1.50 for 15 ounces. Menthol eucalyptus chips (8 ounces, $1.69), chocolate-covered prunes ($1.89 per pound) or grapefruit peel (8 ounces $1.09), macadamia brittle (8 ounces, $1.29), horehound sugar drops, and desert rock candy pebbles (8 ounces, 89¢) are some of the more exotic candies. Other items are homemade fudge, old-fashioned pearl tapioca (69¢ per pound), and candied fruits for baking. Postage is additional.

Harbor Sweets, Box 150, Marblehead, Massachusetts 01945. Free brochure.

Friends and neighbors asking for some homemade candies to give as gifts started this small mail-order business. In genuine cottage industry manner, Harbor Sweets operates out of a home kitchen. Just two products are made. The original is "Sweet Sloop," a sailboat-shaped chunk of almond butter crunch, the mainsail and jib coated with white chocolate, the boat "floating in dark chocolate—pecan spindrift washing her sides." This uniquely shaped morsel is foil-wrapped and packaged in boxes (20 pieces, $6, 40 pieces, $11), glasses, or chowder bowls with nautical motifs. "Marblehead Mints," the newer product, is a thin, chocolate confection flavored with peppermint crunch and embossed with tiny sailboats. An 18-ounce box containing 60 gold-foil-wrapped pieces is $11. Prices are all postpaid.

Hershey's Chocolate World, Mail Order Department, Park Boulevard, Hershey, Pennsylvania 17033. Free catalog.

The ultimate chocolate bar: Hershey's 10-pound giant measures a foot and a half long and costs under $25, including shipping from the Chocolate World at Hershey, Pennsylvania. For about twice the price, there is a mammoth, 25-pound bag of silver-foil-wrapped milk chocolate kisses. (The kisses are wrapped in red, green, and silver foil during the Christmas season.) Another specialty is the toasted almond milk chocolate in 1- and 2-pound gift packages ($3.80 and $6.30), made from about equal proportions of nuts and chocolate. The Hershey catalog also lists some gift packages of its standard-sized candies. All prices include shipping.

Herter's Inc., Route 2, Mitchell, South Dakota 57301. Catalog $1.

Herter's hefty 350-page catalog of outdoor and camping and sporting supplies lists several unusual candies and sweets. There is a 1-pound box of cactus candy made from the original recipe given to Margaret Herter by Sitting Bull (less than $2). It contains no peyote cactus or buds in any form. Another specialty is Buffalo Chip Candy, a confection filled with lingonberries, white raisins, and toffee chips (1-pound bar about $3). Other candies are Black Hills Traders Chocolate Pastel Mints and French Burnt Peanut Candies (both 2 pounds, for about $3). Herter's offers two unusual fruitcakes, one of which is made with wild rice flour and flavored with Benedictine (3 pounds about $4), and the other, "Diamond Lil Toffee and Fruit Cake," which comes with a complete history of the cake (3 pounds about $5). For home candymaking, Herter's has canned invert sugar and concentrated flavorings.

Hotel Sacher, Sacherstube, Philharmonikerstrasse 4, A-1010 Vienna, Austria. Prices on request.

This famous hotel in Vienna will mail its equally famous pastry. What they term the "Original Sachertorte," a rich cake consisting of layers of chocolate cake, apricot filling, and chocolate icing, comes packed individually in an attractive wooden crate wrapped in a cardboard cover. Shipment is by airmail, which takes about eight days. Sizes range from the "piccolo" which serves 4 to the "Number III," serving 12. Prices range from $15 to $24 and include shipment to the United States. The sachertorte remains in excellent condition for three weeks when kept at room temperature.

Istanbul, 900 North Point, Ghirardelli Square, San Francisco, California 94109. Prices on request.

The Greek chewing gum sold by Istanbul may never replace Chiclets, but Middle Eastern pastries should tempt anyone with a sweet tooth. The most popular ones are made from filo dough, crushed nuts, and a sweet syrup. The type of nuts and syrups used can vary, but they are basically the same in every country although with different names. The Greek varieties sold by Istanbul are flavored with honey syrup, and baklava is by far the most popular and well known. It is made from layers of filo, honey syrup, and either walnuts or mixed nuts. The baklava travels well, as do three other filo varieties: trigona, several layers of dough filled with walnuts and cashews folded flag style into a triangle; pistachio delight, a pinwheel or clover-leaf shape filled with mixed nuts and topped with pistachios; and strifto, layers of filo and cashews rolled around a dowel and pushed together to get a crinkly effect. All are 49¢ apiece.

Made from butter doughs are kourabiethes (39¢ each), a very finely textured cookie covered with powdered sugar, and Turkish ladyfingers, which are stuffed with chunk walnuts and honey syrup and sprinkled with crushed walnuts. There is also Greek and domestic lekume ($1.89 per pound), more commonly known as Turkish delight, and stragalia (80¢ for ½ pound), which are dried and roasted garbanzo beans and come plain, salted, or sugar-coated. Other Middle Eastern specialties from Istanbul are a falafel mix from Israel ($1.69); dolmas, stuffed grape leaves (95¢ to $5.95), from Greece and Turkey; and pomegranate juice (about $6.00 a bottle) and rose water (about $3.00) from Lebanon.

Kemoo Farm Ltd., 1718 Wilkina Drive, Wahiawa, Hawaii 96786. Free brochure.

Kemoo Farm mail-orders island confections. Its specialty is a tropical-flavored fruitcake made with macadamia nuts, pineapple, and coconut. A 2-pound cake is just under $10, including shipping. Discounts are offered on 3 or more cakes to the same address.

Kron Chocolatier, 764 Madison Avenue, New York, New York 10021. Free price list.

Kron Chocolatier, one of New York's most famous candy extravaganzas, offers several unique confections. There is the chocolate "eating" card, any short message up to ten words, decorated on solid milk or semisweet chocolate, 6 inches by 8 inches and packed in a wooden gift crate for $15.00, plus $2.50 postage. An 8-by-16-inch-large size is twice the price. Solid milk chocolate letters can be ordered individually ($3.50 each, plus postage) or boxed in a wooden crate to spell out "Love" or "Thanks." A chocolate ruler is an accurate twelve inches long and marked in inches and centimeters. It comes in an old-fashioned sliding-top box for $10.00 postpaid. Pure cocoa powder, another specialty of the Kron family, comes accompanied by specific instructions on how to make the most perfect cup or pot of cocoa ($4.00, plus $1.50 shipping for a 9-ounce jar). The price is the same for 12 ounces of pure, sugarless baking chocolate, while semisweet chocolate chips for baking cost $5.00 for 14 ounces (plus shipping). The Krons share their secrets of chocolate making during evening cooking lessons. The waiting list is sometimes months long.

Krum's, 2474 Grand Concourse, Bronx, New York 10458. Prices on request.

Many a former Bronx resident remembers a special treat at Krum's after spending Saturday schlepping around Alexander's and Loehman's with his or her mother. Childhood memories can be relived by ordering any of Krum's special chocolates and confections which can be sent throughout the world by parcel post or UPS.

Laura's Fudge Shops, 357 East Wildwood Avenue, Wildwood, New Jersey 08260. Free brochure.

Laura's Fudge Shops are famous for their fudge, made with pure whipping cream. You can order the fudge plain or with nuts, marshmallows, coconut, fresh strawberries, peanut butter, pistachios, or assorted. Laura's also makes saltwater taffy ($2.25 per pound), mint sticks ($2.25 per pound), chocolate-covered marshmallows ($4.75 per pound), and the newest item, a chocolate-coated pretzel ($3.00 per pound). Prices include postage.

Leah's Southern Confections, 714 St. Louis Street, New Orleans, Louisiana 70130. Free price list.

Pralines are probably New Orleans' most famous confection. For an extra measure of Southern flavor, Leah's pralines can be ordered in a cotton bale package (15 pieces, $7.95), as well as in tins and gift boxes (1 dozen pralines, not less than 1 pound, $4.75). Other pecan confections include a pecan log (about $4.75 for a 1-pound roll) and toasted orange, rum, crème de menthe, or caramel pecans in 10-ounce tins, all under $5.00. Further New Orleans specialties are 3-pound pails of strawberry or fig preserves ($11.00) fruitcake (a 3-pound cake, around $10.00), and creole fudge (about $4.75). Prices include shipping anywhere in the United States.

Leckerli-Huus, am Barfüsserplatz, CH 4010 Basel, Switzerland. Free brochure.

A recipe that is over four hundred years old is the beginning of a special Swiss spice cookie which is sweetened with honey rather than sugar. Packaged with Swiss precision in 1½-pound boxes, the Basler Leckerli cookie comes in several flavors, including hazelnut and candied lemon peel. The price is $10, payable in Swiss francs.

Liberty Orchards Co., Inc., Cashmere, Washington 98815. Free price list.

In the 1920s two Armenian settlers created an American version of Rahot Locum or Turkish delight, a confection popular in their native land. The transplanted confection comes in three varieties: Aplets (made from tart Washington apples), Cotlets (from California apricots), and Graplets (with a Concord grape flavor). All are made with chopped nuts and coated with powdered sugar; they contain no preservatives. Various combinations and different sizes are sold, such as the 5-ounce boxes for $2.35 and 13¼-ounce boxes for $5.15. Prices include shipping.

Maid of Scandinavia Company, 3244 Raleigh Avenue, Minneapolis, Minnesota 55416. General catalog $1, winter and summer supplements; all sent free to customers who have purchased $15 worth of goods throughout the year.

This is *the* catalog for anyone seriously interested in candymaking or cake decorating. The illustrated, indexed guide of almost 200 pages contains all manner of cooking and baking equipment, with many hard-to-find items. There is molding and dipping chocolate (5 pounds just over $10.00) and esoteric items such as edible rice paper (100 sheets, $4.25), nulomoline (7 pounds, $7.00), marshmallow powder ($2.35 per pound), lecithin ($2.50 a jar), bakers ammonia (95¢ for ½ pound), and semper florentina ($2.25 per pound). The nonprofessional will enjoy such things as crystallized violets, sugar cake decorations for various occasions, gold and silver sprinkles (3 ounces, about $1.50), colored sugars, and paste food coloring far superior to the supermarket variety (8 for $4.00). There is a dietetic chocolate coating and carob coating for candymaking (5 pounds, $7.95) and a chocolate-ice-cream coating which can also be used for making frozen, chocolate-covered bananas. Several products made for bakers and restaurants and not easily obtainable for home use are a pastry mix (2 pounds, $1.45) and a cheesecake mix ($6.25). For making wedding cakes there is a 5-pound white cake mix ($5.75) and also a pound cake mix ($7.25). Honey dough mix makes lebkuchen cookies or pfeffernuesse or gingerbread houses (2 pounds, $3.35). More selections in this large catalog are glacé cherries ($2.20 per pound), almond paste ($1.65, ½ pound), and macaroon paste (about $2.00 per pound), doughnut mix (4 pounds, $4.45), extracts in liqueur and fruit flavors (2-ounce bottles, around $1.25), Hires root beer extract (3 ounces, 70¢), fondant (2½ pounds, $3.50), and hard-candy flavorings. Orders are packed with infinite care and rush orders are given special attention.

Maiffret, Fabrique de Fruits Confits et Chocolats, 53, Rue D'Antibes, 06400 Cannes, France. Prices on request.

Maiffret does a large mail-order business in glacé fruits, shipping them all over the world. Whole lemons, strawberries, pineapples, cherries, melon slices, and the sweet, small tangerines of the Midi are among the many varieties of candied fruits offered. "The lemons taste sweetly, sourly lemony, the figs figgy, even the strawberries are themselves," —so goes Julia Child's recommendation for these handmade, crystallized morsels.

Manukian's Basturma & Soujouk Company, 1720 South Orange Avenue, Fresno, California 93702. Free price list.

Manukian's is the home of two popular Armenian confections. Available by the pound is rojick, a sweet made from dried grape juice and walnuts ($2.75), and bastegh ($2.25), made from a paste of dried grape juice and sugar. Shipping charges are additional.

Mary of Puddin Hill, P.O. Box 241, Greenville, Texas, 75401.

The need for some extra Christmas money prompted a Texas home economics major to bake some pecan fruitcakes from her great-grandmother's secret recipe. The rich fruitcake, made with dates, pineapple, cherries, and Texas pecans, was the foundation of what is now a large bakery business. The original fruitcake is offered in various forms and sizes: a large round ring (4½ pounds, about $15), a loaf cake (3¾ pounds, a little over $10), boxed, bite-sized cakes (28 for about $10), and chocolate-covered miniatures. Vacuum-packed dessert breads, such as eggnog and banana nut, and breakfast breads, like whole wheat prune and pineapple bran, are also sold, all in 12-ounce tins—3 for about $11.

Miss Grimble Corporation, 305 Columbus Avenue, New York, New York 10023. Prices on request.

Miss Grimble, acclaimed time and again in newspaper and magazine articles, has made her name and her homemade desserts as famous as the New York restaurants in which they are served. Although many goodies are baked in her ovens, including the cheesecakes and pecan pies for which she is most known, Miss Grimble mail-orders only 3 items at present; fudge cake (7-inch, $6.50), butterscotch brownies by the pound ($4.00), and a ring-shaped fruitcake packed in a tin ($15.00).

Her fruitcake, 4 pounds of almost solid fruit, is packed full of pineapple, cherries, candied orange rind, a few raisins, and lots of pecans. Miss Grimble's objective appraisal, delivered in her delightful Southern accent; "It's really like candy, it's delicious." It won't be long before all Grimble desserts will be available by mail order, so you might want to inquire from time to time.

Mrs. Herbst Pastry & Strudel, Inc., 1437 Third Avenue, New York, New York 10028. Free price list.

Mrs. Herbst Pastry offers a large selection of cakes, tortes, and strudels, and is experienced in shipping baked goods. Strudels are the specialty and come in a choice of apple, cherry, nut mohn, kraut, and cheese (about $4.00 a strip). At a higher price ($5.25) there is the "special strudel," which has more filling in it. Kuglofs, which are yeast, butter coffee cakes, come plain, cinnamon-raisin, and chocolate-filled in various sizes (from $2.20 to $5.00). There are cheesecakes (about $3.00 per pound), butter cookies (between $4.00 and $5.25 per pound), tortes (dobos, rum, sacher, rigo, Black Forest among the varieties—8-inch, about $8.00; 10-inch, around $12.00), and made-to-order cakes for special occasions.

Charles Muir, Castle Bakery Ltd., 17 High Street, Rothesay, Isle of Bute PA20 9AD, Scotland. Free price list.

The Castle Bakery is an established family concern carrying on a tradition of quality Scottish baking. For export it offers its 100 percent butter Scottish shortbread. The shortbread fingers come packed in two sizes of exclusively designed tins with picture lids and Tartan plaid bases—a most attractive gift item.

Pennsylvania Dutch Company, The Amishman, Mount Holly Springs, Pennsylvania 17065. Free brochure.

The Amishman sells lots of hard candies, such as minihex pops, root beer barrels, and sour balls (85¢ a bag); sassafras, red anise, and spearmint coughdrop-like candies (6-ounce bags, 75¢); and the rum butter, cinnamon, and fruit-flavored bundles of thin sticks popular among New Englanders (50¢ for a 6-stick bundle). Crunches and chewy-type nut candies are cashew crunch, butter-toasted peanuts, pecan logs with caramel-fudge centers, and mountain and saltwater taffy, among others.

The soft-sweet selection is more limited, consisting of assorted chocolate brownie cups (11-ounce box, $3.00), butter mints (8-ounce tin, $2.00), mint cream sticks ($2.25 for a 9-ounce box), and several varieties of nut fudge (at $2.75 per pound).

Salted nuts come in wide-mouth refrigerator jars with hex caps and include salted colossal natural pistachios, smoked almonds, and parched corn, which is said to be a new type and easy to eat ($1.75 to $3.50 each).

Anise cream candy ($2.00 for ½-pound tin) and Happy Amishman or Contented Amishwoman banks, filled with good-luck hex candy, are also featured, as well as a large line of condiments and jellies. A minimum order is $5.00.

Perugina of Italy, 636 Lexington Avenue, New York, New York 10022. Free brochure.

"Baci," the candy specialty of Perugia, Italy, are available by mail from the Perugina candy shop in New York. These individually wrapped "kisses," made from bittersweet chocolate and chopped hazelnuts, come in packages of 5 ($1.75) to 36 (about $10.00) pieces. Perugina has a large variety of Italian confections, including torrone, a nougat candy (18 pieces, $3.75), and chocolates, all in attractive gift packaging. The shop goes all out at Eastertime with exquisite candy eggs and elaborate holiday packaging. Shipping charges are additional.

Plumbridge, 33 East Sixty-first Street, New York, New York 10021. Free leaflet.

Plumbridge describes itself as offering "confections for the carriage trade since 1883," and its list of customers bears out the claim—Rockefellers, Kennedys, the Duchess of Windsor among others. Everything at Plumbridge is made from carefully guarded secret recipes in handmade, nine-teenth-century ways. All ingredients are fresh and no preservatives are ever used.

There are cabinets with five ($30) to nine ($40) trays, each tray filled with a different confection, as well as exquisitely (and expensively) packaged gift assortments whose containers are as much a part of the present as the candies. Spiced pecans are a house specialty, but for children, there is a handmade gingham doll filled with sour balls ($8) and a wicker rabbit basket with chocolate minieggs inside ($12). Tiny pectin jelly beans fill a handmade, yarn rabbit puppet ($10), and handsome wooden trucks haul the chocolate bunny and his load of goodies ($50). Christmas items are equally as imaginative. Postage additional.

Poseidon Confectionery, 629 Ninth Avenue, New York, New York 10036. Prices on request.

Poseidon Confectionery is one of the stores that makes Manhattan's Ninth Avenue a treasury of tastes from all over the world. Varieties of pastries, made with filo dough and filled with a base of almonds, pistachios, and walnuts, include baklava, saragli, kataif, trigona, afali, galactobúrico, and kombehaye. These are all sold by the tray (18 pieces of each average about $7). You can also order Poseidon's homemade butter cookies and filo dough for making your own specialties.

Arnold Reuben, Jr.'s Cheese Cakes, 15 Hill Park Avenue, Great Neck, New York 11022. Free price list.

Apple pie may be the great American dessert, but cheesecake has got to be the great New York dessert. In the city, every culture seems to boast a cheese confection—from the Italian Sicilian cassata to French coeur de crème—and New Yorkers tend to get passionate on the subject. Arnold Reuben makes a cheesecake of 100 percent cream cheese. He will ship them year round and guarantees perfect delivery to any destination. If you get hooked on them, standing orders are accepted for monthly, semi-monthly, or holiday deliveries. Sizes vary from cakes serving 6 ($7.50) to those of 20 portions ($13.50). Prices are postpaid except for Florida, Louisiana, Texas, and the Far West, which require additional airmail charges.

A. L. Roth, 2627 Boardwalk, Atlantic City, New Jersey 08401. Free brochure.

Advance to Boardwalk and get some of Atlantic City's most famous confection—saltwater taffy (about $2.50 per pound). Roth's particular specialties are almond macaroons (24 pieces, about $5.00) and "Macarums" (a 2-pound tin, $6.00), a coconut-and-rum-flavored cookie. Other confections are sold, including a line of sugar- and salt-free dietetic candies. Prices include delivery.

Schatz-Confiserie, Getreidegasse 3, A-5020 Salzburg, Austria. Free price list.

A luscious combination of pistachio marzipan and hazelnut nougat dipped in chocolate is a well-known Austrian confection. Each morsel of "Salzburger Mozartkugeln" is individually wrapped in silver foil emblazoned with a picture of Salzburg's most famous native son. The candies are arranged in different-sized boxes which show an old engraving of Salzburg. Prices range from about $10 to $25, depending upon the size box and whether airmail or surface delivery is specified. The Schatz-Confiserie has had long experience with mail orders and guarantees that packages will arrive promptly. It notes that Mozartkugeln keep fresh for six months.

Schwartz Candies, Inc., 131 West Seventy-second Street, New York, New York 10023. Free brochure.

The Schwartz specialty is "Out of This World Marshmallows," chocolate-covered, flavored marshmallows in a choice of vanilla, mint, maple, strawberry, banana, chocolate, or coffee. There are also various assorted gift boxes of hand-dipped chocolates, nut brittles, and "Broadway Mints," the last being very-thin-layered chocolate and mint squares, which also come in a "Boston" coffee flavor. All confections are handmade and most varieties are $4 per pound, shipping additional.

Stowaway Sweets, 154 Atlantic Avenue, Marblehead, Massachusetts 01945. Free price list.

Stowaway Sweets has been mailing its goodies to Marblehead's seashore visitors for years. They have fruits such as raisins, cherries, and stuffed dates; dark pecans, mocha almonds, and filbert nuts; and caramels, fudge, and chocolates.

Soft centers include almond paste, flavored creams, and plain and ginger penuchi. Rum continental, Swiss filbert, and plum pudding are among the assortment of 15 milk chocolates. If you crave something more chewy, there are vanilla and pistachio nougats, lemon nut, molasses chip caramel and, of course, the old standby, butterscotch caramels. All candies are $4 per pound, plus shipping charges.

For additional sources, see:
Chapter 1. Grains:
    Vermont Country Store, Inc.
Chapter 2. Bread:
    Danish Mill Bakery
    Dimpflmeier
Chapter 8. . . . to Nuts:
    Torn Ranch
Chapter 14. Ethnic Foods
Chapter 17. Health Foods

11. COFFEE, TEA, AND SPICE

Coffee Mills

CHALLENGE CANISTER.

REGAL CANISTER.

Per Dozen

No. 1080—6 ⅝ x 6 ⅝ x 7 ⅝ in., Finely Varnished and Dovetailed Poplar Box, Brown Enameled Castings, Wood Bottom Drawer with Rounded Tin Sides, Solid Chilled Iron Grinders, Set Screw Adjustment on Crank, Holds 1 Lb. of Roasted Coffee..**$9.00**

Weight Per Dozen 40 Pounds.

One-half Dozen in a Box.

Per Dozen

No. 44—Round Air Tight Tin Canister, with Screw Top, Cast Iron Body, Chilled Iron Grinders, Black Enameled, Gilt Decorations, Detachable Japanned Cup, Holds 1 Lb. of Coffee **$7.00**

Weight Per Dozen 44 Pounds.

One-half Dozen in a Box.

SIDE.

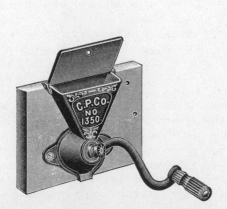

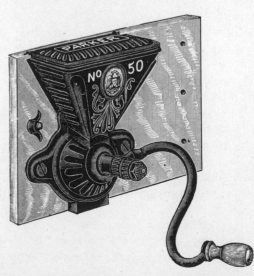

Japanned Cast Iron Hopper, ¾ in. Oil Finished Board.

No.	1350
Hopper at Top, Inches	3 ¾ x 1 ½
Back, Inches	7 ⅞ x 5 ⅝
Weight Per Dozen, Lbs	36
Per Dozen	$5.00

One Dozen in a Box.

Japanned Sheet Iron Hopper, ¾ in. Oil Finished Board.

Nos.	50	60
Hopper at Top, Inches	4 ½ x 1 ⅞	4 ½ x 2 ⅛
Back, Inches	8 ¼ x 6	8 ⅞ x 7
Weight Per Dozen, Lbs.	40	50
Per Dozen	$7.50	8.50

One-half Dozen in a Box.

THE rich smell of freshly roasted coffees, burlap sacks, barrels, and tea chests stenciled with the names of far-off countries, the old-time atmosphere and sensory thrill of the family-run coffee and tea shop are as close as the mailbox. Coffee varieties number in the hundreds, teas in the thousands. Experiment! Variety in coffee is not only in the bean, but also in the roasting, and the difference between the coffees available from the specialty sources listed and mass-market coffee is in the quality of the bean as well as in the care in roasting, freshness, and proper grind.

Many of the sources provide a standing order service by which coffee and tea are sent out automatically at specified intervals; many offer tasting sampler packages of several varieties. There are numerous house blends and unblended teas and coffees with which to experiment, and many companies will blend coffees and teas to your specification and keep the blend on file for you. Although most will grind coffee to order, whole bean coffee and a home grinder are recommended for a fresher brew; some of the catalogs and brochures offer pots, filters, and grinders as well.

Most teas come loose, but there are some companies that offer specialty teas bagged. Both coffee and tea are easily shipped, the charges adding little to the cost. Coffee is no longer a nickel a cup, and with market fluctuations such as they are, it is useless to discuss price. Suffice it to say that the sources in this chapter can provide the finest coffees and teas at about market value, some a bit high in cost, others at prices lower than probably can be found locally, even including shipping costs. The quality of many cannot be surpassed; many of these companies do their own roasting, some are direct importers, all are specialists.

Herbs and spices come in mind-boggling choices. Difficult-to-find varieties are easily procured through the mail. Many of the sources listed either grow their own herbs and spices, import them directly, or specialize and deal in such volume that the freshness of the product (particularly important with herbs and spices) is guaranteed. Quality and freshness are far superior to supermarket varieties of just about any herb. In addition, prices are often lower than local stores, and on most orders shipping charges are negligible. Also offered are many interesting and exciting spice blends and specialty ingredients. Some merchants specialize in herbs for tea, freeze-dried products, or in just one item such as a secret recipe family curry powder.

Aphrodisia, 28 Carmine Street, New York, New York 10014. Catalog $1.50.

Aphrodisia is the kind of store that gives New York's Greenwich Village its charm and attracts shoppers from all over. The store not only stocks a remarkable selection of herbs and spices, artful blends of herbal teas, Chinese, Indian, and Indonesian specialties, and essential oils, but the owner and the staff also maintain a family-like ambiance that makes Aphrodisia a pleasant place to shop. As one customer said, "Whenever I shop at Aphrodisia, I learn something new. One day I just went in for a little oregano for red sauce, and came home with borage, peppermint, and savory to make herb pie. It was delicious."

The catalog, one of the finest we have seen and easily worth the $1.50, is a guidebook for constant reference. All the products offered by Aphrodisia are carefully explained and nicely illustrated, and recipes and suggested uses for herbs and spices in cooking and brewing are liberally and entertainingly punctuated throughout the catalog's 112 pages. Recipes include Kitfo (Ethiopian-style minced meat), using berberi ($1.75 per ¼ pound) and cardamom ($3.75 per ¼ pound—ground); claret cup, made with borage ($1.95, ¼ pound); and Tandoori chicken, using ajma ($1.55, ¼ pound), pomegranate ($1.45, ¼ pound), cumin ($1.35, ¼ pound), and yellow mustard seeds (55¢, ¼ pound). There are recipes for hair rinse (dark, red, or blonde), Christmas potpourri, and scores of other entertaining ideas.

Herb Pie

1 pound potatoes
1 tablespoon butter
1 tablespoon savory
1 head lettuce
½ pound spinach
2 tablespoons borage
2 tablespoons peppermint
¼ cup cream or milk
Pinch cinnamon
Salt and pepper to taste
Freshly grated nutmeg

Boil potatoes until soft; mash with butter and savory; spread along the bottom and sides of a casserole dish (as crust); set aside. Boil a large pot of water; remove from heat; put in lettuce and spinach and immediately remove them with a slotted spoon; drain and allow to cool. Soak borage and peppermint in water for about 5 minutes; drain. Put lettuce, spinach, borage, peppermint, cream (or milk), cinnamon, salt, and pepper into blender; whirl until smooth. Pour into crust and grate a little nutmeg over the top. Bake in 400° F oven for about 10 minutes. Serve hot.

Armanino Marketing Corporation, 1970 Carroll Avenue, San Francisco, California 94124. Free brochure.

Armanino markets a product called "San Francisco Seasoning," which is a blend of spices including freeze-dried shallots, chives, basil, leeks, and garlic ($1.05 per 1¼-ounce jar). Available separately are freeze-dried shallots, chives, leeks, Italian parsley, mushrooms, and green and red bell peppers ($2.50 a tin). A freeze-dried version of pesto, the northern Italian basil sauce, comes in a pouch and will flavor 1 pound of pasta ($1.00 per pouch). Prices include delivery. On orders under $10.00, add $1.00 postage.

Barclays Coffee, Tea & Spice Company, Ltd., 9020 Tampa Avenue, Northridge, California 91324.

Barclays features over 20 kinds of whole bean coffee, always freshly roasted, and more than 30 kinds of tea and herb tea. Teas are shipped in sealed chests, the same technique that has ensured freshness since before the Boston Tea Party. Coffee selections include a special cinnamon roast, a medium-body house blend, Jamaican Blue Mountain, and Kolossi Celebes. Mail orders are shipped the same day that they are received, and coffees can be ground to specification or ordered whole bean. Barclays also has an excellent selection of coffee- and tea-related items, including espresso and cappuccino machines, grinders, and pots.

Celestial Seasonings, P.O. Box 4367, Boulder, Colorado 80302. Free brochure.

Celestial Seasonings is a young company which started in 1970 by handpicking wild herbs growing in the Colorado Rockies. It is now the largest herb tea company in North America, offering herb tea blends in bags or loose, as well as single herbs. Noncaffeinated blends ($3.80 per pound) include "Mo's 24 Herb Tea" containing (you guessed it), twenty-four herbs and having a woodsy flavor tasting like "liquid Colorado." "Red Zinger" ($3.75 per pound), recommended to those trying herb tea for the first time, can be served hot or iced or mixed with fruit juices, and "Pelican Punch" ($3.95 per pound) is a blend of crystal malt, peppermint, carob, blackberry leaves, coconut, licorice, and vanilla and almond extract which was formulated especially for children. Several of the noncaffeinated tea blends would make a healthful alternative to soda pop. Teas come bagged and boxed as well as in bulk.

Celestial's caffeinated blends are maté based, the simplest being a blend of green maté and roasted chicory root ($2.40 per pound). Celestial also has herb and ginseng tablets, ginseng roots and powders, and single herbs by the pound. In order to keep its prices low, the company requires a $15.00 minimum order.

The Ceylon Tea Promotion Bureau, Colombo, Sri Lanka. Free brochure.

Tea can be ordered directly from one of the great tea-producing countries of the world. Although the United States imports over 10 percent of Sri Lanka's annual export crop, high-quality, bulk Ceylon tea is often difficult to obtain in this country because of the increasing popularity of bagged and instant tea. High-quality tea from the better known districts such as Dimbula, Uva, and Nuwara Eliya (grown at six thousand to seven thousand feet) can be ordered in gift packages directly from The Tea Promotion Bureau.

L. A. Champon and Company, Inc., 70 Hudson Street, Hoboken, New Jersey 07030. Prices on request.

Need ten tons of vanilla beans? L. A. Champon and Company is an import broker that sells vanilla beans from Madagascar and other origins. The company also sells in smaller quantities—1 bean for 50¢ (minimum order, 2 beans) or 1 dozen for $5. Both prices are postpaid. They will sell quantities of 10 to 20 tons if necessary.

Chico-San Inc., P.O. Box 1004, Chico, California 95926. Free catalog.

White, unrefined sea salt from Chico-San is crude salt which has been washed with seawater and dried by the sun. A sesame salt (8-ounce bag, $1.05) made from whole roasted and crushed sesame seeds is recommended for use with all foods. Kuzu is a wild arrowroot starch to be used as a thickener for sauces and soups (4 ounces, $1.75). Whole, brown, unhulled sesame seeds are offered by the pound ($1.40). Among the teas are Ohsawa twig tea which is a lightly roasted green tea, and a tea made from powdered lotus root (1¾ ounces, $1.39). A unique dentifrice is Chico-San's tooth powder made from eggplant and salt (1¾ ounces, about $1.00). (Do you have to brush your teeth after brushing your teeth with eggplant??)

O. H. Clapp & Company, Inc., 47 Riverside Avenue, Westport, Connecticut 06880. Free mail-order form.

O. H. Clapp is primarily an importer of teas and it sells large quantities of unblended tea to the major packers in the United States and Canada. The company offers 6 "vintage" teas in small quantities to mail-order customers. There are 4 mainland China teas—jasmine, Keemun, oolong, and Yunnan, in addition to Formosa oolong and Darjeeling. The teas come packed in attractive miniature wooden tea chests ($7.50 each). A sampler of 2 ounces of each of the 6 varieties is also available ($5.00). As a point of interest, Clapp notes that Keemun was the tea that was dumped into the harbor during the Boston Tea Party. Postage and handling $1.00 additional per order.

East India Tea & Coffee, Ltd., 1483 Third Street, San Francisco, California 94107. Free brochure and newsletter.

The East India company appears to be more than a business selling coffees and teas by mail. Would be *exigentes* can start with the coffee sample of 10 different varieties (a tea sampler of 12 types is also available for $6.95) and then learn about brewing techniques from the *East India Packet,* a 4-page newsletter filled with recipes and historical tidbits about coffees and teas. There are 10 different coffees sold and twice as many teas, including some herbal varieties. Pots and brewing accessories can also be ordered, and there is a subscription plan whereby 3 different coffees or teas are shipped monthly. East India accepts telephone orders at (415) 543-5690 with major credit card payment.

Estus, 2186 San Pasqual Street, Pasadena, California 91107. Free price list.

The rage in France several years ago, green peppercorns have become increasingly popular in this country and are generally available canned. Estus sells freeze-dried Madagascar green peppercorns ($3.50) which can be used in a pepper mill, and thereby solves the problem of what to do with the costly leftover little monsters. Other herbs available freeze-dried are tarragon ($2.50), chives ($2.00), and

---

THE GROWTH OF THE COFFEE BEAN

The coffee tree, in reality a shrub, takes about five years to reach maturity. Before fruition, delicate white blossoms appear, similar to jasmine in form and scent. They disappear quickly and are replaced in two months' time by green "cherries" which take about six months more to ripen, turning to red and finally to a deep blackish red. The ripe cherries are handpicked. depulped to reveal the two coffee beans which are then dried and hulled to remove a parchment-like covering and silver skin. Then they are graded for weight and size, and finally hand-inspected to remove impurities and off-color or otherwise imperfect beans. This is the green coffee of commerce which is packed in bags, each weighing 132 pounds.

It takes almost two thousand handpicked coffee cherries to provide enough beans for one pound of roasted coffee. This is slightly more than the annual crop of one average coffee tree.

---

sweet basil ($2.50), all in .28-ounce packets. Herbes d'Provence, a blend of dried herbs from the Côte d'Azur, are put up in rustic terra-cotta crocks—1 ounce, $3.75. Prices include delivery.

Flavorworld, 622 St. Ann Street, New Orleans, Louisiana 70116. 30-page price list, 50¢ plus 24¢ for each mailing.

Flavorworld makes the following offer to its customers: "If you are looking for some particular herb or spice not listed in this catalog, we either have it amongst our vast collection, or can obtain it for you, provided it is legally available anywhere." One would be hard pressed to find a botanical not listed, but don't ask for peyote. Each herb and spice in Flavorworld's hefty price list is described, and uses are recommended. One can learn that cream of tartar (75¢ per pound) is made from pressed grapes, that cubeb berries ($1.85 per pound) can be used as a substitute for pepper and is one of the oldest known ingredients of love potions, that a tea made from fennel berries (82¢ per ¼ pound) supposedly will help control appetite, and that goat's-rue ($1.50 per ¼ pound), usually brewed into a tea,

Crab Boil

1 cup salt
1 tablespoon whole black pepper
1 tablespoon crushed red pepper
4 whole cloves
4 bay leaves
1 teaspoon thyme
2 tablespoons minced parsley
6 whole allspice
½ teaspoon whole celery seed

Combine ingredients and boil in a large pot of water with the crabs. This is an old and traditional New Orleans specialty. For 12 crabs.

is a good soak for tired feet. Also sold are Korean and Manchurian ginseng (whole red root, 1 ounce, $14.00), essential oils, a complete line of Wagner, Jacksons of Piccadilly, and Twinings teas, and specialty foods for Chinese, Japanese, Indonesian, and Malaysian cookery. An impressive selection of coffee, straight growths and blends, is provided, with the blends listing their formula in ounces.

For Your Health, 1136 Eglinton Avenue West, Toronto, Ontario, Canada. Price list 10¢.

The fourth generation now runs this family herb business, which started in 1888 and claims to be the largest supplier of ginseng in Canada. The lengthy price list includes whole and powdered herbs, culinary spices in many varieties, herbal fluid extracts, elixirs, oils, and syrups. There are grapefruit oil ($1.50 per ounce) and dillweed oil ($4.95 per ounce) as well as, yes, skunk oil ($2.95 per ounce). The spices and herbs come in 4-ounce or 1-pound packages. For Your Health is also the exclusive Canadian

Herbal Moth Balls

Use equal parts of rosemary, tansy, thyme, mint, southernwood, and a pinch of ground cloves. Put into cloth bags and store among your clothes.

Mustard Plasters

These can be made by using 1 part mustard powder to 4 parts whole wheat flour and enough egg whites to make a paste. Blend together and apply to desired area.

supplier of Honeyrose brand, nicotine-free cigarettes. Canadian wild rice by the pound ($5.95) is also sold. Postage is additional.

Galerie Van Der Heyde, Pao Pao, Mooréa, French Polynesia. Free price information.

Vanilla beans are cheap and plentiful on the island of Mooréa in French Polynesia, and the owner of an art gallery and curio shop who is not in the food business has undertaken to airmail them to customers in the United States. About $3.50, which includes postage, will bring 8 vanilla beans in a plastic bag. This is about half the price of most local retail sources.

The Good Time Spice Couple Company, P.O. Box 189, Tiburon, California 94920. Free price list.

Old-fashioned, glass-topped canning jars with a rubber ring and wire closure make the handpacked spice line of this company particularly attractive. Its standard culinary spices and unique blended salts are available jarred or in cellophane refill packages. The specialty salts include "survival salt," a mixture of raw sea salt, kelp, sesame, garlic, and parsley, and "garden salt," a blend of sea salt, sesame, kelp, dill, parsley, celery seed, and ginseng, both $2.50 a jar. Squat, French ½-liter canning jars hold a choice of "cafe coconelle," a blend of coffee, chocolate, and cinnamon, "cafe cardanise," coffee, cardamom, and sweet anise, and "cafe clorange," a blend of ground orange peel and cloves that makes a spicy cup of coffee. Five varieties of herbal teas are similarly packaged, as is "mulling spices"—a blend of cinnamon stick, cracked nutmeg, whole cloves, and dried orange peel designed to enhance the flavor of warm wines, ciders, and meads as well as conventional teas and coffees (all about $5.00).

Grace Tea Company, 799 Broadway, New York, New York 10003. Free leaflet.

The Grace Tea Company in Manhattan is a tea importer that buys teas directly from growers or at primary auctions. This enables the company to offer outstanding teas at what it believes are the lowest possible prices. Its tasting assortment ($8.50, in 2-ounce tins) is a good introduction to five English classics: Darjeeling, Keemun, Lapsang souchong, jasmine, and Formosa oolong. It is particularly proud of its winey Keemun ($4.00 per ½ pound), a black China tea produced in the old, slow, hand-fired manner, and the Darjeeling ($4.90 per ½ pound), which it calls the second best in the world. (No. 1 Darjeeling sells for more than $20 per pound, so a slight compromise was made here.) Grace offers several blended varieties, including a house blend ($4.40 per ½ pound) which is available in tea bags (50 bags for $3.90) as well as loose. The literature contains tips on how to brew and store tea. Shipping is additional.

Hilltop Herb Farm, P.O. Box 866, Cleveland, Texas 77327. Catalog 35¢.

Madeleine and Jim Hill retired to a small Texas farm and planned to take life easy and raise a few chickens. Instead they are raising 1700 different herbs which they ship all over the world. Plants for herb gardens are divided into those "for use at the table," "to delight the eye as well as the nose," "for crevices and little pokey places," "for teas and tisanes," and "for dry places—and too far to drag the hose." Dried herbs come in the same startling array. Culinary blends (all $1.15 each, ppd) include "Spaghetti Zip," recommended for anything with tomatoes and ground beef, and "Garamasola," similar to Chinese five spice. The Hills sell salts herbed with chive, dill, curry, garlic, or celery (85¢ for 8 ounces), as well as herbal tea blends and ingredients to blend your own.

The Hilltop Herb Farm uses many of the 1700 or so varieties of herbs they grow for their interesting line of herbed condiments. Wine vinegars flavored with tarragon, rosemary, dill, mint, bargelo, and dilly lemon thyme have "herbal authority and influence" (4 ounces, $1.00 each, ppd). Herbal jellies include apple rose geranium, cranberry basil, hot pineapple, and tomato horseradish. Recommended for serving with meat or cheese is "Cousin Marr's Jalapeno Jelly." Hot sauces to be used with everything are named "Hellfire and Damnation" and "Fire and Brimstone." It is unclear which is spicier. Herb mustard and relishes such as "Granny's Chow-Chow" and "Dixie Relish" are among the many homemade varieties of condiments. All are about $2.00 each plus postage. Recipe sheets are available with some of Hilltop Farm's favorite canning recipes and a book, *From Our Side of the Farm,* tells you what to do with the vinegars and jellies besides the obvious.

House of Yemen East, 370 Third Avenue, New York, New York 10016. Prices on request.

The house blend of coffee at the House of Yemen is named Henry V, not after a dead king but in honor of Henry Bloomstein, a friend of the owner for whom the special

---

Cantonese Salt (Wah Yeen)

> 1 cup salt
> ½ teaspoon sugar
> 1 teaspoon ground cinnamon
> ½ teaspoon five spices powder

In a skillet on top of the stove, heat salt until it is lightly brown. Remove pan from fire and stir in the other ingredients. This is a tasty dip for deep-fried poultry and seafood.

---

blend was originally created. The unnamed blend was shipped to Mr. Bloomstein in Connecticut, he loved it, and gave the new coffee a "five cup rating." Bloomstein Blend didn't sound quite right and so the name became Henry V. Henry Bloomstein orders at least 10 pounds of beans monthly, but smaller orders are accepted for Henry V as well as other straight and blended coffees, such as Yemen's special Turkish blend, and teas in bulk or ¼- and ½-pound canisters. The House of Yemen will also grind and ship fresh, unsalted peanut butter in 1-pound plastic jars, and mail a large selection of dried fruits and nuts and other specialties such as Greek rose petal jam, Hymettus Greek honey, and a 2-pound tin of baklava.

International Spice Inc., 6687 North Sidney Place, Milwaukee, Wisconsin 53209. Free price list.

Many people own a pepper mill and some a sea salt mill as well. But even though freshly ground spices are widely appreciated, enthusiasts who have grinders for nutmeg, cloves, fennel, and white peppercorns, as well as salt and black pepper, are probably few and far between. The International Spice company came up with a new twist in seasonings by sealing these six popular whole spices in attractive plastic minigrinders. The spices stay fresh until ground by rotating the top. Packaged in Lisbon, the world's major spice exchange, they may be ordered individually or in gift assortments—2 for $3, all 6 for $9.

The Kobos Company, The Water Tower, 5331 S.W. Macadam, Portland, Oregon 97201. Free brochure.

David and Susan Kobos roast their own coffees right in their shop in a renovated furniture factory topped by a water tower. A nice selection of straight growths and blends includes several dark roasts such as French espresso, Turkish blend, and Vienna roast. Sampler packages of coffees and teas are available, as well as a large selection of teas in ½-pound tins. When ordering, specify whole bean or particular grind. The Kobos Company is particularly proud of its extensive stock of culinary spices which are offered in bulk and sold by the ounce. Malden English sea salt is sold in 8-ounce or 1-pound packages (75¢). A minimum order is $5 and credit card charges are accepted on orders over $10.

La Norma Coffee Mills, 4416 North Hubert Avenue, Tampa, Florida 33614. Free price list.

Vacuum-packed 1-pound cans of specialty coffee blends are available from The Coffee House. Among the 8 varieties offered are 2 decaffeinated blends, "Coffee House De-Caf" and a more difficult to find "Expresso De-Caf." The espresso, a dark Italian roast, is available regular as well. Another specialty is "Amigos American," an American-style coffee with a Spanish accent, light brown roasts blended with dark espresso. All coffees come whole bean or ground and The Coffee House runs a "Coffee Bonus Club," shipping out your choice at regular intervals. After 20 cans, 2 are sent free and membership can be canceled at any time.

Lawrence Curry, 5044 Fulton Street, Washington, D.C. 20016. Free price list.

A unique blend of imported spices, the Lawrence curry formula has been a family secret for 225 years. An eighteenth-century Lawrence brought it from Madras, India, and later Lawrences, planters in Jamaica, modified it to include the local ginger. Curry powder mixed to the secret formula, which now resides in a Washington safe-deposit box, is sold by direct mail only, initially to family and friends but now all over the world. The curry powder resides in a 4-ounce jar ($3.00 ppd) and can be ordered along with a small selection of other Indian specialties such as Bombay duck (4-ounce box, $3.00), which is a salt-dried fish, a powdered Tandoori marinade (3½-ounce jar, $1.50), and 4 kinds of mango chutney (17-ounce jars, $3.00).

Luzianne Coffee Company, Box 60296, New Orleans, Louisiana 70160. Free price list.

Luzianne coffees, hard to find outside of New Orleans, can be directly ordered from the manufacturer by the case lot. There are medium and dark roasts, with or without chicory. Packed chicory ($12 for twenty-four 6¼-ounce packages) is also sold, along with an instant coffee mix, iced tea mix, and tea bags. Regularly scheduled orders are accepted for delivery at specified intervals. Prices include postage.

Lynchburg Hardware & General Store, Box 239, Lynchburg, Tennessee 37352. Free catalog.

The proprietor of the General Store offers a little bit of everything, and included in the eclectic collection are 3 spices that may be hard to come by in Northern states. There is "red boiling brand" sassafras root chips for open-pot boiling or ground for the percolator (75¢, 2-ounce package). Another standard item in Tennessee is whole leaf Southern sage (⅛ ounce, 55¢). The last is hot red pepper (½ ounce, 55¢) "used at Mary Bobo's Boarding House" and guaranteed to make "a tired taster sit up and say 'Howdy.'"

McNultey's Tea & Coffee Company, Inc., 109 Christopher Street, New York, New York 10014. Free brochure.

McNultey's brochure lists an incredible variety of teas, both straight and blended. Many of them are rare and difficult to find elsewhere. Listed by country of origin, the straight teas include three varieties of Darjeeling (between $5.50 and $10.00 per pound), two of Assam ($4.00 and $5.00 per pound), a long list of China teas, and some interesting Japanese teas such as uji-gyokura, known as pearl dew ($8.00 per pound), and denmai-cha with toasted rice ($2.00 per pound). The tea list goes on and on with special blends and exotic items like wild cherry tea (80¢ per ounce) and peppermint tea blend ($4.50 per pound) and 4 maté-based teas (between 50¢ and 85¢ per pound). Some of these brews are available in tea bags as well as loose. There are herbal tea bags such as rose hips with hibiscus, and the famous chamomile recommended for fever by Peter Rabbit's mother (48 bags, less than $2.00). McNultey's also sells Bigelow's Constant Comment and a selection of Jacksons of Piccadilly's English line.

McNultey's often obtains rare coffees such as Cameroon Elephant Peaberry and India Cherry. Mail-order customers can arrange to have unusual coffees sent at regular intervals, each mailing a different coffee. McNultey's makes no secret of its blended coffees: the brochure gives a list of the beans used in each blend; for example, the mild house blend is made from equal parts of Santos Bourbon, Maracaibo, and Columbian beans. A Swiss freeze-dried instant coffee, Macafino, is available regular or decaffeinated, and a line of Bigelow-flavored instant coffees, such as café cinnamon and café de menthe, come in jars and packets. All orders are shipped out the same day that they are received, and McNultey's guarantees satisfaction.

Café Seville

    Crushed or chopped ice
    Cold, extra-strength coffee
2 tablespoons sugar
¼ cup Grand Marnier
¼ teaspoon grated orange rind
1 cup milk
    Orange slices

Put ice in cup to half-cup level then fill to top with coffee. Combine with remaining ingredients in blender and whip at high speed until foamy. Serve in tall glasses, garnished with orange slice. Serves 2.

Mr. K's Gourmet Foods and Coffees, Farmers Market Shop 430, 6333 West Third Street, Los Angeles, California 90036. Prices on request.

Tea for $70 a pound? Yes! It's called Mandarin pai-ho or Mandarin White Cloud and was originally reserved for the exclusive use of the aristocracy. The tea, described as "a delicate fragile flowery scent, a mild to light body, and an ethereal light amber color" is the leaf bud of the tea plant picked during its first flush in the Congou district of Mainland China. The price? It's hard to imagine, but Mr. K tells us that it takes one woman who has been trained for twenty-five years over two days to pluck one pound of this tea. Pai-ho can also be ordered by the ounce for $4.50, along with 16 other tea varieties at more down-to-earth prices, and a large selection of gourmet-type foods and fancy food baskets.

Murchie's Tea and Coffee Ltd., 560 Cambie Street, Vancouver, British Columbia V6B 2N7, Canada. Free brochure.

In the sidehills of the Himalayas in northern India is the district of Darjeeling, in which are found some 150 distinctive tea gardens specializing in some of the world's most delicate teas. Murchie's claims to be the first in the "free world" to sell these muscatel teas by crop season, garden, and vessel name. If that's your cup of tea, Murchie's has an extensive selection from which you can choose. An importer and blender for nearly a century, Murchie's offers tea both in bulk and bagged. There are also gift-boxed teas in Oriental-design English canisters, minipacks of up to 24 samplers (about $10 for 24), a selection of coffees, and whole or freshly ground spices. Murchie's notes that there is no duty or tax on tea or coffee entering the United States: the Bostonians took care of that a while back.

Natural Food Supplements, Inc., 8725 Remmet Avenue, Canoga Park, California 91304. Free catalog.

A unique line of freeze-dried fruit and vegetable seasonings is offered by this company which produces Sunshine Valley food products. Whole peach, whole lime, whole orange, mushroom pieces, red radish root, and red radish leaves are among the varieties. All are made from orchard-fresh and garden-fresh fruits and vegetables with no additives or fillers, and can be used to add flavor and nutrition to a variety of foods (under $6.00 for 2 ounces). Also available by mail order are Sunshine Valley herb teas and several seasoning blends (all between $1.00 and $1.50) such as a hickory-smoked seasoning made with all natural ingredients; a vegetable seasoning salt made from sea salt and powdered dehydrates of peas, spinach, kelp, horseradish, asparagus, and about ten other vegetables; and a special salt-free blend of kelp, plantain, rosemary, comfrey, marjoram, papaya, and guava.

Nichols Garden Nursery, 1190 North Pacific Highway, Albany, Oregon 97321. Free catalog.

Nichols is a large grower and importer of seeds, and this listing in its catalog is extensive and includes many difficult-to-find varieties. Among the food items offered are a good selection of culinary herbs and seeds. The special herb blends, numbered from one to fourteen (1-ounce packets, 70¢), include a blend for almost any purpose. Among the more unusual selections are a catsup spice seasoning which comes with a recipe for making up to sixteen pints of catsup (95¢ per ounce), an apple pie seasoning which comes from a hundred-year-old New England recipe (migrated to the West Coast), and pork sausage seasoning (two kinds for country or Italian sausage) which also comes from an old New England recipe (4 ounces, $1.60, makes 16 pounds of sausage). These last come with directions on sausagemaking. A selection of herbal and botanical teas is offered, along with several regular tea varieties. Old-fashioned sweet soda water extracts in the tradition of the "J. B. Douglass Saloon" of 1857, in the gold rush country of California, come with recipes and special yeast for natural carbonation. Flavors are sarsaparilla, wild cherry, root beer, and cream soda ($1.85 per jar of extract which makes 55 glasses).

Northwestern Coffee Mills, 217 North Broadway, Milwaukee, Wisconsin 53202. Free catalog.

The catalog is free but "25¢ donations are accepted." Beautifully designed, descriptive, and informative, it is worth an even larger donation. Among the 7 blended coffees are mocha-Java blend, a Hawaiian Kona blend and "Stapleton Restaurant Blend," a favorite of some Milwaukee restaurants worthy of note because of its "forgiving nature when kept heated for long periods of time." Straight growths include Ethiopian Harrar, the highest grown and the best of the Ethiopian coffees, Java Arabica from the Spice Islands, and Mexican Altura. Green coffees are available for those who wish to experiment with roasting their own. There is even a home coffee roaster, but it is only half-heartedly recommended by Northwestern—"it smokes and smells a lot, and is crudely built." Coffee makers, grinders, teapots, and infusers are sold, all fully described and illustrated in the catalog.

A very nice selection of unblended teas is offered, along with blends which are fully described in the catalog. If a customer is interested in a blend that does not appear, Northwestern will create it. (The company prefers that you send a sample, which it will do its best to duplicate or improve.) In addition to the black teas, oolongs, green teas, and scented teas, there are herbal teas, Korean ginseng, and yerba maté ($1.65 per pound).

A complete range of basic cooking spices is sold by the ounce, and they are freshly ground where appropriate. Ask for the special price list for bulk quantities of 1 pound or more. Dehydrated seasonings include mushrooms from South America and some from Europe. Many of the herbs and spices are listed with their country of origin. Chili peppers are available from either Japan or Turkey ($1.40 for 4 ounces); pepper selections include black Tellicherry and black lampong from India, and white pepper from Indonesia (all $1.60 for 4 ounces). Carob powder is sold by the pound ($1.25), as is chicory ($1.75). A company which seems to stress personal service, telephone orders are accepted at (414) 276-1031 or 3278, 9:00 A.M. to 3.00 P.M. Major credit cards.

The Old Mexico Shop, Patio 49, Santa Fe, New Mexico 87501. Free catalog.

The Old Mexico Shop offers primarily handcrafted giftware, with a few food items. The most unusual are the chili pepper wreaths and garlands, bright-red, dried, Southwestern chili pepper pods woven into an 18-inch-diameter wreath or a 4-foot-long garland, each containing about 200 peppers, either one $12.50 postpaid. They make unique Christmas decorations, and the edible peppers can be individually plucked. No processing or sprays are added, and a free cookbook accompanies each order.

Paprikas Weiss, Importer, 1546 Second Avenue, New York, New York 10028. Catalog $1 for annual subscription.

Paprika, the finest quality Hungarian paprika, imported directly from Szeged, the hub of the Hungarian paprika industry, is featured in one of the opening pages of the Paprikas Weiss catalog. This shop began its relationship with the paprika industry when the current owner's grandfather sent back to the old country for the family's supply of paprika. Soon he was getting regular shipments and selling the spice to his Hungarian neighbors, first hawking his wares through the streets and then opening the grocery store that still bears the name called out to him by his early customers, "Paprikas Weiss." Several types of paprika are imported: sweet, which lends seasoning and color to dishes but is mild; half sweet, more pungent and a warm rose color; and hot, which really is and is nearly brown in color. All varieties cost about $5 a pound. Paprikas Weiss carries some 150 other spices, as well as its own imported curry powder blend ($7 per pound) and blue poppy seeds, whole or freshly ground (about $4 per pound). Spices come in 4-inch-high apothecary jars. A selection of gourmet coffees, whole bean or ground, includes some unusual blends such as Israeli aromatic roasted with cardamom, and a special Hungarian house blend. Teas, herbals, and a nice variety of brewing equipment are also described in the catalog.

Rocky Hollow Herb Farm, Lake Wallkill Road, Sussex, New Jersey 07461. Catalog 25¢.

The Rocky Hollow Herb Farm harvests and imports, at last count, 153 varieties of edible herbs and spices. Of special interest are its own culinary blends (1-ounce packages) which include "Oriental Seasoning (90¢), a mix of parsley, ginger, coriander, garlic, sea salt, celery seed, star anise, and Szechuan pepper; "Spice Bread Delight" ($1.00), a combination of sesame, anise, cinnamon, coriander, cardamom, and mace; and "Seafood Seasoning" (90¢), a blend of five spices to be added to melted butter and rubbed on fish. Eight herbal tea blends are described in the catalog. Colonial Tea (1 ounce, $1.05), a supposed favorite of the early settlers of the Wallkill River Valley, is a combination of peppermint, cloves, nutmeg, and citrus peel. Kittatinny Tea (85¢ for ½ ounce) is a fragrant blend of lemon verbena, rosebuds, chamomile, and rosemary. Edible essential oils can be used to add flavor to foods with just a dip of a toothpick. These distilled concentrated flavorings, such as tarragon ($7.00), thyme ($3.00), cinnamon ($3.00), and fennel ($5.60), come in ⅛-ounce vials. Shipping charges are additional.

Claret Cup
(made with borage)

> Juice of 1 lemon, lime, or orange
> ¼ cup powdered sugar
> ¼ cup borage*
> 1 quart wine
> Sliced fruit for garnish

Mix juice and sugar. Steep borage in it overnight. Put into punch bowl along with claret, sliced fruit, and ice.

* Borage: This pleasant herb, with its cucumber-like taste, has an ancient reputation of dispelling melancholy and giving courage. The ancient Greeks put it into their wine.

Rohrs Coffee and Teas, 1692 Second Avenue, New York, New York 10028. Free brochure.

The oldest family-run coffee and tea shop in New York City, Rohrs carries eight basic types of coffee. "What we sell, we sell a lot of, and for that reason you can be sure it is always fresh." The family specialty is coffee blending, and they state that with these eight coffees they can custom-blend to suit every taste. To those who can't find what they want in the brochure, Rohrs makes the following offer: "Tell us what it is or tastes like and we can blend it." Rohrs sells both *genuine* Java and *genuine* mocha coffees and a less expensive Java *style* and mocha *style*. The mocha-Java blend has become extremely popular, and less reputable dealers have been known to substitute cheaper coffees for them. Genuine Java is mild, aromatic, and flavorful, yet not strong bodied on its own; genuine mocha has a winy taste, full-bodied and smooth. The two complement each other delightfully. Rohrs' Java style is Medellin Columbian, rich in its own right, and mocha style is a blend of five South American coffees which offer both richness and taste. Other blends and roasts are described in the leaflet.

Rohrs also has a full line of teas which can be blended to your taste. Available too are green (unroasted) coffee beans, herbal teas, fresh roasted peanuts (about $1.00 per pound), freshly ground peanut butter (about $1.25 per pound), and for the true coffee freak, Rademaker's Hopjes, the coffee candy (a 5-pound tin, under $6.00).

Santa Cruz Chili & Spice Co., Box 177, Tumacacori, Arizona 85640. Free price list.

All the fixings for a spicy dish of chili are available from the Santa Cruz Chili & Spice Co. Chili products include whole and ground chili tepines, piñones, saladitos, green chilis, and mild or hot chili powder. Orders come from as far away as Scotland and Germany for its own brand of taco sauce. A special invention of the owner is chili paste. Originally a chili sauce was made by pounding dried chili pods in a mortar and pestle, but it can be done by making a roux with shortening and flour and adding paste mixed with water. Unlike dried spices, the paste will keep fresh indefinitely until opened, at which time it should be refrigerated. A case of twelve 15-ounce jars runs under $10.

Schapira Coffee Company, 117 West Tenth Street, New York, New York 10011. Free brochure.

"Flavor Cup Coffee," the house blend of Schapira Coffee Company, was for many years the only coffee sold by this established, family-owned business. A blend of Columbian coffees, it is roasted in three styles: brown roast, darker French roast, and the blackest, Italian espresso. Among the other blends now offered are New Orleans, which is a combination of French roast and chicory, and Turkish blend, Venezuelan and dark roast in a powder grind. For the home blender, 7 straight growths are sold.

Schapira has a wide variety of teas, both loose and bagged. "Flavor Cup Tea" is the house blend of India and China teas served by the Schapira family for over sixty years (about $3.50 per pound). There is a tea sampler containing 8 kinds of teas, enough for a potful of each (under $2.00), and a gift-boxed coffee sampler, for which one may choose 5 coffees from among the varieties sold. Joel, David, and Karl have written *The Book of Coffee and Tea*, a comprehensive guide to brewing, selecting, and tasting coffees, teas, and herbal beverages. An autographed copy can be ordered along with your beans for $8.95 plus $1.00 postage.

Shoffeitt Products Corporation, 420 Hudson Street, Healdsburg, California 95448. Free price list.

Tasteless food and the bitter salt substitutes suggested by his doctor after a near-fatal heart attack prompted William Shoffeitt to experiment with salt-free seasoning blends. It took over two years to have them tested and approved by the FDA, but he believes the effort was worth it, since people on low- or no-sodium diets now have a way to perk up their food.

Under the "Pantry Magic" label, Shoffeitt markets 39 different seasoning combinations, 5 of them salt substitutes and 6 "natural seasoners" containing no preservatives or MSG. All are flavored with lemon which acts as a natural flavor enhancer to many foods. The salt-substitute varieties ($1.49 each) include an herb-mix blend, lemon-onion flavor, and lemon teriyaki seasoning. The natural food line ($1.29 each) has a lemon-pepper blend and an all-purpose seasoning. Some of the seasonings are for meat or fish, others are suggested for use as salad dressing mixes or to be added to sour cream for flavored dips. The complete line is available from Shoffeitt individually and in assorted packages.

Simpson & Vail Inc., 53 Park Place, New York, New York 10007. Free brochure.

Simpson & Vail offers 11 different coffees ground to individual specification or whole bean. Among them are a mocha-Java-Columbian blend and a Hawaiian Kona blend. To introduce customers to its coffees, Simpson & Vail provides sampler 6-ounce canisters. Twenty-five teas and tea blends (from $2.70 per pound for a small leaf Ceylon to $4.50 for fanciest blend Darjeeling) are sold, along with 12 varieties of herbal tea (most about $2.00 for ¼ pound). A special iced tea blend that is nonclouding when iced, and mint-in-tea (both $3.50 per pound), a Southern-style blend, are good hot-weather choices. Bagged teas are also sold. Gift combinations include coffees and teas, along with decorative canisters and coffee grinders. Shipping charges are extra.

Specialty Spice Shop, c/o Koll Business Center, 2757 152nd Avenue, N.E., Redmond, Washington 98052. Free price list.

The specialty here for over fifty years is Market Spice Tea, a brew flavored with cinnamon, orange, and spices. The tea, which runs under $4 per pound, should be stored, as should all teas, in an airtight container. To brew Market Spice, rinse a teapot with hot water, use 1 teaspoon per 4 cups of water. Bring fresh, cold tap water to a full rolling boil and brew 3 to 5 minutes. A nice selection of other teas are offered in bulk, along with herbal teas, coffees, essential oils, and a complete variety of culinary spices, which are sold by weight and not prepackaged. There are 9 chili varieties, from hot, mild, and New Mexican to whole or crushed Hontokas chilis. Dried European and Oriental mushrooms are sold, as are carob beans and powder, sugar crystals in a selection of colors, psyllium and chia seeds, and an item called "7th Wonder."

The Spice Market, 94 Reade Street, New York, New York 10013. Free price list.

This is the kind of market that gets "discovered" every day. It's located in an obscure old building nestled among the once-thriving wholesale-food area of Lower Manhattan, just above Wall Street. When visiting The Spice Market, one feels the allure of the past and certainly senses a seriousness about the business of spices. At noon, crowds of workers from the stock markets and metropolitan government centers flood the store. The Spice Market, a long, narrow structure with a higher-than-average ceiling and wood-planked floors, has an old simplicity about it that forces one's attention on barrels of spices that neatly line the walls. Over 200 varieties of herbs and spices are stocked by the market, including many hard-to-find items. It has Chinese (4 ounces, whole, 90¢) and Japanese (4 ounces, whole, $1.10) chilis; rubbed (4 ounces, $1.00), whole (2 ounces, 80¢), or ground sage (8 ounces, $1.60); Spanish (8

ounces, $1.50) or Hungarian paprika (8 ounces, $1.60); and pepper . . . whole and ground, white, black, lemon, red, green corns packed in brine, and green dehydrated. It's a fun place. Postage is prepaid. Minimum order $5.00.

Stash Tea Company, Box 610, Portland, Oregon 97207. Free catalog.

This company's tea and spice catalog comes with a little gift sample of the "tea of the month," a typical example of which is an iced tea blend of sassafras and lemon grass ($3.30 per ½ pound). Another Stash blend is a fruit tea made from lemon grass, hibiscus, rose hips, cherry bark, wintergreen, and orange peel ($3.10 per ½ pound). There is regular jasmine tea ($1.55 per ½ pound) and a spiced jasmine tea blend ($2.80 per ½ pound), along with many popular teas such as Formosa green gunpowder ($1.65 per ½ pound) and English breakfast blend ($2.00 per ½ pound). An attractive wooden box holds 6 of its most popular herbal teas in resealable plastic minibags ($6.50). Fruit-flavored teas ($1.40 per ¼ pound) include apple, strawberry, and lemon tea, and a new item for Stash is boxes of 100 tea bags in 1 of the 7 flavors or as a mixed assortment ($4.25). A nice selection of culinary spices is sold in 2- and 4-ounce packages. Prices include postage.

The Tea Planters and Importers Company, 55/56 Aldgate High Street, London EC3N 1AU, England. Free price lists.

For over sixty years this company has specialized in sending fine quality teas to customers in Western Europe. The selection of teas, which is deliberately small to ensure freshness, is available only by mail order. The 6 varieties offered are unscented blends which rely solely on the natural flavor of the tea. The teas are described as Good English Tea ($4.20), an invigorating morning tea; Fine Ceylon Tea ($4.55), an appetizing lunchtime tea; Finest Ceylon Tea ($4.95), delicious afternoon tea; and after-dinner tea ($5.25), evening tea ($7.35), and drawing-room tea ($8.25), the last two being Darjeelings. Prices, listed in dollars, are reasonable and include shipping charges. The teas are packaged in airtight tins of ½ kilogram. Several trial parcels of 200 grams of 4 varieties are available and cost about $13.00, including postage.

Tony's, 1101 Harris, Bellingham, Washington 98225. Free price list.

Tony's began as a small herb shop, later started to carry teas, and then acquired a roaster, after which it sold freshly roasted gourmet coffees. Next came an espresso machine and then a selection of domestic and imported cheeses (which are mailed only in the winter months). The shop is now owned by Jill Mosher and Michael Ring, who have expanded the types of coffee, tea, and spice available and renovated the shop to serve more coffees as well as special pastries. Coffees include straight growths and blends, among which are "Jill's Java" and "Tony's Blend." A nice variety of teas come loose, by the ¼ and ½ pound. There are herbal tea blends, and individual herbals. Other beverage powders include roasted carob and a dark Dutch cocoa. Culinary herbs and spices are sold by the ounce and include most essential varieties. Mail-order customers are asked to specify UPS or postal service delivery.

White Flower Farm, Litchfield, Connecticut 06759. Prices on request.

The aristocrat of pepper and a connoisseur's coffee blend are the only food items sold by White Flower Farm. The coffee is whole bean mocha-Java and the pepper is Tellicherry black pepper, whole grains of the finest, largest, darkest, and most pungent pepper available, at $5.25 per pound, postpaid.

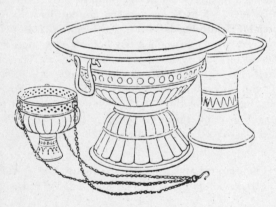

Whittard & Company, Ltd., 111 Fulham Road, London, England SW3 6RP. Free brochure.

For nearly a century, Whittard of Chelsea has offered one of the widest selection of teas in the United Kingdom. There are 5 varieties of Darjeeling, ranging from the least expensive Darjeeling orange pekoe (under $2.00 per pound) to Darjeeling Extra Special Tippy Golden F.O.P. (at about $7.00 per pound). China teas include 3 grades of Lapsang souchong (between $2.00 and $3.00 per pound), which is a large-leafed black tea with a smoky flavor, and 3 Keemuns (from about $1.50 to $2.50 per pound). Among Whittard's most popular items are Breakfast Blend, a strong, full-flavored combination of Indian and Ceylonese growths, and Pelham Mixture, a blend of China teas scented with jas-

mine and bergamot to produce a subtle and delicate aroma. Other special teas include rose-scented tea with petals, peach-flavored tea, and black-currant-flavored tea. **Tisanes** (herbal teas) include lime-tree blossom, verbena lemon scented, and golden maté. Whittard's most expensive tea is peach blossom Formosa oolong at about $10.00 per pound.

Most of the teas are offered in 1-pound canisters, although Ceylon tea comes packed in wooden boxes, and some of the scented and herbal varieties are available by the ¼ pound. Tasting samples of most varieties can be obtained at a small charge. Whittard has a selection of whole bean and ground coffees as well as most interesting coffee sundries such as several varieties of instant coffee, chicory, and pure ground figs (about $1.50 per pound), which give a sweeter, richer flavor to Viennese-style coffee when used about 1 part to 6 parts coffee. Also sold are packages of sugar crystals (under $1.00 per pound), popularly used in England with coffee instead of granulated white sugar. Minimum order is $8.00, plus additional postage and packing charges.

Wide World of Herbs Ltd., 11 St. Catherine Street East, Montreal, Quebec H2X 1K3, Canada. U.S. Address: P.O. Box 266, Rouses Point, New York 12979. Price list $1 with 10 percent discount on first order.

It is hard to imagine that there would be an herb or spice that the Wide World of Herbs doesn't carry. The 13-page

---

Tansy Pudding

Tansy, a symbol of immortality, can be brewed into slightly bitter tea. It was one of the "bitter herbs" of the Bible that the Jews were ordered to eat at Passover time. Tansy and pudding cakes were traditionally eaten to celebrate the end of Lent. The herb was believed to cleanse the body of "bad humours" after the Lenten diet of fish. An old song says, "On Easter Sunday be this pudding seen to which tansy lends the green."

 1 tablespoon tansy
 ½ cup cream
 ¼ cup water
 2 eggs, slightly beaten
 ½ cup soft bread crumbs
 ¼ cup sugar
 ½ teaspoon ground nutmeg

Put tansy, cream, and water into a saucepan; bring to boiling point; cover; remove from heat; let stand.

Combine mixture with other ingredients in a greased casserole and bake in 300° F oven for 1 half hour (or until firm). Serve warm or chilled the next day.

HOW TO STORE COFFEE

There are numerous opinions on exactly how long coffee will stay fresh when refrigerated, frozen, or at room temperature. The consensus is that beans keep longer than ground coffee, that coffee should be stored in airtight, moisture-proof containers, and that coffee (both as beans and ground) freezes well and will stay fresh the longest in the freezer. Beans can be ground directly from the freezer.

---

price list includes two pages of botanicals and two pages of rare botanicals. Rare botanicals include items such as roasted dandelion root, life everlasting powder, broom tops, sheep sorrel leaves, toad flax, unicorn root (true), and unicorn root (false)—all $1.75 for 4 ounces. The less-educated herbalist can order parsley ($1.03), sage ($1.00), rosemary (95¢), and thyme ($1.30)—all in 4-ounce packages. The Wide World of Herbs also sells essential oils, gums, balsams, waxes, dyes, mordants, and Korean ginseng, the last in tablets, sachet tea bags, and whole or powdered roots.

Zabars, 2245 Broadway, New York, New York 10024. Free price lists.

Since 1971, Zabars has been the exclusive East Coast importer of Jamaican coffees. They do not sell these coffees, Jamaica High Mountain Supreme and Jamaica Blue Mountain, to any other retailer or wholesaler. Zabars says it will gladly produce affidavits and documents from the Jamaica Coffee Board to prove that "they are the sole importer and roaster of Jamaica High Mountain Coffee for the entire U.S.A. and of Jamaica Blue Mountain Coffee for the eastern United States."

So much for the pedigree. The Jamaica coffees, rare and highly prized by the coffee connoisseur, are also expensive. Zabars also sells Hawaiian Kona, Tanzania-Kenya Peaberry, and a nice selection of blends. The store advises against blending any of its coffees, with the exception of adding either French-Italian roast or Vienna roast, explaining that blending generally degrades the character of the individual coffees. With most of Zabars' coffees, it would be just a matter of blending blends and the store is probably better at it than you. Zabars imports most of its coffees directly and does all of its own roasting. It notes that coffees will taste different at various times of the year depending upon season, crop changes, and roast variations. Minimum order —5 pounds of coffee which Zabars recommends be kept in the freezer.

For additional sources, see:
Chapter 14. Ethnic Foods
Chapter 17. Health Foods

12. JAMS, JELLIES,
AND CONDIMENTS

IN addition to being savored alone, jams, syrups, condiments, and honeys can serve as that special something with many meals. Included are regional or foreign specialties difficult to obtain elsewhere; many make exciting, unusual, and inexpensive gifts. Beach plum jelly from Cape Cod may be just the present for a displaced Yankee, and there are many who would appreciate a jar of strawberry preserves just like Grandma used to make. Many of the jams and jellies offered are homemade and come in exotic as well as traditional flavors. Most are far superior to supermarket varieties with their additives, heavy sugar, and stingy fruit content. Prices are often competitive. The condiments available include special mustards and soy sauces; chutneys and pickles from India; jalapeno jelly from the Southwest; and Pennsylvania Dutch condiments such as chowchow and pickled watermelon rind. There are organic cider vinegars, herbed vinegars, and special dessert sauces such as a bourbon hard sauce from the South and ginger ice-cream topping from Australia. Many more condiments are available from the shops that specialize in ethnic cooking ingredients and the chapter on health foods also has a selection of such items which have been designed for those who prefer natural ingredient foods.

Alaskan Gourmet, Box 6301, Anchorage, Alaska 99502. Prices on request.

The Alaskan Gourmet specializes in condiments made from wild Alaskan berries, among them sourdough sauce, lingonberry jelly, and cranberry-apple butter. All are put up in 5½-ounce jars, 3 for $9 postpaid.

The Appleyard Corporation, Maple Corner, Calais, Vermont 05648. Free brochure.

The Appleyard Corporation was founded by the late Dr. Hollister Kent and took its name from his mother who, under the name of Mrs. Appleyard, wrote a number of cookbooks and magazine articles. The firm is now owned by two young couples, the Knoxes and the Meyers, who continue to sell under Mrs. Appleyard's name locally made apple cider jelly, tomato chutney (in 9-ounce jars, 2 about $4, 3 about $5), and Cornucopia, a natural dry cereal (3-pound bag about $5). Other products include Vermont maple syrup and cheese and Mrs. Appleyard's cookbooks. Prices include delivery.

Braswell Foods, Inc., P.O. Box 485, Statesboro, Georgia 30458. Free brochure.

This family-operated concern offers an unusual selection of condiments and preserves for about $1.25 per pint. There is artichoke pickle, made from the Jerusalem artichoke, a tuber grown in the mountains of North Carolina, as well as artichoke relish, winter pickle, and red or green bell pepper jelly. Pear preserves are made from fresh fruit, and a plum-raisin sauce is suggested as a complement to roast poultry. Also listed are fig preserves, guava jelly, and rhubarb-raspberry jam.

Broadbent B&B Food Products, Route 1, Cadiz, Kentucky 42211. Free catalog.

Hundred-proof Kentucky bourbon is used to flavor Broadbent's cakes, puddings, and toppings. There is bourbon hard sauce for pudding, cakes, and pies; bourbon sauce supreme recommended for baked apples, plum pudding, and glazing sweet potatoes and ham; and bourbon sundae sauce for, of course, ice cream. Sampler of all 3, between $6 and $7, depending on destination.

Canterbury Cannery, Inc., P.O. Box 17171, San Antonio, Texas 78217. Catalog 50¢.

Canterbury Cannery prides itself on being the first and only full-fledged jalapeno jelly factory in the country, having grown from a small, home-kitchen operation. Sweet and spicy, the jelly is made in small batches with no additives (10-ounce jars). The color of the product will vary from red to green, depending upon the availability of fresh produce. A new item offered by the company is rojo picante (8-ounce jars), a spicy hot sauce made from tomatoes, onions, jalapeno peppers, vinegar, and spices. Either of these condiments is recommended as an accompaniment to roast meat. Three jars of either or a mixed selection costs between $6 and $7. Shipping charges are additional.

The Carolina Mountain Shop, Cashiers, North Carolina 28717. Free brochure.

Homemade preserves, relishes, and sauces made from local mountain fruits and berries are the specialty foods carried by this family-owned shop. Preserves are made by Dot's mother right next door, and include blackberry, wild strawberry with port wine, and huckleberry marmalade. An assortment of six 8-ounce jars is under $8. Damson plum sauce and sweet-and-sour peach chutney are featured among the 12 varieties of relishes and sweet dessert sauces. A selection of either 4 sweet sauces or 4 relishes in 8-ounce jars is about $5.

Chico-San Inc., P.O. Box 1004, Chico, California 95926. Free catalog.

Chico-San, a grower of organic brown rices, offers a traditional Japanese condiment, "Lima Soy Sauce," made in a small rustic factory in northern Japan by the same family for over ten generations. It is a naturally made product, aged for over two years, and contains no chemical stabilizers (under $3.00 a quart). Imported rice malt vinegar is also naturally produced in the traditional Oriental fashion (5 ounces, less than $1.50). Light and dark sesame oil is made from whole, brown, pressed sesame seeds. Yinnes rice syrup is a natural sweetener made from rice water and barley which has a mild delicate flavor and may be used to replace honey (1 gallon, about $12.00).

Cranberry House, R.F.D. 3, Buzzards Bay, Massachusetts 02532. Free leaflet.

From the folks who provide the traditional accompaniment to the Thanksgiving Day turkey come special Ocean Spray cranberry products that are not available in supermarkets or gourmet shops. Their Cape Cod Cranberry House will send cranberry preserves in assorted flavors such as strawberry–cranberry, grape–cranberry, and red raspberry–cranberry, and, yes, cranberry (all 7 flavors in 10-ounce jars, about $10.00 delivered). Jelly made from Cape Cod wild beach plums is also sold, along with cranberry and cranapple syrups. Cran Mix is sweetened cranberry juice without water, designed for making cocktails (32 ounces, $4.25 ppd). There is also pure, undiluted, and unsweetened cranberry juice (32 ounces, $4.00 ppd). Included with the jams in various gift packs, some of them in attractive reusable baskets or woodenware, are cranberry nut and fruit breads. A sampler package will bring 5 varieties ($12.50 ppd).

Estus, 2186 San Pasqual Street, Pasadena, California 91107. Free price list.

The Estus company introduced Moutarde de Meaux Pommery to the United States about twelve years go. The large crock with red sealing wax has become familiar on many gourmet shelves, but if it is unavailable in your locale, it can be ordered directly from Estus ($5.50 for 17½ ounces). Pommery addicts credit its success to the quality of the vinegar and the crushing of the whole mustard seed. The formula goes back to 1632. Also available by mail at the same price are a line of strong Dijon mustards produced in France and packaged in attractive French pickling jars (7 ounces) which permit the mustard to arrive at the table with all the piquancy it had when it left the factory. These mustards come plain or flavored with tarragon, horseradish, green peppercorns, or tomato and paprika.

Franjoh Cellars, P.O. Box 7462, Stockton, California 95207. Free brochure.

Franjoh Cellars manufactures the widely acclaimed working vinegar barrel. The handcrafted, brass-hooped, oaken barrel comes with a working mother and a starter supply of vinegar. Leftover wine of any kind, color, or age is poured into the barrel to provide a perpetual source of natural vinegar with no additives or preservatives. Mother and cask are about $40 postpaid, and Franjoh has a toll-free number, (800) 344-3221, to call to place an order and receive further information.

The Gardens Country Store, Callaway Gardens, Pine Mountain, Georgia 31822. Free catalog.

Muscadine grapes, the local Georgia fruit, serve as the mainstay for many Gardens Store products, among them muscadine grape butter, muscadine syrup, and muscadine sauce and grape jelly. Other varieties of jellies and preserves are elderberry, crabapple, and red plum. The condiment selection includes watermelon pickle, red pepper relish, and pickle peach chutney. These items are all sold in combination packages of 3 or more. An assortment of twelve 2½-ounce sampler jars is about $8, while a package of three ¾-pound jars of muscadine products is about $7. Prices include delivery.

The Ginger Factory, P.O. Box 114, Buderim 4556, Queensland, Australia. Free brochure.

The growing of ginger dates back to antiquity. The plant is indigenous to Asia and grows prolifically in the wild state. At the turn of the century, ginger growing started on the Sunshine Coast of Australia, some sixty miles north of Brisbane. All this is leading up to the Buderim Ginger Factory, the only one in the Southern Hemisphere and the largest of its kind in the world.

The factory processes and sells a wide range of ginger products under the name of "Merrybud," some of which are offered for mail-order export. Among these are crystallized ginger (5 pounds, about $8.50), young stem ginger rolled in sugar, and ginger in syrup (5 pounds, about $7.00), the same product in a thick sweet sauce. Also offered are ginger marmalade, ginger topping, and ginger date nut spread. Merrybud ginger comes gift-packaged and in large presentation hampers. If you are down under, you can stop in at the factory, a national tourist attraction, and snack at the Ginger Bar on hot scones with ginger marmalade and cream, or ice cream with ginger topping.

Herter's Inc., Route 2, Mitchell, South Dakota 57301. Catalog $1.

Among the food items offered in Herter's 350-page catalog of sporting and camping equipment are several unique condiments. There are wild fruit syrups in either blueberry or chokecherry flavors, a concentrated cream of toffee syrup, all in quart bottles for under $2.00, and "Authentic Count Karl Nesselrode Sauce" made of marrons, pineapple, melon rind, and cherries in a heavy sugar syrup (32-ounce jar about $4.00). Herter's 5-Alarm sauce is recommended for those who like a very strongly flavored hot sauce on "hamburgers, hot dogs, meat, duck, venison or in soups, beer or whisky." Three Alarm sauce is available for those with more delicate taste buds (14-ounce bottle of either, about $1.50). Liquid smoke is a bottled product for giving a smoked flavor to meats ($2.00 per pint). Also available is a smoke-flavor cure kit for making your own beef or deer jerky, smoked fish, or smoked fowl. The kit (less than $2.00) comes with instructions and is sufficient for preparing 12 pounds of meat.

Hickin's Mountain Mowings Farm and Greenhouses, Black Mountain Road, Brattleboro, Vermont 05301. Free brochure.

The Hickins love growing things, from the exotic to the traditional. In an average season they have more than 100 varieties of vegetables and fruits, including snow peas, radishetta, lemon cucumbers, and 25 varieties of lettuce. When they are not harvesting vegetables or pampering plants, they are busy preparing their jams, pickles, and baked goods. The jams, jellies, and preserves come in many varieties—wild blackberry, maple-apple butter, lemonmint, to name a few (6-ounce jars, $1.45). A unique item is Hickin's fresh fruit syrups, which are offered in various flavors and are available unsweetened, sweetened with sugar, and sweetened with maple syrup from their own sugarhouse (6 ounces, $2.45). The homemade pickles have a distinct New England flavor, as many of them are also sweetened with maple syrup. A mixture called crookzini is a combination of crookneck, zucchini, and pattypan squashes. There are also icicle lemon cuke pickles, corn relish, kohlrabi dill pickles, stuffed peppers (9 ounces, $2.50; other varieties, $1.45 for 9 ounces), fresh-ground horseradish, tomato ketchup, and maple chili sauce. Gift packages are available in various assortments which include cheese, bacon, and honey, as well as the condiments and jams. Empty spaces can be packed with Hickin's fresh apples—30¢ each. Shipping charges are extra.

Kountry Kitchen, Custer, Montana 59024. Free catalog.

Wild fruits picked in the Yellowstone Valley and old pioneer recipes combine to make Kountry Kitchen syrups and jellies. Chokecherry syrup is bottled and also put up in stoneware jugs (pints about $5). The jellies come in flavors such as buffalo berry, wild plum, and chokecherry (two 7-ounce jars, about $5). All are made without additives or artificial colorings. Prices are postpaid.

Pennsylvania Dutch Company, The Amishman, Mount Holly Springs, Pennsylvania 17065. Free brochure.

Together with a line of candies, The Amishman features jams, jellies, honey, syrup, and condiments. Sweet-sour dressing made from maple syrup ($2.00 for an 8-ounce bottle), horseradish-flavor sauce (8 ounces for $1.50), and sharp mustard sauce (11 ounces, $1.45) are some of the specialties, as are Aunt Lillian's red tomato relish (15½ ounces, $1.75) and Aunt Lottie's pepper cabbage (15½ ounces, $1.35). Also available are salted Virginia peanut butter (12 ounces, $1.75); a number of honeys, two of which are wild huckleberry and buckwheat (1 pound jars, $2.25); country-style apple butter (28 ounces, $2.25) and Brother George's apple butter made without sugar and spices. The last is a recipe brought to this country from England in the 1700s by a small group of people calling themselves the Schwenkfelders (18 ounces, $2.25).

M. M. Poonjiaji & Co., 42, First Marine Street, Bombay-2, India. Free brochure.

Yes, Virginia, there was a Major Grey. Not only did he exist, but this eighteenth-century Bengal Lancer was responsible for the standard recipe for chutney used throughout the world. According to the legend, he standardized Indian chutney to European taste, packed it in wooden casks, and dispatched it to London on clipper ships.

In a spirit of twentieth-century romance, M. M. Poonjiaji & Co. will dispatch your order of "Ship Brand Green Label" Major Grey chutney by registered sea mail. At the time of this writing, $22 will bring twelve ½-pound bottles or cans of Poonjiaji sweet sliced mango chutney, hot mango chutney, Major Grey's mango chutney, sliced mango pickle, lime pickle, combination pickle, or curry, in a choice of powder or paste. Check current prices before ordering.

Saltmarsh Cider Mill, New Boston, New Hampshire 03070. Free brochure.

Pure apple cider vinegar made from unsprayed, organically grown apples is available from the Saltmarsh Cider Mill. Hand-sorted apples are pressed into sweet cider which is then allowed to ferment in charcoaled oak barrels for two to four years. The mature, unpasteurized vinegar, in ½-pint bottles ($6) to gallon glass jugs ($12), contains no preservatives. The bottled vinegar is the only product currently offered for mail order. Apple cider, apple syrup, and apples are available at the mill. Delivery charges are additional.

Savage's Citrus Barn, Inc., Route 1, Box 150, Raymondville, Texas 78580. Free brochure.

The Savages label and sell 18 varieties of preserves, jellies, and relishes made in small batches in the kitchens of their friends. Watermelon rind, old-fashioned fig, blueberry, and dewberry make up the homemade preserve selection. Ringing with Texas-sounding names, their unusual line of jellies consists of jalapeno pepper, ruby red grapefruit, valley lemon, Mexican lime, wild orange, and orange jalapeno. Condiments, such as hot pepper relish, piccalilli, pickled beets, bread and butter pickles, and corn relish, are also available (6 jars, $16 ppd, all one variety or mixed to your selection).

Barbara and Judson Savage are mainly growers of Texas grapefruit and oranges, which they sell in their roadside barn.

Spring Glen Farm Kitchen, Box 518, Ephrata, Pennsylvania 17522. Free brochure, prices on request.

Located in the heart of the Pennsylvania Dutch country, Spring Glen Farm Kitchen offers some of the regional specialties for which the Amish area is noted. There are barrel molasses, apple schnitzel (six 8-ounce bags, $9.01) and Dutch pickles (twelve 15-ounce jars, $13.55). Chowchow is a blend of eleven garden vegetables in a sweet-and-sour syrup. Sweet-and-sour salad dressing, corn relish, sweet pickled beet balls, pickled cauliflower, red cabbage, tomato

relish, and bean and corn salad are also sold. Available only in season are the Dutch treat of sweet, miniature red, green, and yellow peppers stuffed with cabbage (twelve 12-ounce jars, $17.33). Prices include local delivery.

Twist-o Lemon, Revord-James & Company, Golf, Illinois 60029. Free brochure.

Twist-o Lemon is a concentration of oils from the rind of lemons which comes in aerosol (about $5.50) or atomizer-topped bottles (about $7.00). It is pure, undiluted lemon oil, not juice or extract, and is designed for use in flavoring cocktails or on fish, melons, or wherever a bouquet of lemon oils is desired.

Vermont Country Store, Inc., Weston, Vermont 05161. Catalog 25¢.

New England specialty foods ranging from yellow eye beans with pork and brick-oven brown bread to Vermont maple syrup are featured in Vermont Country Store's 90-page catalog, along with many nonfood items.

One can order homemade New England, rum-flavored mincemeat made from a hundred-year-old recipe (3½-pound jar, about $2.00), and pea-sized pearl tapioca in 2-pound bags. Homemade jams and jellies include plum jelly (about $6.00 for 6 jars) made from beach plums found only on the shores of New England waters. Among the selection of confections are maple candies, crystallized candied ginger, and orange peel, along with a colorful array of old-fashioned chewy and hard candies.

Homemade pickles are available in such varieties as green tomato piccalilli, red pepper relish, and sweet mustard pickle (about $6.00 for 6 jars). Rounding out the condiments line are a mild honey mustard, a tarragon mustard, and an especially strong mustard produced from natural mustard seeds grown in Scotland and England and blended with whole spices ($3.25 per jar, 12 ounces).

Tracklements, the English word for herbal jellies made to accompany meats, game, and fowl, are all apple based, made from English Bramsen apples and whole natural herbs, and come in 4 flavors of red currant, mint, sage, and thyme ($2.75 each in 1-pound jars).

Apple cider vinegar, naturally processed and made from organically grown apples, can also be ordered. Vinegar is bought by the barrel from a nearby orchard and put up by Vermont Country Store in imported Dutch ceramic gin jugs ($3.75 per liter).

Susan Wagner, Juan Santamaria Vintage Vinegar, 505 East Eighty-second Street, New York, New York 10028. Prices on request.

Susan Wagner's enthusiasm for sherry wine vinegar led her to import and store three tons of vinegar in her New York apartment during her first year in business. It all started in London during a visit to the home of the Baron and Baroness John Bacholen von Echt, when Susan was served a memorable salad. When she asked the secret, her hostess explained that it was the vinegar made with sherry that tasted unique. After leaving London, Susan stopped at Jerez de la Fronters in Spain where sherry is made and sought a winemaker who could provide such a vinegar.

"It didn't take long to find out," she said, "that most winemakers don't want to admit they make vinegar, even if they do. It's like asking, sotto voce, 'Is there anybody mad in your family?' I did find one or two bodegas that blended vinegar and admitted it, so I ordered a ton and brought it back with me in the passenger baggage section of an airline charter flight." With the help of a group of metal roofers who had been aboard the flight, along with seven taxis, Susan managed to transport her spontaneous purchase to her apartment by eleven that night. The second shipment of two tons was picked up by truck.

Ms. Wagner notes that her vinegar is strong in flavor and therefore lasts longer than other vinegars and improves with age. Bottles containing 1½ pints cost about $5.

Wray & Turnbull, Ltd., 232 Madison Avenue, New York, New York 10016. Prices on request.

Outerbridge's sherry pepper sauce is a traditional Bermuda condiment which comes in either a glass-stoppered cruet ($4.50) or a more utilitarian shaker-type bottle ($2.50). It can be used to season a wide variety of foods, from scrambled eggs and grilled cheese dishes to Bloody Marys and martinis. Wray and Turnbull, the exclusive distributor of this product in the United States, is willing to send a single bottle.

J. Zachary, Rollingstone, Minnesota 55969. Free brochure.

German-style and French-style mustards put up in crocks with metal closures are available for about $3.00 each. Attractive packaging is part of all of the Zachary products—old-fashioned little jugs of honey, maple syrup, vanilla extract, and salad dressings. Special seasoning blends, herbs, and spices come in cork-closed crocks. There are bags of natural red or black popcorn ($3.50 and $2.50), as well as a popcorn-lovers' kit ($12.00) which adds white and yellow dried corns. The colored kernels are claimed to be distinctive when popped and are described as making popcorn either bright white, almost white, soft white, or haze white—apparently important distinctions to the popcorn connoisseur. Zachary also offers popping corn on the cob (from $2.50 to $12.00), a special finishing salt, and pure coconut oil ($2.00).

For additional sources, see:
Chapter 7. From Soup . . .:
   Harold's Cabin
Chapter 11. Coffee, Tea and Spice:
   Hilltop Herb Farm
Chapter 14. Ethnic Foods
Chapter 17. Health Foods:
   Cayol Natural Foods
   Deer Valley Farm and Farm Store
   David Hodas
   Infinity Food Company
   The Natural Development Company
   Natural Foods Supplements, Inc.
   Pavo's

13. HONEY AND
MAPLE SYRUP

"In contemplating the present opening prospects of human affairs, I am led to expect that a material part of the general happiness which heaven seems to have prepared for mankind, will be derived from the manufacture and general use of Maple Sugar."

Letter to Thomas Jefferson from Benjamin Rush,
August 19, 1791

PURE maple syrup, a unique American product easily purchased at New England roadside stands, is readily available by mail order. Most of the maple syrup sources listed in New England, Wisconsin, and New York State (which, incidentally, is the largest producer of maple syrup in the country) do their own sugaring. Prices vary from season to season depending on production. Which grade to buy is often a matter of personal taste, as there are those who prefer the lower (and less expensive) grades generally recommended for cooking, for table use as well. Along with syrup, there are maple sugar candies, creams, and old-fashioned maple sugar.

Honey, straight from the apiaries, comes in many colors and flavors, depending on the source from which the bees gather the nectar. You will find honey in several forms: liquid honey that has been forced from the comb and is free of crystals; comb honey that is sold in the comb just as the bees store it; solid honey, referred to as candied, creamed, or churned, which is partially or wholly granulated; and chunk honey, a combination of liquid and comb honey. Many of the sources will send along ideas for substituting honey and syrup in place of sugar and provide enjoyable recipes for the likes of maple nut pie, honey apple pie, and baked beans made with maple syrup.

Brookman Farms, R.R. 2, Box 157, South Dayton, New York 14138. Prices on request.

The Brookman Farm makes and sells pure New York maple syrup which can be mailed anywhere in the United States. It is available by the pint, quart, half-gallon and gallon, from about $3 to $14, plus shipping charges. Prices of maple syrup vary from year to year, depending upon the luck of the sugaring season.

Brother Adam, O.S.B., Buckfast Abbey, Buckfastleigh, Devon, TQ11 0EE, England. Prices on request.

A very limited supply of heather honey, a somewhat bitter and granular honey, and clover honey are available from Buckfast Abbey. The honey, put up in 1-pound containers, is collected and packed by Benedictine monks. A minimum order is 6 jars, which cost at least $12, including postage.

Clark Hill Sugary, Canaan, New Hampshire 03741. Free brochure.

Pure maple syrup from New Hampshire maple trees is available in pint ($3), quart ($5), and half-gallon jugs ($8). The sugary also produces and mails its jarred maple butter (12-ounce jar, $3) and pure, old-fashioned maple sugar candy in 1- and 2-pound tins ($5 and $9). Postage is additional.

Green Mountain Sugar House, R.F.D. 1, Ludlow, Vermont 05149. Free catalog.

Maple sugaring is a rather uncertain process. Dependent upon the weather, one never knows when the season will begin, how long it will last, or how much syrup can be made. A normal season at Green Mountain produces between 2500 and 3500 gallons of maple syrup. It is available in 4 grades. Fancy ($4.70), Grade A ($4.50), and Grade

---

Sugar on Snow

2 cups maple syrup
Large pan of fresh, clean snow (crushed ice for the Southern clime)

Boil syrup until it spins a long thread when dripped (230° F). Spoon small quantities of hot syrup over ice. Let cool. It should form a soft, waxy taffy.

This is traditionally served with fresh doughnuts, sour pickles, and coffee at a Sugar on Snow Party.

B ($4.30) are termed suitable for use as table syrups. Grade C is used primarily for cooking. (Prices are for quarts and do *not* include shipping.) In general, the lightest color syrups are made at the beginning of the season when it is the coldest; as it becomes warmer, the syrup becomes darker. Grade C is made at the very end of the season. All grades are boiled down to weigh eleven pounds to the gallon even though the darkest colored seem thicker because they are more viscous. The Green Mountain Sugar House is open to visitors all year. Items sent in addition to syrups include maple cream (1 pound about $4.00 ppd), Vermont cheddar, and several gift boxes of New England specialties.

Honey Acres, P.O. Box 250, Menomonee Falls, Wisconsin 53051. Free price list.

Honey Acres features unique packaging of its Wisconsin honeys. There is a reproduction of a square 1876 glass Muth jar with cork stopper (about $7 ppd), and a pair of jars, one filled with clover honey, the other with wild flower (about $5 ppd), come packed in a pine crate with a wooden honey paddle. Each pair comes with a booklet explaining the history of the jars. Other varieties of honey offered include basswood, buckwheat, cranberry, and a blend of clover honey and apricots. These are available in standard jars, pottery jugs, canning jars, and a plastic honey bear dispenser which is a replica of an old-fashioned honey container.

Jack's Honey Farm, R.R. 1, Box 290, Asbury, New Jersey 08802. Prices on request.

Jack sells packaged bees. Jack also sells honey. The primary business of Jack and Marie Lancaster is beekeepers' equipment. They carry a complete line of everything needed to keep bees and produce and package your own honey. The bees are only available in the spring. Honey from their own farm is available all year, along with imported honeys and country-made jams, jellies, and relishes.

Dan Johnson's, Route 1, Jaffrey, New Hampshire 03452. Free price list.

The head of an old-time family syrup operation located in the foothills of Mount Monadnock, Dan Johnson claims that his maple syrup is thicker (by New Hampshire state law) and tastier, than the competition's. It comes from "friendly maple trees," and is packed in attractive jugs from ½ pint ($3.30, or 6 for $18.00) to ½ gallon ($10.50). A card and payment will reserve a first-run order on maple syrup each season. These first-run prices include delivery to area states only. According to Johnson, these first sap runs are noted for their unusual light amber color, heavier sugar content, and higher maple flavor. He believes that the earliest sap contact with the spring buds gives this preferred maple taste.

Having been brought up on maple sugaring, Dan Johnson feels he can impart the following advice to hardy souls contemplating entry into the maple business: "1. Have an unlimited bank account. 2. Don't stop to rest while on a thirsty draft horse near the sap holding tank. 3. Always have one eye on the 'free help' for they become mighty generous when for compensation they sweep the shelves clean of four gallon jugs (for one hour of work!). 4. Avoid hollow trees at the end of a 100 tap tubing line. 5. Place the woodpile on the path to the sugar house; there are some old Yankees left who will arrive at the door fully laden. 6. Avoid abrupt entries into the woodshed after hiring high school girls and boys for help. 7. Most of all come early spring avoid shortcuts with the collection tank over ice ponds. Charlie Bacon had to drain the pond in order to recover his tank and Farmall Tractor."

Lang Apiaries, Route 77, Gasport, New York 14067. Free price list; send stamped, self-addressed envelope.

The natural honey from the Lang Apiaries is produced by its own bees. Lang stresses that it is extracted by stainless-steel extractors or centrifuges and not by heat. The honey, strained but not filtered, is available in 3 varieties—clover, fall flowers, and buckwheat—and comes in 5-pound pails ($6.50 each, or 3 for about $15.00, postpaid and insured to New York City; charges for other parts of the country accompany the price list). The honey comes with recipes for such goodies as honey taffy and pumpkin honey pie. Lang's brochure notes that honey should be stored in a tightly covered container in a dark, cool place. Freezing or refrigeration will not harm it but will hasten granulation. If granules do form, the container can be placed in a bowl of warm (not hot) water until all the crystals melt.

L. L. Lanier & Sons, Wewahitchka, Florida 32465. Free price list.

Tupelo honey is gathered from the tupelo gum trees along the Chipola and Apalachicola rivers of northwest Florida. In early spring, bees placed on elevated platforms along the rivers' edges fan out through the blossom-laden swamps to collect the rare honey. This river valley is the only place in the world where it is commercially produced. Tupelo honey is unique in that it does not granulate, and because of its high fruit sugar content, some diabetics are permitted to eat it. Increased demand for the product has led to more pure tupelo honey being sold than is produced, and the Department of Agriculture of the State of Florida now certifies tupelo honey. L. L. Lanier's honey is certified as pure tupelo, and most of its product, which comes packaged in 5-pound jars (about $8.50 each, or 6 for $45.00, prepaid up to one thousand miles) is sold locally or through mail order.

Old-fashioned Honey Apple Cake

½ cup margarine
½ cup brown sugar
¾ cup honey
3 eggs
2½ cups plus 2 tablespoons self-rising flour
½ teaspoon salt
1 teaspoon baking soda
1 teaspoon cinnamon
1 teaspoon nutmeg
1 cup dried apples cooked and mashed.
½ cup buttermilk
½ cup apple cider

Cream margarine and brown sugar, adding honey and eggs. Add sifted dry ingredients, apples, buttermilk, and cider. Bake in a 9-by-13-by-2-inch pan at 325° F for 35 to 45 minutes.

Penner Apiaries, Route 3, Box 3886, Red Bluff, California 96080. Free price list.

The Penners are primarily beekeepers in Red Bluff, California, but their bees travel every summer to Porcupine Plain, Saskatchewan, where they produce a distinctive Canadian clover honey. The unprocessed, unheated honey is naturally crystallized (solid) and spreads like butter if kept at room temperature. It is sold in 1-pound tubs, 4 tubs for about $7. Shipping is additional east of the Rockies.

Liquid Californian honeys from different floral sources which produce distinct flavors are also available. The flavors include sage, star thistle, alfalfa, orange, and California clover. Gift packages with assorted Tehama County, California, products include dried peaches, prunes, walnuts, comb honey, and olives.

Reynolds Sugar Bush, Inc., Aniwa, Wisconsin 54408. Free catalog.

Yes, there are sugar maples in Wisconsin, and Reynolds Sugar Bush claims to be the largest processor and marketer of maple sugar products in the country. The maple syrup, available in quantities up to a gallon, is packaged in a choice of tins (1 gallon, $15 ppd), squeeze bottles, liquor flasks, plastic jugs, glass jugs, and crockery jugs. Reynolds features a large selection of gift assortments as well as maple products, including maple cream (8 ounces, $3 ppd), granulated maple sugar, and maple sugar candies. A unique gift item is a box of maple sugar candy letters spelling out any message desired up to thirty-nine letters, $6 ppd.

Maynard Rogers, Jr., Swanton, Vermont 05488. Prices on request.

Maynard Rogers, Jr., now runs the maple-sugaring operation started by his father many years ago, and is hoping that one of his children or grandchildren will continue the family tradition, of which he is very proud. Fancy grade, described as the sweetest and "first off the top," runs from about $1.50 for a pint to around $11.00 for a gallon.

Henry and Cornelia Swayze, Brookside Farm, Tunbridge, Vermont 05077. Free price list.

Syrupmaking is akin to winemaking in that no two days' production taste exactly the same. The Swayzes believe that their maple syrup operation differs from others in that they store all of their production in small batches until after the boiling season is over, then select complementary

Baked Beans

4 pounds soldier or yellow eye beans
2 teaspoons baking soda
1 cup maple syrup
1 cup brown sugar
4 tablespoons molasses
1 teaspoon dry mustard
¼ pound salt pork

Wash beans and cover with cold water. Add 2 teaspoons baking soda and bring to a boil. Drain and wash with cold water. Cover with cold water and bring to boil 4 more times. The last time, cook until skin of beans cracks open. Pour drained beans into greased baking dish. Add the sauce ingredients above and top with salt pork, thinly sliced. Cover beans with water. Bake at 225° F with a cover on the casserole for 6 to 8 hours. Be sure to keep adding water if the beans start drying out. (The traditional long cooking process may be speeded up, cooking in a 350° F oven for 3 hours. An old Yankee might be able to tell the difference, but they still come out delicious.) Serves a crowd of people.

flavors to blend when packaging their retail containers. Medium amber Grade A and dark amber Grade B syrup come in pints ($3.30), quarts ($5.00), or gallon ($15.40) plastic reproductions of an old stoneware jug. Shipping charges are additional, and discounts are offered on quantities to one address. Grade C dark cooking syrup has a pronounced caramel flavor and comes only in ½-gallon tins ($6.40). Bulk buyers are offered 5-gallon drums of all grades of syrup, but it is noted that the syrup in these drums, once opened, should be recanned or stored in the freezer in smaller containers. In addition to making maple syrup, the Swayzes raise and keep sheep at Brookside Farm and offer for sale breeding stock, lambs, and handspinning fleece and yarn.

Thousand Island Apiaries, Clayton, New York 13624. Free brochure.

Gathered from the blossoms of many varieties of trees and plants, Thousand Island honey is claimed to have a distinct flavor and fragrance. The honey is not heated to a high temperature, and because it is unpasteurized and un-filtered, most of the pollen grains remain in the natural honey. One can choose from liquid honey (3-pound tin, about $5), honey spread, which is creamed, finely granulated honey (4½-pound tin, about $7), or comb honey (three 12-ounce pieces, $5). Discounts are offered on multiple orders, and postage is additional to most of the United States. The brochure offers a recipe for country "switchell," billed as a favorite thirst quencher at haying time, consisting of 3 or 4 tablespoons of a mixture of equal parts of honey and apple cider vinegar, with water and ice added.

The Wright Farm, Rolling Ledge Maple Orchard, Enosburg Falls, Vermont 05450. Free price lists.

The Wright family produce, pack, and ship their maple products directly from their century-old farm. Grade A (½ gallon, $6.25) or better syrups are packaged in lithographed containers, but Grades B (½ gallon, $5.00) and C (½ gallon, $4.00) are also sold. The Wrights will send to prospective customers samples of Grade B syrup, darker and stronger flavored than the higher grades, and Grade C, very dark and strong flavored, which they recommend for cooking or as a substitute for molasses. The Wrights also sell canned maple sugar (2 pounds, under $5.00) and maple cream (3 pounds, less than $5.00), as well as homemade maple candy (8-ounce box, less than $2.00) and sugar cakes (1-pound box, $2.50). Shipping charges are additional.

Maple syrup is a natural food which is processed by heat concentration of pure maple sap, with no additives or preservatives. The Wrights tell why this syrup costs so much. To make one gallon of pure Vermont maple syrup takes at least four maple trees growing on a mountainside, three gallons of fuel oil or one four-foot-long log burned in the evaporator to boil forty gallons of sap down to one gallon of syrup, and a packing crew to sterilize, filter, grade, seal, and can.

14. ETHNIC FOODS

IF you prefer the exotic viands of the world to familiar tastes, or yearn to experiment in preparing the cuisines of different nations, this is your chapter. Specialty shops in Europe and throughout the United States abound with continental specialties. There are cookies and chocolates from Holland put up in colorful canisters, the masterful trademark of Dutch packaging, and German mustards that so aptly complement bratwurst or mettwurst. From France come elegant foods such as pâtés, cornichons, brandied fruits, and mushrooms marinated in lemon juice and delicate French olive oil. From Britain there are such items as tinned game and kippered pâté, potted meats, calves' foot jelly, biscuits, and, of course, shortbreads and Christmas puddings, and a crock of rock sugar crystals to set out for morning coffee.

You will find a wealth of ingredients available from ethnic shops. Many are small neighborhood shops catering to the interests of the communities in which they are located. They are a mélange of color, exuberant with zesty smells and friendly people. What could be more reassuring than to order food from a shop whose clientele insists on authentic ingredients that he or she knows cannot be fabricated? The Italian shopper who is satisfied with nothing less than olive oil imported from Lucca, Italy, Parmigiano-Reggiano properly aged for strong flavor needed in a good grating cheese, or semolina flour for the weekly making of pasta. The Mexican cook who knows the importance of chilis—the dry red varieties such as ancho, mulato, chipotte, and the hotter green serrano or jalapeno. The Indian cook who makes original curries daily from the creative concoction of up to thirty spices which include fenugreek, cumin, cardamom, garlic, mace, nutmeg, garlic, ginger, and red pepper.

Oriental food—Chinese, Japanese, and the difficult-to-find Vietnamese and Thai ingredients are all here. Everything needed to prepare an Indonesian "rijsttafel," an old-fashioned traditional Ukrainian Christmas supper, or a Scandinavian cold table can be ordered from these specialty shops.

Creole

Creole Cookery, 7740 Florida Boulevard, Baton Rouge, Louisiana 70806. Free price list.

Ready-to-serve foods typical of Louisiana cuisine are packaged in 2 assortments by Creole Cookery. The smaller gift box contains pepper sauce, remoulade sauce, turtle soup, creole mustard, creole gumbo, and jambalaya mix ($11.50

ppd). The larger assortment adds shrimp creole, crayfish bisque, pickled okra, yams, and cane syrup ($17.95 ppd). The gumbo, shrimp creole, and crayfish bisque are recommended to be served over a bed of rice, with a few drops of pepper sauce. The hot pepper sauce is the result of aging fancy Louisiana peppers in oils until the oils disintegrate to a degree that they are soluble in vinegar. These oils are then blended with grain vinegar, wine vinegar, and apple cider to produce the peppery creole seasoning. The gift boxes contain cooking and serving suggestions.

Creole Delicacies Company, Inc., 533 St. Ann Street, New Orleans, Louisiana 70116. Free catalog.

When the solid, down-to-earth plantation cookery merged with the sophisticated skills perfected by eighteenth-century French and Spanish chefs, it resulted in a unique style of food known as creole. Foods typical of this cuisine are available from Creole Delicacies. New Orleans soups include shrimp creole, shrimp gumbo, crayfish bisque, and turtle soup, which come packaged in cartons of 6 or multiples thereof (6 for $10). There is a French Market—style doughnut (beignet) mix, (two 13½-ounce bags, $4 ppd, make about 60 beignets), a New Orleans coffee and chicory brew, remoulade sauce (three 10-ounce jars, $9), cane sugar syrup (carton of four 12-ounce tins, about $7), and a wooden rack holding jars of Louisiana seasonings. Assorted preserves include whole Louisiana figs, and among the dessert items are pralines (10 large candies, under $5) and fruitcakes (a 2½-pound cake, $9). Prices include delivery.

Martin Wine Cellar, 3827 Baronne Street, P.O. Box 15106, New Orleans, Louisiana 70175. Prices on request.

The Martin Wine Cellar, one of New Orleans' noted gourmet food emporia, stocks a wide variety of local as well as imported items. Some of the foods and spices that Martin will gladly mail-order are: locally made Green's soups (about $1 per can) which include smoked sausage and regular gumbo, turtle soup, shrimp creole, and crayfish bisque; spicy red remoulade sauce ($3); peychaud bitters; Pickapeppa sauce from Jamaica (about $1); Louisiana shrimp and crab boil ($1); filé powder ($1); pepper jelly in 8-ounce canning jars; and French imported orange flower water (an essential ingredient in the authentic New Orleans Ramos gin fizz). The Cellar has an extensive display of teas and coffee. Telephone orders accepted (504) 899-7411.

Dutch-Indonesian

Mrs. De Wildt, R.D. 3, Bangor, Pennsylvania 18013. Free price list.

For more than twenty years, Mrs. De Wildt has been supplying mail-order customers with spices and ingredients for Indonesian cookery. On her lists are dozens of varieties of sambal, the hot chili pepper paste used in many Indonesian dishes. A must at any rijsttafel or rice table are krupuk udang, shrimp tapioca wafers which are offered in several sizes for deep frying (large-size, 3½-ounce box, under $2.00). There are many specialty spices such as wild lime leaves (a small bag for about 50¢), and spice blends which come in small jars or in instant, precooked tablets. A special sticky white rice (beras ketan) is available (8 ounces, about $1.00), as are some canned Indonesian foods. There is a small selection of other Oriental foods such as Malaysian chili sauce (6 ounces, about $1.50), Indian pickles, coconut syrup from Hawaii (12 ounces, under $1.00), an anchovy seasoning sauce from the Philippines (6-ounce bottle, around $1.50), and selected Chinese and Japanese ingredients.

Among the Dutch specialty foods offered by mail are imported cheeses, sold by the pound or whole wheel, with such varieties as Edam (4-pound ball, about $12.00), soft and aged Gouda (both about $26.00 for a whole wheel, 9 to 10 pounds; cut cheese about $3.00 per pound), and Leyden cumin cheese. There are Verkade's cookies in economy packages and gift tins, Droste's chocolates, and canned Dutch vegetables. Mrs. De Wildt will combine selected items in custom-made gift packages. Shipping charges are additional.

Dutch Cupboard, 273 North Eighth Street, Prospect Park, New Jersey 07508. Prices on request.

Wooden shoes are surrounded by Dutch imported foods in this specialty shop. There are Dutch chocolates, a special chocolate paste that is made to be spread on bread like jam (about $1), and at Christmastime, chocolate initials at 75¢ each. A selection of Indonesian spices is offered, along with canned vegetables, dry soup mixes, and Dutch breads and biscuits. Mettwurst is the specialty of the house and runs about $3 per pound.

Vander Vliet's Holland Imports, 3147 West 111 Street, Chicago, Illinois 60655. Free catalog.

Vander Vliet's sells all sorts of items imported from Holland, from tulip bulbs to delft earrings and wooden shoes. There is a very large selection of Dutch biscuits and cookies from many of Holland's most well-known manufacturers. There are breads and honey cakes and gingerbread dolls (under $1.00). Candies include hard drops, licorices, and, of course, a wide variety of chocolates which includes unusual items such as a jar of chocolate spread (a little over $1.00 a jar). Other imports are canned vegetables, syrups, soup mixes, cheeses, and a line of fish products such as "fried herring housewife style in vinegar" and smoked conger eel in oil (both about $1.50 per tin). Vliet's also has a selection of ingredients for Indonesian cookery.

Shrimp Sambal Goreng

The rice table or "rijsttafel" is a uniquely Indonesian type of banquet consisting of several main dishes surrounding a communal rice bowl. A typical dish served at such a meal would be Shrimp Sambal Goreng.

- 3 tablespoons vegetable oil
- 2 medium onions, peeled and sliced
- 1 teaspoon minced garlic
- ½ teaspoon sambal oelek (or 1 teaspoon if you like spicy food) *
- 1 teaspoon laos (galangal) powdered†
- ½ cup shredded coconut, soaked in 1½ cups water
- ¼ teaspoon powdered bay leaves (or 2 whole leaves)
- Salt to taste
- 1 cup green beans (or other vegetables) cut into 1-inch pieces
- 1 pound shrimp
- 1 teaspoon tamarind concentrate‡

Heat oil and sauté onions until golden brown. Add garlic, sambal oelek, and laos and cook for 5 minutes. Stir in coconut, bay leaves, salt and water and simmer for 10 minutes. Add green beans; cook for 5 minutes; add shrimp and cook until tender but not overdone (usually about 5 minutes more). Stir in tamarind concentrate and serve hot as part of your rice table.

Note: If you want to make this a vegetarian dish, leave out the shrimp and substitute a pound of your favorite vegetable.

* Sambal oelek is a mashed red pepper sauce which is *very hot*.
† Galangal, a relative of the ginger root, is called "laos" in Indonesian cookery. In imperial China, galangal was often used to scent black tea. Today it is a popular ingredient to blend with other herb teas (such as alfalfa, comfrey, raspberry leaves, etc.) in order to heighten their flavor.
‡ Tamarind concentrate is often used as a substitute for the whole fruit in recipes. It saves time and trouble of soaking, cooking, etc. (Tamarind is a fruit of a tropical tree and is used as a condiment in Middle Eastern, Indian, and Spanish cooking. Because of its sour taste, tamarind is often used instead of lemon juice. The whole fruit is usually available dried and needs soaking before use.)

European

BRITISH

Egertons, Clare House, Lyme Street, Axminster, Devon, England EX13 5DB. Catalog 50¢ by surface mail, $1.50 airmail.

Egertons is a large British mail-order house with a wide range of goods. Prices are quoted in dollars and include delivery to addresses in the United States and Canada. Payment can be made through many of the international credit card systems, which allows the customer to be charged at the prevailing dollar exchange rates. Available for mail-order to North America are coffees, teas, and English preserves, including liqueur preserves such as marmalade with vintage brandy or navy rum. Honeys include "Cornish gold," gathered by the bees of Cornwall, and Devon honey in a pottery tea caddy ($12). There are various assortments of English biscuits and plum puddings, fruitcakes, and Christmas cakes. A wide selection of chocolates and sweets from a variety of confectioners include British specialties such as toffee treacle drops and rose and violet creams (2 pounds, about $17).

For sending gifts within the United Kingdom, the choice widens to almost every food imaginable: smoked trout and salmon, York hams, clotted cream, braces of wild ducks and partridges, apples, pâté, and liquors. Gift hampers from $20 to $70 include several which can be ordered for export. All prices include postage and packing.

R. W. Forsyth, Ltd., 30 Princes Street, Edinburgh EH2 2BZ, Scotland. Free catalog.

The food hall and wine gallery of this large Scottish department store publishes a catalog each year at Christmastime listing the great variety of British foods offered. There is a selection of gift hampers in a wide price range ($5 to $50). Available individually are canned specialties such as whole pigeon in wine sauce (about $4), pheasant in cream sauce (about $6), and quail in sherry sauce (about $2). There are earthenware jars of Stilton cheese (about $2 a pound), pâtés, and malt vinegar, as well as oils, sauces, and pickles. Scottish shortbread from several manufacturers are just part of the selection of tins and packets of assorted sweet biscuits. Scottish heather honey (about $2 for a 1-pound jar), English mincemeat, and rum and brandy butter are more British specialties that can be ordered. Stem ginger in syrup, teas, and jams come in attractive jars and caddies. Among the sweets are chocolates, brandied, crystallized, and glacé fruits, and, of course, Christmas puddings. Prices in general are good. Shipping charges are additional.

Fortnum & Mason, Piccadilly, London W1A 1ER, England. Free catalog.

Fortnum & Mason knows full well that "life can be sustained by bread and water, but is given a sharp, upward boost by the more imaginative combination of caviar and champagne." With characteristic British understatement, the meeting of Mr. Fortnum and Mr. Mason is described in the catalog's accompanying brochure as creating a union "surpassed in its importance to the human race only by the meeting of Adam and Eve." Fortnum & Mason supplied the officers of the Napoleonic wars, sent their concentrated beef tea to Florence Nightingale in Scutari during the Crimean War, had food boxes, their name emblazoned on the sides, carried into the Ashanti capital of Coomassie on the heads of native porters when it was captured by Sir Garnet Wolseley in 1873. Following the British flag throughout the world, Fortnum & Mason stood firm at home as well. According to Charles Dickens, Derby Day was not complete without luxury hampers: "Look where I will—in some connexion with carriages—made fast upon the top, or occupying the box, or peeping out of a window—I see Fortnum & Mason. And now, Heavens! All the hampers fly wide open and green Downs burst into a blossom of lobster-salad." The suffragettes, led by Emmeline Pankhurst, threw bricks through the stately windows in Piccadilly; Fortnum & Mason replied by providing delicacies for the ladies after their subsequent confinement to Holloway Gaol.

Fortnum & Mason specializes in luxury food hampers priced from about $25 on up to over $500, but many of the items are offered individually as well. There are Christmas puddings (F & M's own recipe, 2 to 8 pounds, from about $5.50 to $18.00) and shortbreads (about $2.50), pâtés and caviar, a great variety of honey and preserves, either in standard jars and crocks or in exquisite Coalport or Crown Devon canisters, some as low as about $6.00. Storage jars come filled with mincemeat or brown sugar candy crystals (about $5.25); British cheeses include whole blue (about $2.50 per pound) or red Cheshires (about $6.50 each), blue Wensleydale (around $2.50 per pound), Stiltons (about $2.00 per pound), and Scottish Islays (just over $3.00 each).

Of course there are Fortnum & Mason's famed teas—a gift box of six ¼-pound selections runs about $6.50. Even a jar of hot English mustard has a certain elegance about it if it comes from Fortnum & Mason.

Jacksons of Piccadilly, 171–172 Piccadilly, London W1V OLL, England. Free catalog.

Just down the street from that other British emporium of fancy foods is Jacksons of Piccadilly, grocers and provision merchants to Her Majesty, the Queen, and countless other houses, royal or otherwise. Known for its teas (up to $3 a tin) and elegant food hampers, Jacksons offers a full range of British specialty items, as well as delicacies from around the world. The teas come in many varieties and blends, the hampers are stuffed with shortbreads and Christmas puddings (one 2-pound variety, under $8), jams and jellies. Jacksons of Piccadilly claims to be the first in London to have sold American canned goods, so a customized picnic hamper could conceivably be ordered with a tin of cream of mushroom soup along with the potted prawns.

EASTERN EUROPEAN

Paprikas Weiss, Importer, 1546 Second Avenue, New York, New York 10028. Catalog $1 for annual subscription.

Starting eighty-five years ago as a small neighborhood grocery, Paprikas Weiss now overflows with thousands of specialty food items, including many from Hungary and Eastern Europe. There are over 100 herbs and spices, exotic coffees, and teas. Hungarian china sits just a shelf away from a display of salamis. Cookie cutters, coffee mills, embroidered blouses, Hungarian records, meat slicers, and cookbooks in a dozen languages fight for room on overflowing counters. Among the cookbooks, one called *Hungarian Cookery, Recipes New and Old,* is edited by Ed Weiss, the owner and grandson of the founder of Paprikas Weiss, and contains over 1000 recipes, many of them family specialties. It can be ordered from the catalog for $6.95.

Imported cheeses which can be mail-ordered include Bryndza, a Czechoslovakian soft, white, sheep-milk cheese with a sharp flavor. It comes by the pound ($4.98) or by the 6-pound bucket ($26.98). There is Weiss's own 12-ounce liptaur cheese ball made from cheddar cheese and flavored with caraway and sweet Hungarian paprika ($4.98). A nice selection of imported English cheeses in whole wheels or blocks include Leicester (9-pound round, $45.00), Wensleydale, double Gloucester, and Caerphilly—all in 5-pound blocks for $29.00, and an 18-pound cylindrical cheddar for $75.00. A unique item is Paprikas Weiss's own label of French-style clarified butter. It comes jarred (9¼ ounces) and won't splatter or turn brown when cooked ($4.00).

Paprikas Weiss sends its own brand of Hungarian salami, known as teli szalami or winter salami. It comes in sizes from 1 to 6 pounds. Also sold are Hungarian sausage made from pure pork and seasoned with sweet Hungarian paprika ($4.98 per pound) and a double-smoked Hungarian slab bacon ($3.98 per pound). Imported from Hungary are boneless, cooked, canned hams (3-pound tin $10.00). Among the other meat products described in the catalog are a selection of French pâtés, canned goulash, and stuffed cabbage.

Hungarian strudels come in 1-, 3-, or 6-pound sizes, with a choice of cherry, poppy seed, apple, walnut, cabbage, or cheese filling. Or you can bake your own. . . . Paprikas Weiss offers ready-to-use strudel dough ($1.50 per box of 4 sheets), completely prepared fillings, and even the little goosefeather brushes recommended for the delicate task of spreading warm melted butter over the fragile dough. Each package of dough comes with recipes. Other freshly baked Hungarian-style desserts include walnut or poppyseed roulade ($6.98), apricot or raspberry linzer tarts ($12.00 a dozen), patko, which are horseshoe-shaped, yeast-dough pastries filled with walnuts or poppy seeds ($10.00 a dozen), and Hungarian tea biscuits (friss vajas pgacsa), which are similar to Scottish scones (12 for $7.20). There is canned, Hungarian-style chestnut puree to make Mont Blanc, or gesztenyepure as it is known in Hungary. The catalog describes a chestnut ricer to make the puree light and fluffy. Among the vast selection of sweets are chocolates, hard candies by the pound, plum puddings, and English biscuits, as well as baking supplies such as imported unfilled cake layers, orange and rose waters, extracts, and candied fruits and peels. Naturally grown organic foods include Paprikas Weiss's dried beans, seeds, peas, whole-grain flours, and stone-ground cereals—all sold by the pound from barrels. Truffles, jams, honeys, the makings of an authentic Hungarian fish soup, and, of course, paprika from Szeged can be ordered, along with the freshly made pastas and pots and pans and on and on and on.

H. L. Roth & Son, Lekvar-by-the-Barrel, 1577 First Avenue, New York, New York 10028. Free catalog.

Located in New York's famed Yorkville section, Lekvar-by-the-Barrel is crammed full of not only its Hungarian specialties, but marvelous baking equipment and imported delicacies from around the world. Large barrels are filled

Apple Strudel

    2 or 3 medium-size green apples, peeled and cut
        into small cubes
    ¼ cup sugar
    ⅛ cup chopped nuts
    ¼ cup raisins
    ¼ teaspoon cinnamon
        Grated rind of half a lemon
    ¼ pound butter or shortening
    2 sheets ready-to-use strudel dough
    ½ cup dry bread crumbs or crushed cornflakes

Preheat oven to 400° F. Mix together in large bowl apples, sugar, nuts, raisins, cinnamon, and lemon rind. Melt butter or shortening. Open package and unfold strudel dough sheets carefully. Place 1 strudel dough sheet on damp cloth. Using pastry brush, paint dough sheet lightly with melted butter or shortening. Sprinkle with bread crumbs or cornflakes. Place second strudel dough sheet directly over first sheet. Paint second sheet with butter or shortening. Sprinkle with bread crumbs or cornflakes. Place mixture on edge of dough sheet nearest you, in one strip. Roll like a jelly roll, by lifting up edge of damp cloth. Place on buttered pan and paint top lightly with butter. Mark individual portions with sharp knife. Bake 25 to 30 minutes, until golden brown. Serve at once or allow to cool. Note: Unused sheets of dough may be kept in freezer. Allow to thaw before using.

with grains, flours, rice, and dried beans. There are red and green lentils, black turtle beans (98¢ per pound), peas (whole and split, yellow and green, all less than $1.00 per pound), and French flageolets ($2.40 per pound), the traditional accompaniment to roast lamb. By the pound there are buckwheat flour (98¢), chestnut flour, chick-pea flour ($1.19), and a special strudel flour (Retes Liszt, 59¢). Lekvar also sells the strudel dough ready-made (4 sheets, about $1.00). Nuts for baking and eating come shelled whole or ground, and include such varieties as black walnuts (about $4.00 per pound), hazelnuts (about $2.50 per pound), and Brazil nuts (around $2.00 per pound). Among some of the other Hungarian specialties of this shop are egg drops (tarhonya, $1.29 per pound), a potato substitute which is prepared by browning the egg drops in shortening, adding boiling water, simmering until tender, and seasoning. Also sold are spaetzle noodles ($1.29 per pound) and other varieties of egg noodles. Rices include basmatti, Italian rice, Texas patna rice, and a yellow rice seasoned with saffron.

Of course there is the barrel of lekvar (prune butter). The thick prune puree, a Hungarian specialty is used as a filling for strudel or palichinka, the crêpe dessert, or just spread on bread. It is homemade and comes by the pound ($1.59) or in an 8½-pound tin ($8.75). Also sold are apricot ($1.89 per pound), apple, and plum butters. There are Hungarian jams in several flavors, including the popular sour cherry (about $1.50 for a 1-pound jar). A large selection of honeys include a kosher Israeli honey and a Central American coffee blossom honey—both under $2.00 for a 1-pound jar.

A very complete selection of herbs and spices include Mama Roth's special goulash blend ($1.45 for ¼ pound), Hungarian paprika (about $3.00 per pound for sweet, medium, or sharp), and poppy seeds, whole or freshly ground (both about $2.50 per pound) and used by Hungarians for their famous poppy seed cake, strudels, and noodles with poppy seeds. At Christmastime, there are German and Hungarian specialties such as lebkuchen, marzipan figures among which are the traditional marzipan pigs, and chocolate tree decorations wrapped in colorful foil (from 35¢ to $1.30 each). Available year round are many baking items such as paste food coloring, almond paste, multicolored

Varenyky (Pyrogi Dumplings)

Dough: Mix 2 cups flour with 1 teaspoon salt. Add 1 egg and ⅔ cup cool water. Knead lightly. Cover with kitchen towel and set aside.

Potato filling: Mash 4 large, cooked potatoes. Add 1 large chopped onion sautéed in ½ cup vegetable oil. Season with salt and pepper. Cool.

Sauerkraut filling: Rinse 1½ pounds sauerkraut with hot water to remove salt. Rinse cold. Squeeze dry. Chop fine. Sauté 1 large onion in ⅓ cup oil. Add sauerkraut. Sauté covered 10 minutes. Season. Cool.

Cheese filling: Combine 2 cups farmer cheese, 4 ounces cream cheese, 1 egg, salt. Add a little sour cream if mixture is too dry.

Fruit filling: Fresh berries, pitted cherries, plums, or stewed prunes can be used. Sprinkle lightly with flour to thicken juice.

To form Varenyky: 1. Roll dough thin. Cut rounds with inverted water glass. 2. Hold round in palm. Place spoonful of filling in center. Fold in half. 3. Press edges to seal. 4. Lay on dry kitchen towel and cover.

To cook: Drop into large pot of boiling water a few at a time. Boil rapidly about 4 minutes. Lift out into colander and rinse with hot water. Drain. Coat with melted butter. Keep hot. Serve with sour cream. Delicious as leftovers. Sauté in butter until golden and crisp.

sugar crystals, and candied rose petals (about $1.00 an ounce). Lekvar-by-the-Barrel stocks a selection of Brazilian, Indonesian, and Chinese imported foods, as well as teas, coffees, and dried and candied fruits.

Surma Book and Music Co., Inc., 11 East Seventh Street, New York, New York 10003. Free leaflets; prices on request.

Surma is a small shop chock-full of books, notepapers, records, and exquisitely handcrafted Ukrainian items such as embroidered shirts and trimmings and batiked Easter eggs. During the Christmas season, Surma provides its out-of-town Ukrainian neighbors with foods necessary to prepare the traditional Ukrainian Christmas supper. The owner, Mr. Surmach, says that "after the kids grow up, marry and move to the suburbs, the Ukrainian traditions become a bit fuzzy." In order to help, Surma offers a set of beautifully illustrated recipe cards (30¢ each) representing the twelve meatless courses of the traditional supper. Kutia, for instance, the first and most indispensable of the twelve courses, is a mixture of shelled wheat, honey, and ground poppy seeds.

Among the foods that Surma will mail are shelled wheat berries (50¢ per pound), poppy seeds (whole, $1.50 per pound, or ground, $2.00 per pound), buckwheat groats (50¢ per pound), millet (65¢ per pound), Carpathian imported dry mushrooms (caps, under $4.00 per ounce, or whole, under $2.00 per ounce), and thick, long, whole vanilla beans at 25¢ each.

FRENCH

Delpeyrat, Sarlat-en-Périgord, France. Prices on request.

Rare aromatic fungi from the soil of Perigord sparkle in Delpeyrat's special foie gras and truffles. The foie gras is also available packed in earthenware crocks, handpainted, and signed by the artist. A very special gift at very special prices.

J. A. Demonchaux Co., 225 Jackson, Topeka, Kansas 66603. Free brochure.

Demonchaux has two brochures, one of gourmet garden seeds and the other of French, gourmet-type foods. The bi-

lingual food descriptions include a page of pâté varieties, ranging from the most expensive goose liver pâté with truffles (7½ ounces, $20.00) to a small tin (2¼ ounces) of hare pâté for $1.00. Snails come with or without shells (3 dozen extra large, about $7.50) and special escargot plates (about $3.00), holders ($1.10), and forks (65¢) are also sold. There is a nice selection of French vegetables such as salsify (15-ounce can, $1.60), also known as oyster plant because of its similar flavor to the shellfish, and endive (15-ounce can, $1.80), sorrel (13-ounce can, $1.30), and flageolets, which are sold dried ($1.85 per pound) as well as tinned ($1.35, 15 ounces). Condiments include a selection of mustards, petit cornichons (½-pound jar, about $3.00), the traditional tiny pickle served with pâtés, and various vinegars. There is a small choice of biscuits and pastry shells, petit babas (12 mini cakes for $2.10), French chestnuts, and bonbons. Candied fruits in cognac (between $7.00 and $8.00 a jar) are available in several varieties, and there is a special giant French lollipop for $1.10.

Fauchon, 26, Place de la Madeleine, Paris-8, France. Free brochure.

Fauchon is to the gourmet what the big rock candy mountain would be to a six-year-old child. The famous shop in the Place de la Madeleine in Paris is a feast for all the senses. One marvels at the fresh fruit and vegetables—can they be real, they are so perfect? The smell of the tiny crimson fraises du bois and the snowy white velvet peaches gives them away. The shelves and counters abound with chocolates, teas, mustards (green peppercorn mustard, shallot and chervil mustard, orange mustard, lemon mustard, and then there is mint mustard and honey mustard and pink pepper mustard, herbes de Provence mustard and traditional mustard, all in 7½-ounce jars, ranging from about $1.25 to $2.50)—a ball park frank never had it so good. Herbs come in earthenware crocks with the Fauchon name emblazoned on them (a good snob appeal item, but also wonderfully fresh, a little over $1.00 each). Of course there are pâtés, and again the selection is overwhelming—blackbird or lark, pheasant, deer, partridge, and then hare and thrush and baby wild boar. Fauchon's general catalog, printed in French, is extensive and includes exotica like Rice Krispies and Heinz ketchup. The export brochure, in English, lists those foods most popular with Americans, among them the pâtés, mustards, teas, honey, and jams. There are Fauchon's vegetables, such as miniature mushrooms (about $1.00, 15 ounces) and green kidney beans (1 pound, 14 ounces, less than $1.00), and whole truffles (.90 ounces, about $8.00) and truffle pieces (.90 ounces, about $5.50), and snails, and French sardines (less than $1.00), and dried mushrooms (morels, 3½ ounces, about $12.50; cèpes 3½ ounces, about $6.00), and pureed fruits with which to top sherbets, and glazed chestnuts (14 ounces, just over $10.00), and fruits in syrup or in liqueur, and cheeses in cans and biscuits in tins and plop, plop, fizz, fizz.

Hediard, 21, Place de la Madeleine, Paris-8, France. Free catalog.

Sharing the Place de la Madeleine with another famous establishment of epicurean delights and an almost as famous church, Hediard, "magasin d'alimentation de luxe," has been catering to the gourmet tastes of discriminating Parisians since 1854. Originally Hediard specialized in importing unusual products that no one else dared offer at the time—spices and exotic fresh fruits carefully imported by boat from Africa, Asia, and South America. Hediard imported the very first pineapples to come to Paris, offering them in honor of Alexandre Dumas. The original Hediard family continues to run the business, but there are now nine branches and over 500 products with Hediard's own label—jams, jellies (under $2.00 a jar), syrups, mustards (under $1.50 a jar), paves aux fruits, and marzipans. Each year a Christmas catalog is printed which describes some of the thousands of items available from Hediard. They range from foie gras, truffles, and lime juice punch to glass jars of fruit and vegetables such as perfect baby tomatoes and endives (about $1.50). There are Christmas baskets attractively combining many of these items, and if you happen to be in Paris in December, you can buy fresh wild strawberries on the Place de la Madeleine.

Le Jardin du Gourmet, Les Echalottes, West Danville, Vermont 05873. Catalog 50¢.

Most of the business of Le Jardin du Gourmet is in seeds and plants but it offers, in addition, French imports from graisse d'oie to bouillabaisse. There are bilingual descriptions of the imported seeds, which are a bit more exotic than garden-variety radishes. Leading the list of food items are such delicacies as a selection of pâtés, unusual canned vegetables (salsify, snow peas, green and white flageolets), and snails. Dried green flageolets, the traditional bean accompaniment to roast lamb, are also sold (17 ounces, $1.65). Varieties of mushrooms (chanterelles, morels, cèpes) come canned and dried. Other specialty foods include a stone crock of "Fire Cherries," soaked in brandy ($9.00, 17 ounces), many varieties of chestnuts (pureed, whole, vanilla flavored, glacé), and quenelles in several varieties. Getting a

little more international, Le Jardin has a selection of Indian chutneys, some Mexican and Indonesian ingredients, Christmas puddings from England, and herb teas from Germany. Soups range from dried French imports to real turtle soup from England to kangaroo tail soup from Australia (about $1.00). From France comes cassis (black currant) syrup (about $4.00, 24 ounces), and from Hawaii, white coconut syrup. Somewhere in between is gefilte fish and Israeli grapefruit marmalade (under $1.00). Shipping charges are additional.

Maison Glass, 52 East Fifty-eighth Street, New York, New York 10022. Catalog $1.00.

Maison Glass, one of Manhattan's posh East Side delicacy shops, publishes an impressive 70-page catalog in September of each year. Hundreds of distinctive foods are featured in the catalog, including pâté de foie gras, tinned and freshly smoked fish, fresh caviar, meats and game birds, wild birds, smoked birds, imported foods, and ingredients of all kinds for special dishes. A terrific selection of imported cheese, coffee, tea, and spices is also offered.

Lobster with cognac and crabmeat squares with curry (about $3) are among a selection of frozen hors d'oeuvres that also includes individually sized portions of cheese, mushroom, and spinach quiche (around $2). Maison Glass stocks a wide array of confections, ranging from French lollipops to Harlequin stuffed oranges, as well as creamy cheesecake, around $6 for a 24-ounce cake, and a special cheesecake low in cholesterol for about $7 (25 ounces).

Mail orders are given special attention and are usually shipped the same day. Maison Glass asks your indulgence at Christmastime, since gifts are custom made, packed on the premises, and require sufficient time for expediting. Monthly accounts can be opened and BankAmericard is honored on purchases of $15. For out-of-town shipment, there is also a $15 minimum order. Telephone orders are accepted at (212) PL 5-3316.

GERMAN

Bremen House, 200 East Eighty-sixth Street, New York, New York 10028. Free catalog.

A wide variety of gourmet specialties can be ordered from Bremen House, a German specialty food shop in Manhattan's Yorkville district. There is a large selection of traditional German cookies, cakes, stollen, and marzipan specialties. Christmas stollen comes in several varieties and sizes, expertly wrapped for freshness (2-pound stollens for $5.50 to $14.00, depending on the brand). There are spiced pfeffernuesse cookies (7 ounces, $1.10), marzipan novelties which include the traditional good-luck pig packaged in a tiny wooden crate ($1.75), and a number of continental chocolates and biscuits. A large selection of honeys and jams include varieties from around the world. From Holland there is salt herring (4-pound keg headless matjes herrings, $7.25) and from Scandinavia a variety of fish products. European-style wursts and meats include Westphalian hams, touristenwursts, and lachsschinken, that tender smoked pork with a flavor reminiscent of smoked salmon, all between $4.00 and $5.00 per pound. Tins of vegetables include giant white asparagus (about $5.00 for a 15-ounce can) and special mushrooms such as cèpes and pfifferlinge (both about $4.50 for 8-ounce tins). There are mustards from Dusseldorf and Dijon (under $1.00) and canned game from Poland such as roast wild boar in juniper sauce ($3.00, 14 ounces) and deer goulash with chanterelles (31 ounces, $5.00). The catalog offers subscriptions to German magazines and cuckoo clocks and opera records and German colognes. A minimum order from Bremen House is $10.00, and shipping charges are additional. A service for sending gifts to East Germany is also offered.

Schaller & Weber, Inc., 1654 Second Avenue, New York, New York 10028. Free price list.

Schaller & Weber is a mini-supermarket chock-full of German and other Old World delicacies. Unfortunately the only price list currently available is for Schaller & Weber's meat products—over 3 dozen varieties. They range from frankfurters and speck blutwurst (beef blood sausage with fat), both $2.29 per pound, to the popular Black Forest-style smoked products such as Westphalian-style ham ($4.19 per pound) and whole lachsschinken, smoked pork loin wrapped in pork fat ($5.69 per pound). A minimum order on the meats, which are sold by the pound, is $10.00. If you know what you want in terms of syrups, jams, breads, and condiments, they can probably be included with a meat order. Write with requests.

ITALIAN

Italian Importing Company, 104 Sixth Avenue, Des Moines, Iowa 50309. Prices on request.

This family-operated business is a wholesale-retail store stocked full of food imported from several parts of Italy.

Although the company does not publish a catalog, it has been mail-ordering its foods for some time. It has over 20 varieties of pasta (50¢ to 60¢ per pound) in bulk form, ranging from Foratini to Elena Piccalla to folded spinach noodles. There is also semolina flour for making pasta. Olives ($1.10 to $1.40 per pound) include green Italian style, and dried, black, oil-cured. Among the selection of Italian spices available is the company's own recipe of mixed Italian spices (35¢ an ounce or $4.00 per pound). Italian sausage, either garlic-flavored or medium-hot ($1.20 to $1.45 per pound), Genoa salami ($3.29 per pound), pepperoni ($2.25 per pound), or D'Annanzia salami, with hot or black pepper ($3.29 per pound), and a variety of Italian cheeses. Cheeses include Pecorino Romano (the most expensive at $4.20 per pound), Argentine Sardo, provolone, Asiago, and Fontinella—all about $2.50 per pound. Many tinned specialties such as Contadina-brand pizza or spaghetti sauce in gallon containers are also stocked.

Aside from Italian prepared foods and ingredients, Mexican and Spanish items extend the choice of hard-to-find items. You can order, for instance, chili powder, chili ancho peppers, comino seed or powder in bulk, Mexican chocolate, whole, green Spanish tomatoes, salsa supreme, salsa ranchera, and salsa victoria, as well as Mexican oregano and dry beans.

Westphalian Rolls a la Danoise

Westphalian ham, with its distinct smoky flavor, lends itself to innumerable preparations. Here it is filled with a refreshing cream cheese, cucumber, and radish mixture, but it is equally good when rolled around cooked cold asparagus and poached leeks. Serve Westphalian ham as a topping to finely sliced ripe pears, or with honeydew or cantaloupe melon.

    1 8-ounce package of softened cream cheese
    3 tablespoons sour cream
    ½ cup finely minced cucumbers
    ¼ cup finely minced scallions
    ½ cup finely minced radishes
    3 tablespoons finely minced dill
      Salt and freshly ground pepper
    6 to 8 slices of Westphalian ham
      Garnish with sprigs of parsley, radishes, cucumber
      slices, 6 to 8 dill gherkins

In a bowl combine the cream cheese, sour cream, cucumbers, scallions, radishes, dill, salt, and pepper. Blend well with a fork. Place a spoonful of the mixture on each ham slice, roll up the slice, place on serving dish, and garnish. Serve chilled but not cold with finely sliced buttered pumpernickel and cold beer.

Manganaro's, 488 Ninth Avenue, New York, New York 10018. Free catalog.

Mange, mange. Manganaro's has everything (or so it seems). The maker of the 6-foot-long hero sandwich, which unfortunately can be delivered only in New York City, sells just about everything for Italian feasting and then some: cold cuts, hams, cheeses, antipastos, soups, vegetables, bread sticks, pastries, cakes, cookies, and more than 500 different sizes, shapes, and brands of imported and domestic pastas, Manganaro's is one of the country's larger importers of Italian meat products and one of the few that will mail them anywhere in the United States, or the world for that matter. Imported and domestic prosciutto is offered in bulk or sliced paper thin for serving (from $2.50 to $7.00 per pound). Other cured meats include mortadella, coppa di Piacenza, and pancetta, an Italian-style cooking bacon—all between $3.50 and $5.00 per pound. There is imported citterio salami ($6.50 per pound) and sopressata ($4.80 per pound), a chewy pork sausage to be eaten out of hand accompanied by chunks of bread. The minimum order is ½-pound cuts, and all meat shipments are carefully wrapped to preserve texture and ensure freshness.

Cheeses particularly suited for grating include pecorino Romano, ricotta Siciliano, fiore Sardo which comes from Argentina and, of course, Parmigiano. Mild Italian cheeses include Bel Paese, fontina, fonduta, taleggio, and Friulana, a cheddar-type cheese imported from Venice. For heartier appetites there are cacciocavallo, ragusano, pepato, and incannestrata, the last distinguished by its braided basket wrapping. All the cheeses are between $3.50 and $5.00 per pound. There are many other cheeses, as well as all the makings for the most elaborate antipasto.

Manganaro's offers a selection of Italian cakes and sweets suitable for mail order. Panettone, the high, fluffy, semi-sweet holiday cake, is lemon-flavored and stuffed with raisins and citron. It has particularly good storing quality. A 1-pound cake is $4.25; a 4-pound one, $12.50. Available in several sizes is Colomba, the popular, dove-shaped Italian Easter cake. Amaretti, the dry, crisp Italian macaroons, come in tins or boxes (1 pound, $5.50; 5 pounds, $21.50). Pandoro, a specialty cake from Verona (1 pound, $4.25; 2 pounds, $7.50) and Panforte di Siena (1 pound, $4.40), a slim, round, flat cake thick with candied citron, orange, sugar, and almonds, are two other selections suitable for mailing. Manganaro's sells a variety of Italian chocolates, nougats, and brandied fruits, and makes up confectionery baskets packed with selections of pastry and candies ($35.00 and $65.00). Orders are taken by mail or over the telephone —(212) LO 3-5331—and charge accounts are invited. Mange.

Modica's Latticini, 6319 Eighteenth Avenue, Brooklyn, New York 11204. Prices on request.

With little capital, sheer nerves, and lots of love, Mr. and Mrs. Modica have created one of the more exciting and complete neighborhood Italian food shops in New York. Fresh foods, homemade specialties, and Italian imports from Palermo, Sciacca, Aprilia, and Succa fill the shop. Modica's has a reputation for top quality and it is said to have the best pizza rustica in this Italian neighborhood.

Appetizing Italian salamis and sausages strung by chain and rope from the ceiling and rafters lend to the charm. Jellied cured beef ($1.29 per pound) and prosciutto imported from Aprilia (under $6.00 per pound) can be ordered, as well as domestic-made and -cured specialties. These include sweet or hot dry sausage, Genoa salami, pepperoni, and sopressata, a sweet sausage flavored with wine and black peppers.

Italian specialty cheeses such as smoked mozzarella ($2.29 per pound), mozzarella made with prosciutto ($3.29 per pound), and mondegas ($2.29 per pound) made with a butter ball in the center are available from Modica's. Plasticcurd (pasta filata) cheese varieties can also be ordered, as can incannestrata ($4.79 per pound) with pepper added, and cacciocavallo, a cured cheese with a smooth, firm body similar to provolone with less fat and not smoked as is provolone. Bel Paese, an uncooked, soft, sweet, mild Italian table cheese, blue-veined Gorgonzola, and toplino, a semisoft, mild provolone are among the selections the Modicas will send (all just over $3.50 per pound).

Eggplant appetizer (caponata), melanzane eggplant in oil (about $1.50, 16 ounces), tangy eggplant, and eggplant rollettes (8 ounces, $1.19) stuffed with bread crumbs and anchovies are among a vast selection of tinned imports. Also available are imported antipasto; pasta con sarde, a complete seasoning for macaroni with sardines ($1.29, 15 ounces); and pesto à la Genovese, a sauce made from fresh basil, olive oil, and cheese (65¢). Canned fish items include mussels on the half shell, fillets of anchovies, or sardines in salt.

Dried beans such as split and whole fave, lupini, and cannelini are sold, along with dried chestnuts and imported dried mushrooms. Olive oils from Lucca and Sicily include Francesconi, Madre and Amastra brands ($8.50 to $13.00 per gallon). And in the condiment line, the store stocks Gaeta and Sicilian dry-cured olives, both under $2.00 per pound. Other specialties the Modicas often mail are anisette sugar and nutella, an Italian fudge packed full of finely chopped hazelnuts.

Ramsey Imports, Inc., P.O. Box 277, Ramsey, New Jersey 07446. Free brochure.

Italian Polli brand condiments and Mennucci brand pastas (ranging from 69¢ to $1.25 for 14-ounce packages) can be ordered as single items from Ramsey Imports, exclusive U.S. agents for these products. Available is a line of 25 packaged pastas which include fidellini nest (loosely intertwined noodles in the shape of a ball). Among the selection of other Italian specialties are pepper salad in strips or whole (from about $1.50 to $3.00) antipastos (7 ounces, about $2.00), wild mushrooms ($2.00 for 3½ ounces), pickled mixed vegetables, and pesto spaghetti sauce ($1.00, 3½ ounces).

Tagliatelle with White Truffles

    4 quarts water
    5 tablespoons salt
    1 pound tagliatelle (or other Italian egg noodles)
    1 ounce white truffles
    ¼ pound (1 stick) sweet butter, at room tempera-
        ture
    1½ cups freshly ground Parmesan cheese

Heat a large earthenware casserole or baking dish
in a slow oven.

Bring water to a boil and add salt. Cook the tagliatelle until done (but still slightly firm).

While noodles are cooking, pour ¼ cup of truffle liquid into a small saucepan and heat but do not boil. Using a sharp knife, cut the truffles into slices ⅛ inch thick.

At the instant the noodles are done, remove the heated casserole from the oven. Drain noodles into a colander and, before they have a chance to drain thoroughly, pour them into the heated casserole. Add the heated truffle broth.

Immediately start adding large pats of butter until all the butter is added. Toss quickly and add spoonfuls of cheese. Toss until thoroughly blended. Quickly add truffle slices, toss again, and serve immediately with additional freshly grated Parmesan cheese. Yield, 4 servings.

It has cheeses—Brie, Tilsit, havarti, kommonost (all about $4 per pound); homemade liver pâté (3-pound loaf, about $19); Russian and Iranian caviar (from $110 to $130); smoked salmon from Denmark (about $20 sliced, $16 whole); Danish salamis (from $4 to $7); and confections—Danish stollen (about $4 for a 3½-pound cake), butter cake, almond tarts (just over $3 per pound), and Anthon Burg chocolates (about $10 per pound), said to be the finest in the world. Homemade delicacies prepared daily by three chefs for Old Denmark's famous salad bar are all available for shipment anywhere in the country. The selection includes such salads as potato (just over $1 per pound), vegetable, summer, lobster (the most expensive at just under $2 per pound), or crab, artichoke, mushroom, herring, meat, Danish caviar dip, and dessert fruit salad. If you are in Manhattan, you might be interested to know that a sampling of the salad bar is served each afternoon for a set fee.

SCANDINAVIAN

Nyborg & Nelson, Inc., 937 Second Avenue, New York, New York 10022. Prices on request.

This is a small grocery and delicatessen full of imported foods from Scandinavian countries. It has crackers, cookies, mixes for baking, dehydrated soups, and jars and tins of lingonberries (under $3.00), glögg mix, a drink concentrate to mix with wine, aquavit, or gin, goat cheese (about $2.40 per pound, and yellow peas in a 2-pound burlap sack ($1.49). Included among the selection of fish and fish products are fish balls—haddock in fish bouillon—(about $2.50 a jar), fish cakes in gravy or bouillon (8 ounces, $1.49), herring in various sauces (less than $1.00), anchovies, and smoked cod caviar paste in a tube, plain or with dill ($1.49 each).

Old Denmark, 133 East Sixty-fifth Street, New York, New York 10022. Prices on request.

An interesting and complete line of imported Scandinavian specialties is available from this unique little shop.

Plattar
(thin pancakes)

    2 eggs
    2½ cups milk
    1½ cups white flour
    ½ teaspoon salt
    1 to 2 teaspoons sugar

Mix ingredients in a jug with a pour spout. Whisk the egg with a little of the milk, add the flour, and whisk to a smooth batter. Stir in the rest of the milk and add the salt and sugar. Heat pancake pan slowly, brush with melted butter, stir batter often, and pour a thin layer into heated pan. When pancake looks matt (dry), turn over and cook until light brown. Serve with lingonberries or fruit preserve.

Frestelse

2 large onions
5 potatoes
Tin of Scandinavian skin- and bone-free anchovies
2 tablespoons butter
1 cup medium cream

Peel and slice onions, and sauté until light brown. Peel and shoestring cut potatoes. Arrange ½ of the potatoes in buttered baking dish, place anchovies and ½ of the sauteéd onion on top. Dot with butter, pour in ½ the cream and anchovy liquid. Place remainder of potatoes and onion into dish. Bake in preheated 435° F oven until potatoes are golden brown. Pour on remainder of cream and bake until potatoes are tender. Total time about 40 minutes.

Scandinavian Foods, 244 Main Street, Farmington, Connecticut 06032. Free price list.

A varied and exciting selection of Scandinavian smorgasbord delicacies can be ordered from this shop. Fish products range from whole cod roe and Norwegian brook trout to caviar paste in tubes. There are imported cheeses, candies, rye flour, cardamom and other spices, almond paste, pearl sugar, and even glögg. Rose hips are offered in bulk, and there is a selection of dried fruit for making fruit soup. The shop's bakery has homemade cookies, Swedish limpa, vort limpa, and cardemunring. Specialties of Scandinavian Foods include homemade herring sylat, kalvsylta (jellied veal), Danish leverpastej (liver pâté), rullepolse (rolled and tied with herbs at about $5.00 per pound), and korv (a homemade Swedish sausage at $2.50 per pound). These and other items can be assembled in gift packages to your specification. A very good selection of Scandinavian iron cooking pans includes krumkaka, plet irons, visps, and lefser grills.

Indian

Foods of India, 120 Lexington Avenue, New York, New York 10016. Free price list.

Foods of India offers a 5-page price list of everything needed in the way of Indian groceries. There are many varieties of dhal (the edible seeds of leguminous plants such as lentils, peas, and beans), rice, and flours which are sold by the pound. Of course there is a complete list of spices, including all those necessary to make your own gar-masala. Masala is the paste made from ground spices which is the basis of a curry. Garam masala usually contains peppercorns, cloves, cinnamon, cardamom, black cumin, nutmeg, and mace. Commercial curry powders are usually not as good, in that cheaper ingredients such as white cumin, coriander, and poppy seed are often used in disproportionately high amounts, along with fillers such as rice flour. Commercial powders make all dishes taste the same, rather than offering a unique combination of spices, freshly ground, for each different recipe. Foods of India also offers oils, several instant mixes, poppadums (crisp bread wafers usually made from rice and lentil flours, most between $1.00 and $1.35 a package), dried fruits and nuts, pickles and pastes of various manufacturers, snacks and sweets, and miscellaneous items such as Indian magazines, cookbooks, hair oil, jaggery (which is unrefined brown sugar, about $1.00 per pound), and silver leaf for very special dishes ($1.80 a packet). These are made by beating pure silver into very thin leaves. They are edible and used for decoration.

House of Spices, 76–17 Broadway, Jackson Heights, New York 11373. Free catalog.

House of Spices promises that frequent use of its catalog will give you "health, wealth, vigour and over all happiness!" It certainly will give you a wide variety of Indian and Pakistani foods and ingredients from which to choose. There are all major brands of pickles, dhals (dhals are over 50 varieties of lentils and pulses), rice and flours by the pound, poppadums, canned vegetables, fruits and nuts, and, of course, spices. Listed as "after dinner delicacies" are pan (kathan, pan bahar, pan masala), chuna for pan (all between $1 and $2), and the real fresh pan, whose listing is followed by the note "banned item for import—sorry." Betel nuts and spices are wrapped in pan (or paan) leaves (betel) which are served and chewed as a digestive after a meal. House of Spices sells a selection of Indian cooking utensils as well and notes in the catalog that "no orders are small—all orders are welcome with pleasure."

India Gifts and Foods, 1031–33 West Belmont Avenue, Chicago, Illinois 60657. Free price list.

India Gifts and Foods is a good Midwestern source for all the necessary ingredients of Indian cookery. A 4-page list

---

Red Pumpkin and Salted Roe Patia

3 onions, sliced finely
Ghee
4 red chilis ⎫
6 cloves garlic ⎬ grind to a paste
½ teaspoon cumin seed ⎭
1½ pounds red pumpkin cut into pieces
1 roe, salted and cut into 1-inch pieces
½ cup tamarind water (thick) —to make this, soak
    1 tablespoon tamarind in ½ cup and squeeze
    out the pulp
1 tablespoon jaggery
Salt to taste

Fry onions in the ghee until transparent. Add the ground chili-garlic-cumin paste and cook for a few minutes. Add the pumpkin pieces and cook until half done. Add the roe and cook until tender. Mix tamarind water and jaggery together and add the tamarind mixture to the patia. Keep on the fire for a few minutes. Remove from the fire and serve hot with rice and lentils. Serves 4 to 6.

---

includes everything from spices to dhal, flours and poppadums, teas, and oils, sweets and syrups. There are many varieties of pickles: lime pickle, shredded mango pickle, lemon chili pickle, and turnip pickle, among the dozens and dozens (most under $2). Vegetables include difficult-to-find Indian varieties such as karala, a bitter gourd; parval, an Indian vegetable which looks like a gherkin; and drumsticks, which is a long hard bean with a delicate flavor. Celery is sometimes used as a substitute. There is also a selection of cookbooks, along with incenses, hair oils, soaps, and cooking utensils such as idli vessels (steamers) in a choice of 3, 4, or 6 layers (from about $8 to $14) and a very inexpensive jalebi maker (about $1). Jalebis are the crisp, deep-fried sweet served soaked in syrup.

India Spice Store, 126 Lexington Avenue, New York, New York 10016. Free price list.

The India Spice Store, which claims representatives in London, Paris, Cairo, Nairobi, Karachi, Dacca, and Bombay, is an importer, grinder, repacker, and distributor of domestic and imported spices. Located in New York City's Indian grocery row, its price list includes over a dozen specially blended curry powders and a long list of imported spices. Among them are many specialty spices such as asifoetida (2 ounces under $1). Asifoetida is the gum resin of a Persian plant which is used as a flavoring and is also known as "food of the gods" or "devil's dung" (depending upon what one thinks of its rather peculiar odor). There are also fenugreek (seed, powder, or leaves), poppy seeds (blue or white), mustard seed (black or yellow), and sesame (with or without skin, black or white). All are about 50¢ for 4 ounces, except the fenugreek which is about $1 for 4 ounces. Curry leaves are also sold, less than 50¢ per ounce. Yes, there are such things as curry leaves, although they have nothing to do with "curry powder." Curry leaves, a mild seasoning, is the leaf of a plant called mithi neem in northern India, kariwepillai in southern India. The rest of the list offers rices, dhals, seeds, flours, and mixes, as well as every major brand of poppadums, pickles, and chutney. A minimum order of $10 is required.

Indian Super Bazaar, 11128 Georgia Avenue, P.O. Box 1977, Wheaton, Maryland 20902. Free price list.

Two and a half pages list everything essential to Indian cookery, from spices to beans, dhal, flours, poppadums, pickles, and chutneys. There are also nuts, fruits, oils, canned products, and miscellaneous ingredients such as rose water (about $1.25 for 6 ounces) and unsweetened coconut flakes (just over $1.00 per pound). There is kum kum which is promised not to spill (less than $1.00), China grass for dessert (75¢ for ½ ounce), incense, and kadais, which are the iron frying pans used by Indian cooks.

Dhal Khatti

½ pound lentils
Pinch baking soda
2 tablespoons cooking oil
1 medium onion, peeled and sliced
2 teaspoons cumin seeds
1 teaspoon powdered ginger
½ teaspoon cayenne
Salt to taste
1 medium potato, peeled, boiled, and diced
1 teaspoon tamarind concentrate
1 teaspoon garam masala
Parsley for garnish (optional)

Soak lentils overnight; boil with baking soda in a lot of water; cook until tender; strain and reserve water. Heat oil and sauté onions until golden brown, add cumin, and cook for another 2 minutes. Put in lentils, ginger, cayenne, salt, and some of the stock. Cook for 5 minutes over low heat; add potato and a little more of the stock; cover and cook for another 5 minutes. Stir in tamarind and garam marsala.

Kalustyan's, 123 Lexington Avenue, New York, New York 10016. Price list 13¢.

Among the many Indian grocery items listed by this established business are curry powders, spices, nuts, teas, canned goods, poppadums, flours, and mixes. Kalustyan's house blend garmasala is less than $1 for 2 ounces. Dhals include chana (a variety known also as gram or chick-pea), mung, dry or oily toor, and urad (black beans)—all less than $1 per pound, as are moth beans and masure dhal, which are red lentils. Listed under "Liquids—Oils, Syrups and Ghee" are pure butter ghee, coconut cream, mustard oil, and jasmine-scented hair oil. They are all about $2 for 16 ounces, but be careful what you cook.

Trinacria Importing Company, 415 Third Avenue, New York, New York 10016. Free price list.

The only price list currently available from Trinacria is for Indian foods, although other foods can be ordered. There are many varieties of pickles and chutneys: various kinds of mango, lemon, green chili, mixed gunda and date, lime, brinjal and bamboo in different brands—most under $2.00 a jar. There are all the essential spices, and some blends such as a Tandoori mix (about $1.50), rasam powder (under $1.00), and garmasala (about $1.50 a tin). Dried poppadums come in a packet (about $1.50) and dhal (lentils) are available by the pound in several types: tur, chana, assur, mung, and urad (all about 60¢ per pound). Just about everything needed for Italian, Middle Eastern, and Indonesian cookery, as well as hundreds of European gourmet items, are stocked by Trinacria. Address mail orders and requests for particular items not mentioned in the available price list to John of Trinacria.

Middle Eastern

Athens Pastries and Imported Foods, Inc., 2545 Lorain Avenue, Cleveland, Ohio 44113. Prices on request.

Pastries and countless Middle Eastern foods are available from this shop. Bakery goods include baklava, kataiji (honey-dipped strudel dough filled with ground nuts), nut cookies (dipped in syrup and covered with chopped nuts), and butter cookies (covered with confectioner's sugar and filled with chopped almonds). Feta cheese and olives come packaged or in bulk, as does kassari, also known as "flame cheese," which is made from goat and sheep milk. There is bulgur wheat for making pilaf or tabooli (the Middle Eastern parsley salad), tahini for making various dips and spreads, as well as dolmas (grape leaves), to stuff or already stuffed.

Hellenic American Broadcast, 2365 Mission Street, San Francisco, California 94110. Prices on request.

A specialist in Greek imported foods, Savas Deligiorgis will answer inquiries on prices for desired items. Among the many foods in the store are filo dough for making baklava or spanakopitta with spinach, feta cheese, olive oils, grape leaves for dolmadakia, Greek honey, loukoumi, and volvi, which are Greek wild onions in vinegar.

Kassos Brothers, 570 Ninth Avenue, New York, New York 10036. Prices on request.

Kassos Brothers carries all the essentials for Greek cookery as well as many delicacy items. Offered in bulk are pilgouri (cracked wheat, 49¢ per pound), koukia (fava beans), fakes (lentils, 65¢ per pound), and rovithia (chick peas, 75¢ per pound). There are at least a dozen kinds of olive oils, Greek pickled products such as Salonica peppers, vine leaves, and stuffed eggplant, and a large selection of olives (from $1.00 to $1.40 per pound), including Greek colossals, calamatas, chios, and green cracked tsakistes. Imported and domestic tarama comes in jars, and for dessert there is a selection of Greek pastry at $4.00 per tray, confections, halvah ($1.50 per pound), and imported figs, including calamata string figs at less than $1.00 per package and Smyrna pressed figs ($1.50 for a 1-pound package). Write requesting the prices of items wanted; Kassos Brothers has a wide, wide selection.

Sahadi Importing Company, 187–189 Atlantic Avenue, Brooklyn, New York 11201. Free catalog.

Brooklyn's Atlantic Avenue, a shoppers' paradise, is filled with Middle Eastern food stores, small Syrian pastry shops, and a dozen or so restaurants serving Lebanese, Egyptian, and Moroccan specialties. In the middle of all this is Sahadi's bazaar of Middle Eastern foods and gifts. Over 500 items imported by Sahadi and packaged under its name are listed in this 20-page catalog. All the spices and ingredients necessary to prepare Middle Eastern cuisines are available. Homemade pastries (from $3.25 to $3.50 per pound), candies, nuts, and dried fruits, preserves, syrups, condiments, and cheese extend the selection. You will find many ready-to-serve tinned specialties such as baba ghannouj (an eggplant dip), tahini tartar sauce (for fish or falafel)—both $1.20, and couscous (1-pound box, $1.00). If you are of the mind to grow your own Middle Eastern vegetable varieties, Sahadi has imported seeds from Syria . . . white Syrian squash ($1.20 per pound), parsley (similar to Chinese parsley, 25¢ per ounce), or rashaad seeds (50¢) among others.

Skenderis Greek Imports, 1612A Twentieth Street, N.W., Washington, D.C. 20009. Prices on request.

Many of the specialty foods of Greece can be mail-ordered from Skenderis. The store stocks a wide variety of hard cheeses ($2.00 to $3.75 per pound), olives (black, calamata, green, throumbes, oil-cured—all between $1.00 and $1.50 per pound), pickled Salonica peppers ($1.00 per pound), and baby eggplants ($1.50 per pound), honey ($2.75 per pound), tahini ($2.00 per pound), hommos ($1.89 per pound), rose water, filo dough ($1.50 per package), and more. Do you want to roast a lamb in your backyard and live in the area? Skenderis has an auto-psistaria. If you like kefalaki (lamb's head), it has them all year round. For dessert there is baklava, 50¢ a piece, and loukoumi, Greek delight at $2.00 per pound. Telephone inquiries (202) 265-9664 or 265-9667.

Syrian Grocery Importing Company, 270 Shawmut Avenue, Boston, Massachusetts 02118. Prices on request.

The Syrian Grocery is a direct importer of groceries and artifacts from the Middle East. It carries items such as couscous (just over $1.00), grape leaves in jars or in bulk, dried fruits (from $1.25 to $2.00 per pound), Turkish delight (from $1.30 to $2.20 per pound), a selection of Syrian spices, including Syrian allspice at $3.00 per pound, Turkish coffee, and backgammon tables. There is no catalog but prices will be quoted upon request. Postage charges are additional.

Oriental

The Asian Express Company, P.O. Box 375, Pelham, New York 10803. Free price list.

Fresh ginger? Fear of Oriental cooking? Along with its price list, The Asian Express Company includes a listing of the most popular Chinese and Japanese dishes with their ingredients, a helpful hint for the improvising cook or those unfamiliar with Oriental foods. Recipes for the dishes can be obtained for 10¢ each. Canned and dried Chinese and Japanese ingredients, as well as the fresh ginger (8 ounces, $1.10), are available.

East Wind, 2801 Broadway, New York, New York 10025. Free price list.

East Wind sells a very complete assortment of Chinese foods and ingredients, each listed with the origin or brand. Canned goods range from bitter melon (59¢), pickled cabbage (70¢), to 4 varieties of bamboo shoots from 65¢ to $1.50 for spring shoots). Red beans, mung beans, and soybeans are all under $1.00 per pound. There are dessert items such as white peaches (95¢) and lychees ($1.50) in

---

Barrie Chi's Fish in Hot Bean Sauce

   1 pound fish fillets (flounder or sole)
   1 piece of ginger
   3 cloves of garlic
   3 scallions
     Peanut oil for frying
   2 tablespoons superior soy sauce
2½ tablespoons shao hising wine
   2 teaspoons sugar
   6 tablespoons hot bean sauce
   1 cup chicken bouillon
   1 tablespoon rice vinegar
   4 teaspoons cornstarch

Cut the fillets into rectangles of approximately 3 inches by 1 inch.

Mince the ginger and the garlic and dice the scallions.

Deep-fry the fish pieces in heated peanut oil in the wok until they are uniformly golden.

Drain the fish pieces and pour the oil from the wok, leaving about 1 tablespoon oil in it.

Return the wok to the stove, with the garlic, ginger, scallions, soy sauce, wine, and sugar.

Add the hot bean sauce and stir-fry for about 1 minute.

Add pieces of fish, then bouillon, and cook on a small flame until the sauce is reduced by about a third.

Add the vinegar and cornstarch, which has been mixed with 3 tablespoons cold water. Mix well and serve.

---

syrup. Dried products include lotus root starch ($1.70 per pound), tiger lily buds ($1.25 for 8 ounces), dried seaweed (3 ounces, 90¢), and sweet rice flour (1 pound, $1.20). There is a line of China teas and some interesting preserved dessert fruits like red dates (8-ounce box, 95¢) and sweet roasted walnuts (7-ounce can, $1.15) from mainland China. Shipping charges are additional.

House of Rice, 4112 University Way, N.E., Seattle, Washington 98105. Prices on request.

The House of Rice runs a series of gourmet cooking courses in Chinese, Indian, Japanese, and Indonesian cookery and sells many of the ingredients necessary for these cuisines. A small line of Vietnamese and Thai foods has been added recently, and includes edible rice paper, fish sauce, Thai rice vermicelli, rice chips, and curry mixes. Hawaiian products have been popular, among them frozen poi and frozen coconut milk and papaya juice.

Katagiri & Company, Inc., 224 East Fifty-ninth Street, New York, New York 10022. Free price list.

Established in 1908, Katagiri claims to be the oldest Japanese food store in Manhattan. Its extensive listing of Japanese foods and cooking ingredients includes a wide variety of soy sauces, pickles, spices, dried seaweeds, noodles, fish products, teas, dried vegetables, canned goods, miso, and confectionery.

Omura Japanese Food and Gift Shop, 3811 Payne Avenue, Cleveland, Ohio 44114. Prices on request.

These very nice people do not have a price list or brochure, but regularly ship Japanese canned goods and spices as well as some interesting fresh foods. (The latter can be sent only during the colder weather.) Their complete line of Japanese foods includes frozen rice cakes, popular around the New Year season, rice crackers, instant noodles, soup mixes, beans, and fish cakes. Fish cakes can be ordered fresh or canned in 2 varieties. Kamaboko, a steamed cake, can be eaten plain or cooked, and satsumage is deep-fried and ready to eat. Three types of satsumage are available: shrimp, gobo (burdock root), and regular (similar to the gobo with the addition of carrots). Finally, Chinese seasoned pork sausage is available.

Saigon Market, Inc., 3147 Wilson Boulevard, Arlington, Virginia 22201. Free price list.

Until about a year ago Minh Chau Gallagher, a very accomplished Vietnamese cook, had to import from Paris the rice paper necessary for the outer wrapping of her spring rolls. Slowly these and other Vietnamese ingredients have become more readily available in the United States. Many of them are the same or very similar to those used in other Oriental cuisines; others, such as ca muoi, salted elephant plant ($1.55 for 8 ounces), are uniquely Vietnamese. The Saigon Market offers many of them to mail-order customers, including nuoc mam ($1.39 for 10 ounces), the bottled fish sauce which is the essential ingredient in the dipping sauce served with spring rolls. (See recipe on opposite page.)

Uwajimaya, Sixth Avenue South and South King Street, P.O. Box 3642, Seattle, Washington 98124. Free price list.

Uwajimaya describes itself as a one-stop Oriental supermarket, offering Oriental vegetables, taro root, bamboo shoots (59¢), mustard greens ($1.10); seafoods, octopus, swordfish, abalone ($4.29), squid, eel, crab, geoduck; and fresh vegetables, ginger root, sato imo (sweet potato), and tororo imo. There are also instant noodles and sauces from the Orient, cookware, cosmetics, toys, and Japanese periodicals and books. The store carries many items other than those listed in the 4-page, mail-order price list, and inquiries are invited for information on products not listed. Prices FOB Seattle.

Vietnam Center, Viet My Corp. Mail Order Dept., 3133 Wilson Boulevard, Arlington, Virginia 22201. Free price list.

Sources for Vietnamese foods in this country have long been difficult to find. This Virginia store puts out a four-page price list of Oriental foods which include many of the difficult-to-obtain Vietnamese items. The list is in

---

Chawan Mushi

This is a famous custard recipe. The Japanese name means "steamed bowl."

4 eggs
4 cups dashi (cooled)
1 tablespoon shoyu sauce
4 teaspoons salt (see Note)
Dash MSG
4 or 5 dried mushrooms (see Note) or matsutake (canned mushrooms), bamboo shoots, or water chestnuts
1 kamaboko cake, sliced thin, or 6 ounces raw chicken, boned and sliced thin, *plus* 12 medium shrimp, raw (clean and soak in some shoyu sauce for ½ hour before using; drain before adding to custard)
Watercress, parsley, and lemon peel (optional)

The first 5 ingredients are basic for the recipe. The other ingredients may be varied to suit one's taste. Beat the eggs slightly (there should be no foam). Add the cooled dashi, shoyu, salt, and MSG. Arrange the other ingredients in 6 individual bowls, pour the prepared custard mix over them, add a few leaves of parsley or watercress for green color, set the bowls in a pan of very hot water, and bake in oven at 325° F until custard is set. Serve piping hot as soon as done. A small piece of lemon peel may be placed on top of each custard.

Note: Soak mushrooms in water for ½ hour, cut them into small pieces and boil them in the dashi, shoyu, and salt for 10 minutes. If you use ham (which the Japanese never do), omit or reduce the salt. Bamboo shoots or water chestnuts should be washed, peeled, and sliced into small pieces.

Minh Chau Gallagher's Vietnamese Spring Rolls
(Cha-Gio)

    5 black Chinese dried mushrooms (Tong Cu)
    2 heaping tablespoons dried tree fungus (Muc-Nhi)
    ½ ounce bean threads (transparent noodles) (Mien)
    1 package dried, thin rice paper imported from
        Thailand (Banh-Trang)
    10 canned water chestnuts (or Chinese yam if avail-
        able) (Cu Dau)
    ½ medium-sized onion
    ½ pound ground pork (butt)
    6 ounces crabmeat flakes or minced shrimp (pref-
        erably Maryland blue crab meat)
    1 egg yolk
    1 tablespoon fish sauce (Nuoc Mam)
        Freshly ground pepper and salt to taste
        Lettuce leaves, fresh coriander, and mint leaves

Soak mushrooms, dried fungus, and bean threads in hot water at least ½ hour before cutting. Spray water on the rice paper and wrap in a wet towel for at least ½ hour before use. This will dampen the rice paper, making it easy to handle, since rice paper breaks easily when it is dry. Dice water chestnuts or Chinese yam, onion, and black mushrooms very small. Cut dried fungus into very thin threads and cut the bean threads into 2-inch strips. Mix all the above ingredients with ground pork, crab or shrimp, egg yolk, fish sauce, salt, and pepper. Cut the rice paper with a scissor into two. Then fold the half-cut rice paper in half again. Put about 2 teaspoons of the filling on the right angle, then fold it over and wrap it the same way as a Chinese egg roll. Deep-fry the rolls on low flame until golden brown. Serve with lettuce leaves, fresh coriander, and mint leaves and dip into Prepared Fish Sauce.

PREPARED FISH SAUCE

    16 tablespoons fish sauce (Nuoc Mam)
    10 tablespoons water
    3 tablespoons lime juice
    1 clove garlic mashed and chopped very fine
    2 tablespoons sugar
    1 red hot pepper

Mix all the ingredients together and serve as a dip for the spring rolls wrapped in lettuce leaves and fresh herbs. Taste it; if it is not salty enough, add more according to taste.

Vietnamese with some English translations. Among the distinctively Vietnamese foods are Cha que and Cha lua ($6 per pound) which are cold cuts, the Vietnamese equivalent of bologna. Another specialty is Nem chua, sour pork (under $1), which in Vietnam is eaten raw wrapped in fresh banana leaves.

Wing Fat Company, 33–35 Mott Street, New York, New York 10013. Free price list.

The Wing Fat Company puts out a very businesslike listing of the canned goods, dried items, teas, sweets, and other Chinese ingredients which it will mail-order. There is a good selection of sauces—hoisin (1 pound about $1.50), plum (a little more), oyster (lots more; about $4.00 for 16 ounces), barbecue ($1.65 per pound), and various bean sauces and soy sauces, including black mushroom soy from mainland China ($1.60 for a 21-ounce bottle), as well as other Chinese and Japanese varieties. Wing Fat will send wonton skins (thick for dumplings and thin for soups, under $1.00 per pound) and egg roll skins (thin Shanghai style, 10 pieces, just over $1.00; and Cantonese style for deep frying, 2 pounds, about $1.25) only during the cooler months and then only at the cutomer's own risk. Fresh ginger is available according to market price, and Chinese vegetable seeds and mung beans and soybeans for sprouting (75¢ per pound) are also sold. Minimum order is $5.00, and postage charges are additional.

Tex-Mex

Cal-Foods, 195 South Twenty-eighth Street, San Jose, California 95116. Prices on request.

Cal-Foods stocks a fairly complete line of ingredients for Mexican cooking, many items of which are imported from Mexico. In the San Jose community, Cal-Foods is especially noted for homemade flour tortillas, which can be ordered in amounts of 2 dozen or more, under $1, plus postage.

Caliente Chili Inc., P.O. Drawer 5340, Austin, Texas 78763. Free brochure.

Billed as the world's most famous chili, "Wick Fowler's 2-Alarm Chili" is made from the recipe used by the late Wick Fowler in the World Champion Chili Cookoff events held annually at Terlinqua, a ghost mining town in west Texas. Not a typical chili mix, a package of 2-Alarm Chili contains nine ingredients in seven individual packets. These are added to two pounds of meat and a can of tomato sauce. Two packages are $2.50 ppd; 24 packages, $26.00. The result—Texas chili adjusted to individual taste —false alarm to 4-alarm. "Distinguished Chiliheads" listed in the brochure include Dan Rather, Elizabeth Taylor, Elliott Roosevelt, the LBJ family, Walter Cronkite, Ben Hogan, Leon Jaworski, Honcho Crouch (who?) and the Executives of Jockey Menswear (what?).

Casa Moneo, 210 West Fourteenth Street, New York, New York 10011. Free list; prices on request.

Casa Moneo sells cast-iron tortilla presses and absolutely everything else needed for Mexican cookery. There is an incredible list of chili and chili products in all sized cans and brands: dried ($6.00 per pound), powdered ($2.10 per pound), pickled, sliced, chopped, diced, mild, hot. There are Mexican beans and beer, chocolate, sauces, nuts, and spices. Casa Moneo also stocks Cuban and Puerto Rican foods. Write to Casa Moneo and ask for price quotes on what you want; the odds are that the store carries it.

Cowboy Kitchen, American Micro-Fare, Inc., 4560 Leston Avenue, Dallas, Texas 75247. Free brochure.

At the rate it's going, mail-order chili may soon compete with mail-order hams as the most popular food to order. Cowboy Kitchen's product comes frozen accompanied, like several other chilis, with a pedigree. It is "the official 'bowl of red' of the annual Republic of Texas Chilympiad" that takes place annually in San Marcos, Texas. Among the chili aficionados who have given their endorsement to Cowboy Kitchen Chili are Barry Goldwater, Abe Fortas, and Lyndon B. Johnson (whose family, incidentally appears on a competitor's list as well). The chili, made with chunks of meat and without beans, can be ordered separately (12 pounds of chili in 1-pound packages $45) or in combination with hot tamales and meat, cheese, or bean burritos (all between $40 and $45). All assortments are packed in dry ice to guarantee safe arrival.

Ray's Brand Products, Inc., 1920-22-24 South Thirteenth Street, Springfield, Illinois 62705. Prices on request.

Arguments about chili recipes have been known to raise passions to the level one would associate with an international skirmish. Perhaps it is regional chauvinism that leads to violent arguments on how best to prepare this popular dish. Ground meat or chunks? To bean or not to bean? Green pepper? Chopped onions on top? Cheese? Wash it down with beer or Mexican style with chocolate? Most of these discussions take place in the Southwest, but a small but persistent chorus is being heard from Illinois, praising the virtues of Ray's Chilli. (Ray spells chili with two lls, so now there can be arguments about that, too.)

From a home kitchen product, Ray's Chilli has developed into a business that still uses the original recipe but measures ingredients in tons instead of pounds. Available with beans or without, or in a variety called Chilli Mac with spaghetti, Ray's products are shipped, in cases of 6 cans anywhere in the United States by UPS. Chili without beans, 6 for about $10.00; chili with beans and Chilli Mac, $6.50 per case. Prices include shipping.

Rio Grande Foods, Route 4, Tilden, Texas 78072. Free price list.

More on the chili controversy, this time from Texas. A new company specializing in "Tex-Mex" food informs us that chili is not Mexican per se, but was invented by Mexican cooks who had moved north of the border. Tex-Mex chili, which is offered in two styles, with or without beans, uses, of course, a "secret combination of twelve spices, herbs and aromatics." From a family recipe perfected over the years, the chili is made with coarsely chopped *not* ground beef. Strictly a luxury product for the chili gourmet, it contains no cereal fillers or preservatives and is available exclusively by mail order (case of six 15-ounce cans, $12.00 with beans, $16.00 without). Serving suggestions include a side of scrambled eggs and toast, Texas style, or topped with a plop of sour cream and finely chopped onion. Also sold is chili con queso (case of six 8-ounce cans, $6.00), a spicy cheese and chili pepper mixture to be used as a sauce or as a dip with tostadas or corn chips. A sampler order of 2 cans of chili with beans and 2 of cheese dip is $6.00. Add $1.75 per item for UPS charges.

Chorizo with Eggs and Chili

2 chorizos (Spanish sausage)
1 tablespoon onion, chopped
2 eggs
¼ cup green chili sauce

Mash and heat the chorizos in a well-greased heavy skillet. Add onion and mix. Turn heat low and add lightly beaten eggs and chili sauce. Stir eggs from bottom of skillet as they become firm. Cook to desired firmness. Serve at once with toast. Panecitos (Mexican hard rolls), halved, buttered, and toasted, are excellent to serve in place of toast. Serves 1.

FRESH GREEN CHILI SAUCE

8 to 12 chili pods
1 medium ripe tomato
½ teaspoon salt

Peel chili; remove stem, seeds, and veins. Peel tomato. Chop chili very fine. Cut, then mash tomato with hands until it is almost a liquid. Combine chili and tomato. Add salt. This sauce will keep covered in the refrigerator 4 to 5 days.

Variations: (1) 1 clove of mashed garlic, or (2) ½ cup finely chopped onion, or (3) 1 tablespoon olive oil (reduces the pungency of the chili), or (4) 2 tablespoons vinegar for a tart sauce, or (5) 2 tablespoons vinegar, 4 tablespoons brown sugar, and 1 teaspoon cinnamon for a sweet sauce.

For additional ethnic sources, see:

Creole

Chapter 10. Cakes, Cookies, and Confections:
    Leah's Southern Confections
Chapter 11. Coffee, Tea and Spice:
    Luzianne Coffee Company

Dutch Indonesian

Chapter 10. Cakes, Cookies, and Confections:
    Chocolaterie "Dauphine"

European

Chapter 3. Fruits and Vegetables:
    Paul A. Urbani Truffles
    M. V. Wine Company
Chapter 4. Meat and Poultry:
    Fred Usinger, Inc.
Chapter 9. Cheese:
    Frigo Cheese Corp.
    J. M. Nuttall and Company
    Paxton Whitfield Ltd.
Chapter 10. Cakes, Cookies, and Confections:
    Conditorei Kreutzkamm
    Charbonnel et Walker Ltd.
    Charles Demel and Sons
    Ferrara Foods and Confections, Inc.

Hotel Sacher
Leckerli-Huus
Maiffret
Charles Muir Castle Bakery
Schatz-Confiserie

Indian

Chapter 11. Coffee, Tea, and Spice:
    Lawrence Curry
Chapter 12. Jams, Jellies, and Condiments:
    M. M. Poonjiaji & Company

Middle Eastern

Chapter 2. Bread:
    Toufayan Bakery
Chapter 4. Meat and Poultry:
    Manukian's Basturma & Soujouk Company
Chapter 10. Cakes, Cookies, and Confections:
    Istanbul
    Manukian's Basturma & Soujouk Company
Chapter 11. Coffee, Tea and Spice:
    House of Yemen East

Tex-Mex

Chapter 11. Coffee, Tea and Spice:
    The Old Mexico Shop
    Santa Cruz Chili & Spice Company

15. KOSHER

SOURCES for kosher foods are either hard or easy to find, depending on the community in which you live. In this chapter can be found companies which will mail selections of kosher meats, individually packaged and wrapped for the freezer, along with complete meals, frozen challahs, salamis, and even kosher aspirin. Remember . . . you don't have to be Jewish to love . . . challah? bagels? bialys?

Freeda Kosher Vitamins, 110 East Forty-first Street, New York, New York 10017. Free catalog.

Kosher vitamins for almost every need are described in the large Freeda catalog. Items such as liver tablets are made from glatt kosher freeze-dried liver (100 for $4.95). Vitamins are vegetarian in formula and contain no sugar or starch preservatives or artificial flavorings. There is even a complete line of pharmaceuticals prepared especially for Passover, including aspirin tablets.

Katz's Delicatessen, 205 East Houston Street, New York, New York 10002. Prices on request.

Katz's, one of New York City's oldest delicatessens, established in 1898, has been sending salamis to campers, college kids, servicemen, and displaced New Yorkers for generations. The brand? Katz's, what else? Hard salamis are recommended for overseas shipment and either hard or soft for deliveries in the United States. The kosher salamis range in size up to their largest of 5 pounds ($2.20 per pound, plus postage). Other delicatessen can be sent air freight. A New York tradition.

Kineret Kosher, Row D, Office 434, N.Y.C. Terminal Market, Bronx, New York 10474. Prices on request.

Primarily a wholesaler and distributor to stores, Kineret will accept orders from groups wishing to purchase in bulk. Its unique line of kosher frozen foods includes main courses and desserts as well as such items as gefilte fish ($1.49 per pound) and mini frozen challah which puff up and bake into crisp, full-sized loaves (about $1.00 per pound). Prepared fish products such as fish sticks, batter dipped fish, and fish cheeseburgers range from 69¢ to $1.49 per pound. There are several complete dinners in aluminum trays (99¢ to $1.59), such as flounder in lemon sauce with peas and mashed potatoes. For dessert there are doughnuts—jelly, glazed, and cake—from 99¢ to $1.19 a package. A grocery line is being added which will offer 4 varieties of salad dressing, barbecue sauce, and several flavors of puddings.

S & S Strictly Kosher American Meat Service Ltd., 7 Hagra, Rehovot, Israel, or S & S Strictly Kosher American Meat Service Ltd., c/o Silverstein, 557 Avenue Z, Brooklyn, New York 11223. Free brochure.

This company offers a specialized service: by writing either to the New York or the Israeli branch, one can arrange to have kosher American-cut meats delivered to someone in Israel. A box of 20 pounds of fresh beef, including rib steaks, roasts, flanken, stew, and ground meat, is individually packaged and labeled in English—about $50, delivered. "The corned beef is made on our premises using a special recipe that Rabbi Spring brought back from New York City." A special gift for a homesick New Yorker in Israel. S & S also prepares lamb, beef, veal, turkey, and chicken.

Signature Prime, 143 South Water Market, Chicago, Illinois 60608. Free catalog.

Zion Kosher pure beef products are packaged in 7 different gift selections, ranging from $20 to $80. An example is the "Delux Deli" assortment which includes salami, bologna, dinner franks, cocktail franks, knockwurst, Polish sausage, snack sticks, corned beef, and pastrami, plus the hardcover *Hadassah Cook Book*.

Sinai Kosher Sausage Corp., 1000 West Pershing Road, Chicago, Illinois 60609. Prices on request.

Sinai offers fine-quality kosher food products and kosher freezer-wrapped meats in consumer-size packages for the home freezer, together with a selection of delicatessen products. Write or phone to (312) 927-1810 for further information and prices.

16. MEALS BY MAIL

FEELING lazy and luxurious? Here you will find the largest menu in the world. Whether you prefer a classic New England shellfish dinner delivered in a pot, fancy foods for formal dining, or hors d'oeuvres for two or a large cocktail party, it is all here. There are pâtés and delicious breads, interesting soups, main courses from beef Wellington to stone crab claws, and many desserts. You can even have a watercress sandwich sent right to your office.

Captn's Pick, 702 Fulton Market, Chicago, Illinois 60606. Free brochure.

Do-it-yourself seafood meals can be sent by the Captn's Pick seafood house. Such a meal includes fish and shellfish and all the ingredients for preparation, along with instructions for easy and quick home assembling. "The New England Classic" (about $40) consists of lobster, long-neck steamers, and corn on the cob; "A Great Catch" (about $30) is an assortment of seafood, plus ingredients; and "Bouillabaisse" (about $35) is described as follows: "Legend has it that bouillabaisse was prepared by angels for the three Marys who found themselves shipwrecked on a barren French beach." All serve 4.

Other prepared selections are seafood hors d'oeuvres, one assortment of which includes 48 coconut shrimp, shrimp 'n turf, seafood cromezque (filled crepes), and crab puffs (about $42 for 4 pounds). Breaded shellfish and stuffed fish varieties also appear on the list.

Smoked items which can be sent include "colossal" shrimp (3½ pounds, about $30) and whole fish such as lake or rainbow trout and eel. Escargots with snail butter (3½ pounds, about $30), imported fresh beluga caviar ($100 for 7 ounces), and many prepared shellfish varieties can be ordered individually without the dinner trimmings. Oysters come raw on the half shell (about $20 for 2 dozen), Rockefeller, Bienville (with shrimp and mushrooms), Mornay, Provençale, and casino (all about $20 for 20). Soft-shell crab in season, Hawaiian mahi mahi, and whole dungeness crab are sold frozen, as are the imported frog legs.

Clambake International, Inc., 161 Harvard Street, Suite 11, Allston, Massachusetts 02134. Free brochure.

For displaced New Englanders and shellfish lovers everywhere, Clambake International will send to your door a native New England meal in a pot, ready to cook. The menu: four 1½-pound live Maine lobsters, 4 pounds of Ipswich steamer clams, 4 servings of New England–style clam chowder, and corn on the cob (in season), about $11 per person, minimum order of 4 servings. If this is too much to handle, Clambake will send a cook along as well and cater your meal for you in your home, on the beach, in the ball park, or in Central Park. Dinners, sent air freight, are guaranteed to arrive fresh, the lobsters alive and kicking. All are packed in a cooking/shipping container, with the necessary paper products and lobster crackers. It is stressed that you should allow ten days for shipping arrangements.

Contemporary Marketing, Inc., 790 Maple Lane, Bensenville, Illinois 60106. Free price list.

Contemporary Marketing features the Bon Appetite weekend-for-two gourmet package. A weekend menu can be shipped directly to your home, apartment, summer cottage, ski lodge, or boat for Friday and Saturday nights. Here is what you receive: four 6-ounce, ground New York strip steaks for grilling, 2 portions of chicken Kiev stuffed with wild rice, 2 baked potatoes stuffed with cream cheese and herbs, 15 assorted hors d'oeuvres, rice pilaf, and Escoffier steak sauce. The cost for all this is about $30, including shipping. Telephone orders are accepted at (800) 323-2408. Illinois residents call (312) 595-0461.

Meatique, 758 Madison Avenue, New York, New York 10021. Free price list.

Prepared appetizers, entrées, and desserts are the specialty of Meatique. Everything can be oven-heated for an almost instant dinner party. The selection covers a fairly wide range of tastes, and each item can be ordered for one or a crowd.

Within Meatique's offering of some 30 items, one can order crab puffs, seafood crepes, rumaki, or quiches; entrées such as beef loaf Wellington, honey-dipped chicken, or stuffed seafood crepes; and a variety of desserts, including chocolate or coffee mousse, and apple-raisin or pineapple-apricot crepes for a little less than $1 a portion.

Apart from the prepared entrées is a line of quality meats dominated by steaks and chops, but also containing beef and veal for stew, calf's liver, fillet tips, and crown roast. Cooked Gulf shrimp are available for a little over $4 per pound in an unspecified size. All items can be ordered separately, as long as the complete order is a minimum of $25.

Omaha Steaks International, 4400 South Ninety-sixth Street, Omaha, Nebraska 68127. Free catalog.

Omaha offers a large menu by mail, featuring everything from fully cooked prime roasts to kosher hors d'oeuvres. It has fancy foods such as "crèpe a la reine," with a filling of mushrooms and diced chicken, and sautéed in a sherry cream sauce; a crepe sampler; and "cannelloni a la milanese," with a filling of seasoned pork, veal, chicken, mushrooms, and cheese—all are about $25 for 24 portions. Among the selection of 5 fully cooked roasts is a 13-pound prime rib roast, cut to include only the first five ribs—about $60; a 3-pound boneless veal saddle roast—about $32; and a 7-pound, boneless leg of spring lamb—about $41. There are also ready-to-serve cured meats such as a 2-pound hickory-smoked chicken—about $13; and a 4-pound, fully cooked, kosher-style corned beef—about $21. More fancy prepared entrées include pheasant, stuffed Cornish game hens, and breast of chicken Cordon Bleu, ranging from $32 to $40. If you are in need of kosher snacks for a crowd, you can order beef turnovers, stuffed mushrooms, and potato knishes; 160 pieces run about $45. Omaha Steaks also features (uncooked) roasts, steaks, and chops, items for which they are well-known.

Saltwater Farm, York Harbor, Maine 03911. Free catalog.

Two prepared combination Florida shellfish dinners are available from the Maine lobster people. There are Southern lobster halves stuffed with crabmeat and blue crab cocktail claws (under $50) or stone crab claws with a shrimp ring and cocktail sauce (under $60). Both dinners serve 6 and include a homemade Key lime pie, the sending of which probably requires a more masterful approach than the making of the pie itself.

Wickford Shellfish Company, 67 Esmond Avenue, Wickford, Rhode Island 02852. Prices on request.

A complete Rhode Island clambake (as opposed to a New England clambake or a Massachusetts clambake or a Maine clambake) is packed in its own can and shipped air freight at about $6.00 per serving. Each serving of a Rhode Island clambake includes chicken, lobster, steamers, fish fillet, onions, carrots, potatoes, and link sausage. Minimum order is a 2-serving can. Air-freight charges are $4.50 per can.

William Poll, 1051 Lexington Avenue, New York, New York 10021. Free catalog.

William Poll, one of Manhattan's fine gourmet shops, has an entire catering service by mail order. Pâté maison by the pound ($7.00), cocktail crabmeat quiche by the dozen ($6.50), tarama (fish roe mixed with olive oil, lemon juice, eggs, and bread—6 ounces for $3.00), and cheddar-chut (a mixture of cheddar, chutney, and seasonings—6 ounces for $3.00) start out the selection of close to 200 prepared foods. Pints of soup include avgolemono (Greek egg lemon soup—$3.50), bouillabaisse ($6.00), and pea soup with Madeira wine ($3.50). For entrées there are baked spring lamb with fresh string beans and tomatoes, coq au vin, and Athenian Stew—all about $6.00 per portion. Seventy-five different sandwiches range from a ham, cucumber, and watercress combo to a BLT.

Fresh white or black truffles and fresh foie gras with truffles can be ordered in season, and terrines or block-form tins of foie gras are stocked all year. Baked goods that can be ordered include Mr. Poll's own thin sliced breads such as light Russian pumpernickel, Westphalian pumpernickel, and rye (all under $1.00 per package), as well as such specialties as French croissants (45¢), brioche (45¢), baguettes (50¢), and pistollettes (rolls—$1.25 a package).

Overnight shipments of all items can be provided upon special request—from a single serving to a dinner party of baked hams, cheese platters, smoked fish, and hors d'oeuvre trays.

For additional sources, see:
Chapter 4. Meat and Poultry:
    The Bruss Company
    Irving Levitt Company, Inc.
    Omaha Steaks International
    Pfaelzer Brothers
Chapter 6. Fish and Seafood:
    Burdine's
Chapter 14. Ethnic Foods: Scandinavian; Old Denmark
Chapter 15. Kosher:
    Kineret Kosher

FINE LUNCH BY DOG TRAY.

17. HEALTH FOODS

WHILE some of us may have a health food store nearby, most of us do not have access to the farmers who produce naturally grown foods. Here you can order from farmers who produce naturally grown grains, fruits, and vegetables; and from one livestock farmer, you can order organically raised beef. There are, also, several sources specializing in one or a few unusual products; seaweed products from Ireland and carob pods from California are among the selection. To give a reasonable distribution, we have included general health food stores that for the most part carry a complete selection of health foods, as well as foods for special dietary requirements and allergies. Many of these stores offer a nutritional counseling service.

Although we have tried to include specific health food sources in this chapter, you will find additional sources for most foods in their respective chapters.

Lee Anderson's Covalda Date Company, P.O. Box 908, Coachella, California 92236. Free price list.

If Lee Anderson had his way, the date would replace the potato chip as the national munchie. His naturally sweet, organic date products include dried, TV-snack date chips (4 pounds, under $9.00), a date-almond confection made of dates rolled in unsweetened coconut, and stuffed dates with a choice of nut, pineapple, or ground coconut and sesame butter fillings (5 pounds, about $20.00, in a gift box). Creamed dates is a spread of honey and dates (2 quarts, about $11.00) and "Mom's Mix," made of ground sunflower, sesame, and flax mixed with date sugar, is suggested as a topping for cereals and baked goods (about $4.50 per pound). Prices included delivery.

Barth's of Long Island, 270 West Merrick Road, Valley Stream, New York 11582. Free catalog.

Barth's catalog offers a general range of natural foods, including many of its own brand products. Dried instant soup mixes come in 8 varieties such as vegetable, carrot, and chicken, and are made without any additives (4-ounce jars, $1.25, make 20 servings). Among the other selections are Barth's peanut mix ($1.50 per pound) containing peanut varieties especially selected for home grinding, herbal teas, vacuum-packed nuts and seeds, canned black cherry

juice ($2.00 a pint), and a variety of carob products. Maldon sea salt can be bought through Barth's ($2.00 a pound).

Carob Products, P.O. Box 5084, Walnut Creek, California 94596. Free brochure.

Carob fruit and products made from this brown, bean-like pod, often referred to as St. John's bread, are available from Bee Williams, owner of Carob Products. One can order the whole pod, carob fondue, and carob candy. There is also carob powder and sweeteners and flavorings such as carob honey and carob molasses. Whole pods run about 65¢ a pound; all other products are about $1.

Cayol Natural Foods, 811 La Salle Avenue, Minneapolis, Minnesota 55402. Free catalog.

Cayol Natural Foods, a retail store in the heart of Minneapolis, puts out a 76-page catalog featuring organic foods, natural vitamins, minerals, some soaps (yogurt), cosmetics, and a large selection of health-oriented books. It offers a good selection of cereals and pastas, grains and flours, a seven-grain bread (about 80¢ a loaf), and bread mixes (2 pounds, under $2). There are lots of snack items from which to choose (cookies, coconut and carob products, candy, seeds, and honey-dipped fruits). You will find oils such as almond, coconut, apricot kernel, and sesame among others. Raw milk goat cheese can be ordered in season (10 ounces, about $2). Most popular health food brands are stocked, as well as lesser known names such as jams and jellies from The Healthians of Escondido, California. Shipping is additional.

Deer Valley Farm and Farm Store, R.D. 1, Guilford, New York, 13780. Free catalog.

In the rolling hills of Chenango County in the center of New York State, Deer Valley Farm operates a large organic farm that produces lots of good things to eat. You will find nuts and nut butters, unsulfured fruits, home-grown herbs and spices, many teas, grains, seeds, and beans (from hard wheat, about 30¢ a pound, to black-eyed peas, about 42¢ a pound), cereals and meals, whole wheat and vegetable pastas, honey (including North County cut comb, 12 ounces for $1.30), spreads, jellies, jams, and more.

There are dairy products such as butter, made from fresh cultured cream for about $1.59 a pound; whey, sold in bulk at 42¢ a pound; and yogurt in freeze-dried grains, tablets, or dry culture (about $2.49 a package). Cheeses include cheddar, Muenster, and Swiss. Whole milk cheddar, from New York and Wisconsin, is made from late May or June milk, only. Varieties include raw milk cheddar with caraway seeds, medium-aged, white cheddar, and washed curd cheddar with low salt content; all run a little under $2.00 a pound.

Processed fruits, vegetables, and juices, many of which are put up on the farm, include frozen sauerkraut—about 55¢ a pound; pure vegetable juice "with a fresh-uncooked taste"—$1.60 for a 17-ounce bottle; and a good selection of

HEALTH-FOOD SUBSTITUTES FOR . . .

Bread crumbs: Soy grits (absorbs liquid in the same way as bread), wheat germ.

Butter: Corn germ oil (for use in baking and cooking), nut butters, tahini paste (finely ground sesame seeds).

Chocolate: Carob confections for snacking; carob powder or flour for drinks and cooking (it has a flavor closer to chocolate when toasted before using). Three tablespoons carob powder combined with 2 tablespoons water equal 1 square of chocolate.

Coffee: Pero and Yano (made from grains), herbal teas.

Milk: Nut milk (made from raw nuts and water), soy flour and water (made from ground soybeans and water). Both should be combined with a natural sweetener if the taste is not palatable to you.

Pepper: Paprika.

Protein: Miso (made from soybeans and often used in soups), raw nuts, nut milk, vegetable protein (concentrated), soy grits, brewer's yeast (Torumel brand has a milder flavor than some others), wheat germ, and white rice substitutes.

Rice (white): Organically grown, short-grain brown rice, rice grits (coarsely ground brown rice), wild rice. buckwheat, bulgur wheat. For use in soups, stews, etc.: soybeans (almost complete protein), millet, barley grits, and gruenken (unripened green wheat kernels that have been dried).

Salt (refined): Earth or sea salt, both unrefined and rich in minerals; vegetable salt (made from dried vegetables that have finely ground).

Soy sauce (most brands contain MSG): Tamari sesame paste with the addition of water.

Sweeteners: Date sugar or syrup, maple syrup, sorghum, carob syrup, unrefined honey or molasses, malt syrup (less sweet than most other sweeteners), fruit concentrates (particularly apple), and blackstrap molasses (combine with other syrups; it has a bitter flavor, but is high in nutrients).

Tea: Herb combinations with mint or peppermint.

Thickeners (in place of cornstarch and white refined flour): Unrefined flour, arrowroot (in equal amounts as for cornstarch), agar-agar (use 2 tablespoons to each 2½ cups of liquid), Irish moss (also called carrageen; used in thickening desserts), rice cream, wheat cereal, tapioca starch, potato flour, and plain gelatin.

Vinegar: Naturally processed apple cider vinegar, wine vinegar, or lemon juice.

---

foods all packed in number 303 tins. There are unsweetened peaches, about 70¢ each; cream of pea soup, about 75¢ each; and spaghetti sauce with meat, about $1.35 each.

From the Deer Valley bakery on the farm you can order whole-grain bread, cookies, and cakes, all made from organically grown whole wheat flour, raw milk, and eggs that come from the farm. Yeast-raised breads and pastries are sweetened only with honey, maple syrup, or unsulfured molasses, and many items are made without salt. Among a selection of over 50 items, there is whole wheat sponge cake and angel cake, butter cookies, three-grain bread, and whole-grain raisin bread. Cornell-formula pizza topped with tomatoes and cheese, about $1.35 for a 13-ounce size, is available, as well as whole wheat frankfurter and hamburger rolls or buns, about 75¢ a package—an all-American lunch, made from natural ingredients.

If you are in the vicinity, Deer Valley Farm invites you to visit and provides picnic facilities for outings.

Ener-G Foods, Inc., 1526 Utah Avenue South, Seattle, Washington 98134. Free brochure.

Ener-G Foods, a wholesaler of Jolly Joan allergy, dietetic, and low-sodium foods and wheat and gluten-free products, will mail-order these items to individuals in single units or by the case. Most of these products are mixes, allowing those on special diets to enjoy bread, cakes, pancakes, cookies, pies, biscuits, and muffins. Recipes for preparation are on each box. Among the selections are rice (regular or low-sodium), potato, corn, barley, and oat mixes, as well as rice 'n rye bread mix. Pancake mixes come in 3 varieties: stone-ground whole wheat, wheat, and soy. A number of cereals, rice flour, and rice polish are also available, as are Jolly Joan egg replacer and instant soy milk powder. Almost all individual items are less than $1 each.

Herb Products Co., P.O. Box 898, 11012 Magnolia Boulevard, North Hollywood, California 91601. Catalog 25¢.

The Herb Products catalog lists hundreds of botanicals for almost any purpose. The "Therapeutic Index" following the lists includes laxatives (buckthorn, $1.55 for 4 ounces; mandrake, $2.35 for 4 ounces; mountain flax, $6.20 for 4 ounces) and aphrodisiacs (damiana, $1.45 for 4 ounces; muirapuama, $2.85 for 4 ounces; sawpalmetto, $1.45 for 4 ounces). All herbs, culinary as well as medicinal, come in 4-ounce or 1-pound packages. If you do not know an herb by its English name, ask for it by any name you know it by—Latin, German, Ukrainian, Polish, Lithuanian, Chinese—Herb Products Co. says it will have it or can get it if it is available at all. The catalog lists a complete selection of essential oils, and contains a great deal of advice such as: "Do not get angry; do not worry; do not fear . . . they kill. Eat alkalinizing foods and you will not do any of these," and "Do not wear cheaply colored underwear. . . . Do not wear dyed fur against the skin." Postage is paid on orders over $20.00. Specify cut, powdered, or whole when ordering herbs.

David Hodas, Pleasant Plains Natural and Organic Foods, P.O. Box 190, 1708 Lakewood Road, Toms River, New Jersey 08753. Free price list.

This family enterprise run by Mr. Hodas and his sons offers a selection of natural foods. They have dried fruit (between $2.00 and $2.50 per pound)—papaya, peaches, pears, and pineapples; shelled seeds and nuts—black walnuts ($2.60 per pound), filberts ($2.00 per pound), and dry

Rose Hip Soup

1 cup seedless rose hips
1 quart water
2 tablespoons honey
8 cassia buds
½ teaspoon ground cinnamon
Yogurt, sour cream, or whipped cream

Soak rose hips in water overnight. The next day, put them into a saucepan along with the water, honey, cassia buds, and cinnamon. Simmer for about ½ hour. Remove from heat, cool slightly, whirl in blender until smooth. Chill and serve with cream or yogurt. Serves 4.

vegetables—great northern lima beans, green soybeans, and popcorn (all between $2.50 and $2.75 for 5 pounds); and many grains and stone-ground flours—rice (70¢), soy (50¢), or rye (40¢), flour, hulled barley (55¢) or barley flakes (55¢) and buckwheat (65¢) for sprouting (prices are per pound). You will find juices, apple cider vinegar, syrups, pastas (artichoke or buckwheat spaghetti), and butters such as Joyua tahini, sesame and sunflower tahini, and almond butter. The Hodases also have some natural cheeses available, among them Monterey Jack, Norwegian Swiss, and Kefir cream cheese (under $1.00).

Infinity Food Co., Inc., 157 Hudson Street, New York, New York 10013. Free catalog.

The Infinity Co., is something unique—health foods in wholesale quantities at wholesale prices with a minimum of $100.00. What started with a flour mill in the living room of Howard Miller's Greenwich Village home is now a large operation that has everything from nut butters to homeopathic tissue salts—over 300 products in all. In particular, a very good selection of whole grains, rice, beans, and seeds, flour, meal, and cereal is offered. There are aduki beans (12 pounds, $9.00), apricot kernels (5 pounds, $3.00), black turtle beans (12 pounds, $6.36), chick-pea flour (50 pounds, $30.00), a mixture of bran and wheat germ (5 pounds, $5.00), couscous (55 pounds, $45.00), and chicken feed (50 pounds, $3.25). Flour mills are bought, sold, repaired, and stones are dressed. Ginseng (in all forms), herb teas, mineral water, soda, and juices such as apple-pomegranate (twelve 32-ounce bottles, $10.00), pear, and ruby-red grape (12 bottles, $14.00) are among a wide variety of beverages. Infinity also carries pastas, dried soups, salad dressings, olives, snacks, preserves, date syrup, and honey ranging in flavors from thistle to eucalyptus. A small collection of Japanese products includes miso, agar-agar, tamari, tiziki, nori (sheets), and wakame. Truck deliveries to New York boroughs and New Jersey are made weekly at no extra charge. In addition to the Infinity catalog, mailers are sent out every so often featuring the latest items, along with specials.

Lee's Fruit Company, P.O. Box 450, Hobby Hill, Leesburg, Florida 32748. Free brochure.

The "Famous Grapefruit Diet" and the Lees' story, *A Look Behind the Compost Pile,* accompany their organic citrus price list. Oranges and grapefruits are sold by the bushel ($15.75), ¾ bushel ($13.50), and ½ bushel ($9.90), postpaid to states bordering the Mississippi. Orange blossom honey is shipped with citrus only for about $1.25 per pound. Lee notes that in order to pass the maturity test early, commercial growers spray their grapefruit trees with arsenate of lead to counteract the excess acid in the fruit. Lee does not and consequently must wait until the fruit is ripened naturally, normally around mid-November. An automatic shipping plan at stated intervals is also offered at a 3 percent discount on a seasonal order.

Herbed Tomato Juice

3 medium tomatoes
½ teaspoon kelp
1 teaspoon chia seeds
    Dash Worcestershire sauce

Blend until smooth and creamy and pour over ice in tall glasses.

The Natural Development Company, Box 215, Bainbridge, Pennsylvania 17502. Free catalog.

Natural Development specializes in a vast variety of organic seeds for gardening. Among the food items available for mail order are a line of Loma Linda meatless canned foods made from soy beans. Also sold are edible seeds and grains such as hulled white sesame seeds ($5.00 for 5 pounds), bran flakes (3 pounds, less than $1.00), and hulled unpearled barley (5 pounds, $2.20). For sprouting there are corn, wheat, alfalfa seed, mung beans, soybeans, and buckwheat—ranging from 20¢ to $2.00 a pound. Natural and organic flours include whole wheat (10 pounds, $2.70), rye, and corn, an eight-grain cereal, and an eight-grain pancake flour—all between about 25¢ and 75¢ per pound. "Kleen" raw sugar comes in 5-pound bags ($3.75) and up. Some Pennsylvania Dutch specialties include peach butter (1-pound jar, $1.54), butter mints (11 ounces, $2.10), and scrapple (1-pound tins, $1.50). Shipping charges are additional.

Natural Food Supplements, Inc., 8725 Remmet Avenue, Canoga Park, California 91304. Free catalog.

All of the Sunshine Valley food products produced by this company are made from whole foods using seeds, pits, skin, and fibers of organically grown fruits and vegetables. The company has pioneered in subzero, freeze-dried foods and offers unique items such as almond meal with powdered pineapple. Varieties of nut spreads made with the freeze-dried fruits include walnut with orange, raw Spanish peanut spread with papaya and tangerine, and cashew walnut spread with avocado and peach. The nut spreads come in 1-pound jars ($6.00). Also available by mail are wheat germ oil ($5.00 per pint), cider vinegar ($1.75 per pint), and a multipurpose oil made from corn germ, sunflower, sesame, olive, avocado, apricot kernel, and wheat germ oils ($3.00 per pint). Imported fruit concentrates to use as a syrup on cereals or desserts or as a beverage base come in several flavors (about $10.00 for 4 ounces). Also sold are seeds for sprouting and planting, dry soup mixes, natural-ingredient fruit and nut cakes, and powdered fruit concentrates for baking or flavoring yogurt, among other uses ($2.00 to $3.00 for 8 ounces). Postage charges are additional.

Northern Health Foods, Box 66, 13 South Fourth Street, Moorhead, Minnesota, 56560. Free price list.

In the fertile Red River Valley of Minnesota is a health food shop experienced in mail-order service. All orders over $4.00 are shipped prepaid and the prices are reasonable. The shop's current mailing offers specials on unprocessed wheat bran at 60¢ a pound, jumbo, hulled, raw sunflower seeds for $1.13 a pound, raw embryo wheat germ, 50¢ a pound, and a sprouter which fits on jars, along with samples of alfalfa, mung, and wheat for $1.98. The specials vary with the mailings, as do the recipes tucked inside. (We received one for crunchy granola cereal.) An additional discount of 3¢ a pound is offered on any item ordered in quantities of 5 pounds or more.

North Penn Health Food Center, 1313 North Broad Street, Lansdale, Pennsylvania 19446. Prices on request.

A homemade doughnut which is baked rather than fried in fat is the specialty of Mr. Wade, owner of North Penn Health Food Center. His doughnuts, similar in taste and texture to muffins, are made with organically grown wheat ground fresh each week, full fat soy flour, fresh eggs, raw sugar, applesauce, soy oil, molasses, pure lemon and vanilla extract, nutmeg, cinnamon, aluminum-free baking powder, and sea salt. Mr. Wade alters the plain doughnut with fruits such as blueberries, apple bits, and pure apple concentrate, sun-dried currants, and toasted coconut to produce other varieties. A minimum order is 3 dozen, at $1.35 per dozen, plus postage. A complete line of standard health foods are also available for mail order.

Dorothy I. Page, The Breezeway, P.O. Box 117, Sun City, California 92381. Free brochure.

Describing herself as "71 years of age, scarcely 5 feet tall, and weighing 95 lbs. dripping wet, trying to conquer an acre of ground," Dorothy Page guesses that some may think her "tetched." She raises organically grown vegetables and offers for mail several food supplements, including organic seafoods and a concentrated alfalfa extract (270 tablets, $5). Bat guano (a little over $3 per pound, ppd) can also be ordered by mail (not to be eaten).

Pavo's, 57 South Ninth Street, Minneapolis, Minnesota 55402. Free catalog.

Pavo's publishes an indexed consumer catalog listing thousands of nationally known health foods available from it by mail order. Featured are Pavo's own grains and cereals (brown rice, long-grain, 77¢ per pound; potato flour, $1.19 per pound; buckwheat groats, $1.49 per 1¼ pounds; alfalfa leaf flour, $1.52 per pound; soy carob flour, 98¢ per pound; peanut meal, 8 ounces, $1.05) and its pasta products made from semolina wheat and soy (artichoke noodles, whole wheat macaroni, spinach ribbons—all in 7-ounce packages for about 75¢). Pavo's cold-pressed oils come in many varieties, as do its herbal teas, dried and honeyed fruits, and nuts. High-protein, foods, sugar-free foods, low-sodium foods, foods for allergy diets, and juicer machines and blenders can all be found in the catalog.

Seaweed Ltd., Kylbroghlan Moycullen, County Galway, Ireland. Prices on request.

Seaweed Ltd. is a company specializing in the production of health products which are either seaweed or based on seaweed. Food products include packets of carrageen, a seaweed which when boiled in water produces a viscous liquid which sets to a jelly when cooled. It is used as a thickening agent in making jams and jellies. Dillisk, also in packets, is an edible seaweed often served raw as an appetizer or used for flavoring and thickening stews and soups. In Ireland it is often boiled with new potatoes, fried with rashers and sausages, or added to salads and sandwiches. Seaweed Ltd. also

offers a powdered-seaweed food supplement, a bath salt, a shampoo ("which shows up all the natural highlights which all women-folk desire"), and a footbath, all based on seaweed.

Shiloh Farms, Inc., Sulphur Springs, Arkansas 72768. Free catalog.

Shiloh Farms, a well-known name in the health food business, distributes some 400 products to over a thousand retail stores across the United States and also runs a mail-order service. Since the catalog is not just for mail order, but also for use in buying directly from two completely stocked warehouses, many items listed cannot be shipped, among which are meats, poultry, frozen products, and juices.

Among the great selection of foods that can be ordered are carrots by the 25-pound bag (about $8.50), and oranges by the bushel for about $16.00, several varieties of dates and date confections, shredded coconut, dried fruits such as apples and bananas as well as raw shelled nuts, peanut butter, raw sweetening agents, bee pollen, and pure sesame protein. Alpahorn, a combination of cheddar, colby, and longhorn types, and mild or sharp New York cheddars can also be ordered during the colder months. The bulk of Shiloh's products are grains, seeds, flours, and baked goods. Many are from Arrowhead Mills, which no longer mails to individuals. Raw, unprocessed bran, rice flour, barley and soybean grits, flax meal, and chia seeds popular among the Southwest Indians as an energy source are just a few of Shiloh Farms' wide assortment. There is soft whole wheat pastry, rice, and triticale flour, rye grain, hard-berry wheat, and sunflower meal. Over 40 baked items include sourdough rye bread, corn-soy muffins, banana loaf, whole wheat hamburger buns, sesame seed cookies, and whole wheat or white pizzas.

Most items are sold in case lots of 12 units per case. A 20 percent discount is offered to co-ops and buying clubs on orders of $200.00 and up. Telephone orders are accepted at (501) 298-3297.

Walnut Acres, Penns Creek, Pennsylvania 17862. Free catalog.

Walnut Acres, a large organic farm of 360 acres, has been in the business of growing, preparing, and shipping whole, unchemicalized natural foods by mail for over

---

Mocha Blancmange

Before making up any carrageen recipe, weigh out the required quantity of carrageen, stir briskly in hot water, remove from the water immediately, pick over and proceed according to the recipe. This preliminary step removes the sea salt which is left adhering to the carrageen, to serve as a preservative.

½ cup carrageen (Irish moss)
3 cups milk
2 squares unsweetened chocolate
1 cup sugar
¼ cup boiling water
2 teaspoons strong black coffee

Put the milk into the top of a double boiler; add moss, and cook without stirring for about 30 minutes. Melt chocolate in water, add sugar, and boil for 2 minutes; add to moss mixture. Add coffee. Mix well. Strain, mold, chill. Serve with whipped cream.

twenty-six years. Foods in every category are listed in this twenty-three page catalog. There is also a section on "helpful household things" such as dietary gram scales, a sprouter and sprouting jar wire; a list of natural toiletries and cosmetics; a gardening section; and a food supplements and booklist.

Walnut Acres refers to itself as an overgrown home kitchen producing handcrafted natural foods. Many foods grown on the farm are prepared in Walnut Acres' kitchen and put up in tins. Such items include soups, sauces, meat, poultry and fish products, fruits and vegetables, and, homemade from the bakery, cookies and plum pudding. Prices are quite reasonable. An open invitation stands to visit the farm, especially during Open House held yearly in midsummer.

Wolfes Neck Farm, Freeport, Maine 04032. Free brochure.

Organic beef from animals that are not force-fed results in a natural product with less fat than most beef. Details of Wolfes Neck's organic cattle-raising procedures are fully described in its literature. The animals are slaughtered in a Federally inspected abattoir, aged for about two weeks, cut, wrapped, and flash-frozen. Air shipments are offered to any sizable airport in addition to less expensive truck deliveries throughout New England. The beef comes in 42-pound boxes. Butchering and packaging are designed to provide a fair share of 1-inch to 1½-inch steaks and 3 to 5-pound roasts, as well as ground meat. Organ meats, stew beef, and soup bones are available, and the stew beef and ground beef are separately wrapped in 1-pound packages.

The hindquarter carton currently selling for about $80.00 contains approximately 30 pounds of steaks and roasts and 12 pounds of ground meat. A standard 42-pound carton has fewer steaks and roasts and more ground beef plus stew meat. It sells for a little over $40.00 at the time of this writing. Organically raised lamb is also sold and runs about $1.65 per pound. If interested, request Wolfes Neck Farm's *Butchering Instructions* for more details about butchering and packaging.

Wonder Natural Foods, 11711 Redwood Highway, Wonder, Oregon 97543. Free price list.

Wonder Natural Foods is located near the Siskiyou National Forest in a purple geodesic dome which also houses the Wonder Pollen Collective and East Earth Herbs. The collective obtains pollen from the wilderness areas of North America and from Spain. Bee pollen from chamomile and blackberry flowers of Spain and from wildflowers of Canada comes in 1-pound packages ($7). Ginseng roots can be ordered in a number of varieties which are all thoroughly described in a ginseng information booklet (25¢). Available are Chinese ginseng flowers for tea, Chinese dong kwai (female ginseng). Korean ginseng concentrated extract, and Fo-Ti Tieng slices, among other varieties.

For additional sources, see:
Chapter 1. Grains:
    Chico-San Inc.
    Leon R. Horsted
Chapter 2. Bread:
    Hearty Mix
Chapter 3. Fruits and Vegetables
Chapter 4. Meat and Poultry:
    Mel Cordes
    Nodine's Smokehouse
    Teel Mountain Farm
Chapter 8. . . . to Nuts:
    Koinonia Partners
Chapter 9. Cheese
Chapter 11. Coffee, Tea, and Spice
Chapter 12. Jams, Jellies, and Condiments:
    Chico-San Inc.
    Saltmarsh Cider Mill
Chapter 13. Honey and Maple Syrup
Chapter 14. Ethnic Foods:
    Eastern European; Paprikas Weiss
Chapter 15. Kosher:
    Freeda Kosher Vitamins

18. FOODS FOR CAMPERS

IN this last chapter we set aside our search for fine food and exotic delicacies and move into an entirely different realm of eating . . . "expedition food." Whether your expedition is a weekend backpacking trip, or a three-week hike along the John Muir trail, or a full-scale assault on Everest (Sherpas and all), the food you take with you is of crucial importance. Most importantly, it must be lightweight and nonperishable. Secondly, it must be nutritious, providing the proper amounts of protein, fats, and carbohydrates. And lastly and of secondary importance it must be relatively edible (although everything tastes good in the mountains, right?).

The principal method for reducing weight and stopping spoilage is the removal of water. This is accomplished either by dehydration or the process of freeze drying (a space program spin-off). In any case the water awaiting you in the mountains is added to the dried food at the camp to restore it to a rough approximation of its former self.

Since regular food stores offer little in the way of wilderness foods, and since camping stores often stock only a limited selection, we have collected a number of original sources for lightweight, nonperishable food. Freeze-dried and dehydrated foods are available in complete meals, as well as in separate items such as fruits, vegetables, and meats. And for additional flavor and nutrition in soups and stews, there is beef-, ham-, and chicken-flavored vegetable protein made from dehydrated soybean flour.

Some popular brands such as Rich-Moor and Mountain House cannot be obtained directly from the manufacturers. For this reason, we have included a number of backpacking stores in the listings from which these products are available. These stores generally provide an annual backpacking equipment catalog which includes their food products.

Of course, there are other backpacking foods besides the freeze-dried products. Interesting foods suitable for backpacking can be ordered from other sources listed throughout the book. For instance, there are dehydrated and concentrated foods such as Chinese and Japanese ramen soups, dried mushrooms, fish, and shrimp, as well as a tremendous choice of fresh herbs for flavoring meals and making nutritious teas. Quick-energy candies and high-protein drinks are available from health-food stores; and nuts, dried fruits, and trail snacks can be obtained from fruit and nut growers. In Chapter 1, "Grains," you will find numerous varieties of grains and seeds for breakfast and snack concoctions, as well as compact breads such as pumpernickel (which when tightly sealed will keep for two weeks in the wilderness). There are also many sources for sausages, beef and buffalo salami, and jerky, all of which are excellent foods for backpacking.

Sam Andy Foods, 826 La Para Avenue, Palo Alto, California 94306. Free brochure.

Sam Andy says that it is the world's largest dehydrated food company. Judging from the tremendous selection of fruits, grains, vegetables, animal protein, plant protein, and premixed concentrate items featured in the brochure, this may well be true. Foods are available in small foil pouches and #10 cans (about ¾ of a gallon). Sam Andy suggests that a substantial amount of money can be saved, especially if one uses backpacking foods often, by purchasing #10 cans and packing one's own individual servings. For that extra-long trip you've been planning into the wilds of Alaska or such, canned items are packaged with little oxygen or water and will last in storage for decades.

The selection seems worth exploring. Featured under dairy products, for example, are eggs with milk (96 eggs, $12.20), dried egg yolks (462 servings, $16.95) as well as whites, cheese, milk, sour cream, butter (168 tablespoons, $9.50), and margarine powder (168 tablespoons, $5.70).

Chuck Wagon Foods, Micro Drive, Woburn, Massachusetts 01801. Free brochure.

During World War II, Chuck Wagon Foods supplied the armed forces with tropical chocolate, malted milk tablets, biscuits, and fruit and nut pemmican to be used as emergency rations. After the war the company assembled food rations for industry, and since 1957 it has produced dried and dehydrated foods for recreational purposes.

Seventy-five varieties of food include breakfast items, fruits, vegetables, soups, chowders, main dishes, desserts, baking mixes, and beverages. A selection of specialty items other than staples includes strawberry and apricot tear sheets (pure fruit unrolled and eaten—50¢ each), a plastic pouch of peanut butter (7½ ounces, $1.20), meat product bars, and jelly or cheese spreads (6 servings less than $1.00).

Waterproof and buoyant concentrated emergency food

kits (about $3.00), a number of complete meal packs (4 servings, between $4.00 and $6.00), several pot meals, called budget pouches (all about $3.00 for 4 portions), and a $10.00 sampler of a complete breakfast, lunch, and dinner for 2 are other Chuck Wagon offerings. Chuck Wagon specializes in getting orders out fast.

Dixie Beehive Foods, 1890 Forge Street, Tucker, Georgia 30084. Free catalog.

IFCO is an international cooperative producer of dehydrated and freeze-dried foods marketed under the label of Dixie Beehive Foods. It features a tremendous assortment of items, ranging from hors d'oeuvres to desserts, and sandwich spreads to main dishes. Just about everything one needs to sustain a balanced diet, plus snacks, spices, and dried dairy products, are available from this company.

Dehydrated foods, packed in #10 cans, cost less per ounce of reconstituted food than wet pack foods. Unopened cans have an indefinite shelf life, and can be reconstituted with the use of hot water in a few minutes or with the use of cold water in several hours.

Freeze-dried compressed foods, a complete line of fruits, meats, vegetables, eggs, salads, and complete meals, are for the most part completely cooked and require only boiling in water before eating. Some may be eaten without dehydrating. A sample case of six #2½ cans is $18; the variety pack of 12 cans runs about $33, while a year's supply is about $350.

Dri-Lite Foods Inc., 8607 Canoga Avenue, Canoga Park, California 91304. Free brochure.

Some 300 freeze-dried foods manufactured by Dri-Lite are listed in this brochure. A wide choice of staples, such as breakfast mixes, main-course entrées, vegetables, and soups, is accompanied by a selection of fruit varieties, spreads and snacks, beverages and desserts.

Specialty items featured by Dri-Lite are freeze-dried pork chops (2 ounces, $2.99), beefsteaks (2 ounces, $3.99), and cubed beef, ham, and poultry for adding to stews and other dishes (1¼ ounces, $2.20). No-cook, freeze-dried products packaged to serve two, Dri-Lite's newest items, include precooked eggs ($1.77), turkey chowder ($2.85), and Neapolitan ice cream ($1.17). Complete meals for 2 and 4 are also available, as well as HM products, which range in choice from "kwik" lunches to trail-pack cookies.

Herter's Inc., Route 2, Mitchell, South Dakota 57301. Catalog $1.

Campers will find several food items of special interest to them in Herter's hefty, 350-page catalog of sports and outdoor equipment. There is bacon plus, a lightweight, bacon-flavored protein (the equivalent of 3 pounds of fried bacon, $1.39); a high-energy fruit bar (box of 24, $7.12 or 34¢ each); and Kendall Mint Cake ($1.69), a

---

SPROUTING SEED ON THE TRAIL

Among the lightest and most nutritious foods you can take camping are beans for sprouting. Before the trip, start the beans sprouting. Then fill a clear plastic bag with the sprouts and tie onto your pack, remembering first to fit the mouth of the bag over a small-sized embroidery hoop to allow in the necessary air for continuation of the sprouting. The beans should be rinsed in a cold stream or lake two or three times a day.

---

lightweight, candy-type food bar which was used as the primary high-energy snack food by the Druo expedition while hiking in the High Sierras for 194 days. Also sold are Herter's Hudson Bay freeze-dried foods, which come in varieties from beef stew (6 to 8 servings, $13.97) and chicken chop suey (6 to 7 portions, $10.63) to vegetables to chocolate ice cream (14 to 20 servings, $6.97). The ice creams, the catalog notes, are usually eaten dry but can be added to cold water for a nourishing drink. All of the freeze-dried foods come with complete instructions for preparation and are packed in #10 containers. Another item which may be of interest to backpackers is the powdered concentrate of imitation maple syrup ($1.49, makes 16 ounces of syrup). It is lightweight and can be reconstituted by adding boiling water.

Oregon Freeze Dry Foods, Inc., 770 West Twenty-ninth Avenue, P.O. Box 1048, Albany, Oregon 97321. Free brochure.

Oregon Freeze Dry Foods, manufacturer of Mountain House and Tea Kettle brand freeze-dried products, has available to the individual by mail a "sampler case" of 9 foods identical to those distributed nationally for about $21 per case. A case contains beef with rice, sausage patties, precooked eggs with real bacon, chicken pilaf, chicken and noodles, compressed peas, compressed shrimp creole, pineapple and strawberry ice cream. There is a limit of 1 case per person.

Perma-Pak, 40 East 2430 South, Salt Lake City, Utah, 84115. Free catalog.

Some 200 low-moisture, lightweight foods have been processed and marketed by Perma-Pak for over twenty years. Two separate catalogs are available; the larger stresses crisis kits for emergency use, low-moisture foods, and freeze-dried foods packed in cans for long-term storage. The selection includes a wide variety of items ranging from chili to freeze-dried chocolate ice cream. *Camplite,* the second catalog, is strictly for campers and backpackers and features dehydrated and freeze-dried foods in 2- and 4-person packs—all between $2.00 and $7.00 for complete meals. Aside from dinners and breakfast dishes, Perma-Pak offers a choice of meat-flavored protein soups, syrups, spreads and gravies, fruits and vegetables, juices and drinks, breads and biscuits, salads and desserts. Some of the unique items among the 75 foods listed are instant apple and peach preserves, seedless grapes, tomato juice crystals (less than $1.00 for 2½ ounces) onion skillet bread (6 ounces, under $1.00), Yukon biscuits (8 for less than $1.00), and no-bake pies (7 ounces, $1.20).

The Smilie Company, 575 Howard Street, San Francisco, California 94105. Free brochure.

The Smilie Company puts up its own brand fruits and vegetables in 1-pound bulk packs and also features some 150 lightweight foods from most outdoor food manufacturers. Smilie vegetables include 13 varieties, among them dehydrated cabbage shred (1 pound, $3.20), tomato flakes (1 pound, $3.80), diced potatoes (1 pound, $1.40), freeze-dried green beans (1 pound, $9.60), and corn (1 pound, $5.30). One ounce of vegetable is said to equal a single serving. Apricot nuggets (1 pound, $4.20), instant apple slices (1 pound, $3.20) and applesauce (1 pound, $2.00), grapes (1 pound, $2.40), and a pack of mixed fruits make up the Smilie brand selection of fruits. Telephone orders are accepted at (415) 421-2459.

Speedy Chef Foods, Inc., 2395 Middlegreen Court, Lancaster, Pennsylvania 17601. Free brochure.

Speedy Chef Foods manufactures a variety of freeze-dried foods such as textured vegetable protein and a number of main dishes, most of which contain vegetable protein. Among a selection of 13 items are baked beans with ham-like protein ($1.40 for 5 ounces), chicken almondine, and wine-flavored mix ($1.35 for 5 ounces), as well as candied squash with nutflake topping and chowder base—both under $1.00.

Mail orders are accepted from most states, but not from

FREEZE-DRIED VERSUS DEHYDRATED

Dehydrated foods are not a new phenomenon. We have been using them for a long time. Cake mixes, dried soup mixes, nonfat milk, instant potatoes, and breakfast cereals are all dehydrated foods. Dehydration ovens remove 98 percent of all moisture from the food, and as the moisture is removed, the food shrinks in size. The shriveled outer covering contracts and tends to protect nutritive values for longer periods of time.

Advantages: Lower cost. Costs less per serving than dried or off-season fresh foods; far less than freeze-dried. Reduced storage space. Long storage life.

Disadvantages: Longer reconstituting time. Less initial food value than freeze-dried because of evaporated mineral salts.

Freeze-dried foods, a relatively new development, are sliced or processed, immersed or sprayed with a preserving agent, and frozen. The frozen foods are then placed in a vacuum chamber and heated. The frozen moisture in the food then changes directly to gas vapor without melting into water first. This water vapor escapes from the frozen food, leaving the cellular structure essentially the same. The food is thus lightweight and porous. When immersed in water, it rapidly soaks up the water, and is reconstituted and ready for use in a short time.

Advantages: Faster to reconstitute than dehydrated. More convenient. Higher initial food value.

Disadvantages: More expensive and bulkier than dehydrated food. Also, the porous cellular structure allows more rapid degradation of nutritive values and of flavor. Within six months, nutritive value is lower and depletes faster than dehydrated products.

MEAT-FLAVORED VEGETABLE PROTEIN

The latest food technology "miracle" is the meat-flavored vegetable protein—dehydrated chunks of soybean flour, etc.—which when added to soups or stews looks and tastes remarkably like chunks of beef, chicken, or ham (depending on which kind you use). They are actually quite good (relatively speaking) and help enhance a dull camp meal. Nobody knows how they are made.

Massachusetts, Rhode Island, New York, New Jersey, Pennsylvania, Maryland, or Washington, D.C., where Speedy Chef products are widely distributed to retail stores.

Stow-A-Way Sports Industries, 166 Cushing Highway, Cohasset, Massachusetts 02025. Free catalog.

This is a general backpacking store which carries its own Stow-Lite brand foods originally developed and formulated for the space flights with the assistance of the U.S. Army. Also available are major brand freeze-dried foods in single packs and #10 cans.

Featured among the selection of Stow-Lite brand foods are complete packs for breakfast, lunch, and dinner, along with beverages packaged to serve 4, from about $3 to $7.

These complete food packs are planned for a balanced diet with the use of calorie counts based on *Composition of Foods,* the Department of Agriculture handbook #8. A wide choice of beverages, breakfast, one-pot meals (around $3 for 4 servings), fruits and vegetables (all between $1 and $2 for 4 servings) is also available. The Stow-Lite line is rounded out by canned fruit and pecan cakes (60¢ to 65¢), gingerbread and brownie mix (less than $1), and buttery flavored shortening or oleomargarine in a #1 can (also under $1). A variety of 25 trail aids put out by several manufacturers adds to the list of items included in Stow-A-Way Sports' outdoor food and equipment catalog.

Westland Foods Corporation, 1381 Franquette Avenue, Concord, California 94520. Free brochure.

The flavor of real bacon without the waste or weight can be had with Westland's Campin' Bacon, a precooked, vacuum-packed product which needs no refrigeration, even after it is opened. Designed for campers and backpackers, it is available in individual- or family-sized tins and in bars. One pound of this product ($7.50) is the equivalent of three pounds of raw bacon.

LIST OF SOURCES

INDEX